Have you ever wondered why you're so busy, where your time goes, or how much your time is really worth?

This book will radically alter your understanding of the nature and value of time. Authored by leading experts in social, economic and environmental sciences, it explains how moving towards shorter, more flexible hours of work could help tackle urgent problems that beset our daily lives – from overwork, unemployment and low well-being, to entrenched inequalities, needless high-carbon consumption and the lack of time to live sustainably.

Time on Our Side challenges conventional wisdom about what makes a 'successful' economy. It shows us how, through using and valuing time differently, we can reclaim the time to care for each other, follow our dreams and enjoy each moment.

About this book

"Time is the one resource in human life that is absolutely scarce. Discretionary time has also been shown to be a major determinant of perceived well-being. The unorthodox, empirical-minded and change-oriented authors who have contributed to this volume weave issues of time allocation and time use to those of labor and employment, growth and productivity, gender and care, life style and consumption, money and time, and environmental/climate sustainability. The result is a coherent, comprehensive, and highly suggestive account of ideas and policies whose time has come."
Claus Offe, Emeritus Professor of Political Science, Hertie School of Governance, Berlin

"To a lot of people, the idea of reducing work hours will seem like a modern heresy. But working long hours doesn't necessarily equate with more productivity and it certainly doesn't equate with a fulfilled life or a better environment. In this book, the contributors think the unthinkable – a standard working week of 30 hours or less – and show that it is quite possible to conceive of a world in which more people work less with all kinds of benefits that follow on. This remarkable volume could be the start of a quiet revolution in attitudes to life and work."
Professor Nigel Thrift, Vice-Chancellor and President, University of Warwick

"This important volume places time at the heart of a range of vital political issues including the environment, socio-economic inequality, gender equality and care. Most fundamentally, it underlines the significance of the politics of time for how we fashion a good life and a good society."
Baroness Lister, Emeritus Professor of Social Policy, Loughborough University

"With the publication of this outstanding set of essays, **nef** brings to the public an extraordinarily rich range of insights into how we could all make much better use of our time. If you want to know how environmental sustainability, social justice, and gender equity can all be enhanced through shorter paid working hours, then take the time to read this stimulating book."
Peter A. Victor, Author and Economist at York University, Toronto

"Time is money... except it isn't. This exploration of the politics of time and the asymmetries between clocks, work, wages, the seasons of the day and the cycles of life is vivid and vital."
Beatrix Campbell, writer and broadcaster, London

Time on Our Side: Why we all need a shorter working week

Edited by Anna Coote and Jane Franklin

Contributors: Barbara Adam, Valerie Bryson, Ian Buck, Tania Burchardt, Molly Conisbee, Anna Coote, Mark Davis, Angela Druckman, Anders Hayden, Bronwyn Hayward, Tim Jackson, Dominque Méda, Martin Pullinger, Juliet Schor, Andrew Simms, Robert Skidelsky

nef
economics as if people
and the planet mattered

First edition published in hardback in Great Britain in 2013 by
nef (the new economics foundation)
3 Jonathan Street
London
SE11 5NH
www.neweconomics.org
E-mail: info@neweconomics.org
Telephone: +44 (0)20 7822 6300

The moral right of Anna Coote, Jane Franklin, Barbara Adam, Valerie Bryson, Tania Burchardt, Molly Conisbee, Mark Davis, Angela Druckman, Anders Hayden, Bronwyn Hayward, Tim Jackson, Dominque Méda, Martin Pullinger, Juliet Schor, Andrew Simms and Robert Skidelsky to be identified as the authors of this work has been asserted by them in accordance with the Copyright, Designs and Patents Acts of 1988.

Every effort has been made to trace or contact all copyright holders. The publishers will be pleased to make good any omissions or rectify any mistakes brought to their attention at the earliest opportunity.
British Library Cataloguing in Publication Data: a catalogue record for this book is available from the British Library.
ISBN: 978–1–908506–39–9
Registered charity number 1055254

economics as if people
and the planet mattered

The new economics foundation supports The Forest Stewardship Council [FSC], the leading international forest certification organization. All **nef** book titles are printed on FSC certified paper.

FSC	MIX
	Paper from responsible sources
www.fsc.org	FSC® C013056

Cover design and art direction danfarleydesign.co.uk
Typeset by Tetragon, London, NW1 7JE
Production management Eddepro, West Sussex RH12 3DQ
Copy edited by Juno Baker
Printed and bound in Great Britain by TJ International, Padstow PL28 8RW

Contents

Introduction: A new economics of work and time

Anna Coote

Most of us live by the clock and the calendar. Weekday clock time tells us when to get out of bed, have breakfast, get the kids to school, go to work, leave work, pick up the kids, go home, make dinner, watch television, get the kids to bed, go to bed. We're allowed to do different things on Saturday and Sunday, on bank holidays and usually in two or three weeks of the summer months.

Each hour, measured by the clock, is the same for all of us: made of 60 equal minutes and pacing out the day in 24 equal measures, at all times of the year and in all parts of the world. Each year, measured by the Gregorian calendar, is the same for all of us: made of 365 days, each comprising the same number of hours and minutes, divided into the same number of weeks and months. We take all this for granted as though it were as natural as the sun rising in the East.

Time that is divided into discrete, globally consistent units can be measured and counted uniformly. The units become a tradeable commodity. We are all familiar with the saying: *time is money*. We sell our clock measured hours for wages and – in theory, at least – the more hours we sell the more money we get. But most of us have little or no control over how our time is valued, or how much of it we must trade to earn a living. It has become 'normal' to spend between 35 and 45 clock hours in paid work each week, for somewhere between 45 and 48 weeks of the calendar year.

The rest of our time is assigned no monetary value whatever. It is not officially tradeable and, according to conventional economic wisdom, it is just a lost opportunity.

Some questions arise. How 'natural' is clock time? How accurately does it reflect the way we actually experience time? How 'natural' is the 40-hour paid working week? How accurately does it reflect the time we actually need to exchange for money? How much money is enough? Is our time worthwhile only when it is sold? How do we experience and value the time we do not sell?

And what would happen if we exchanged less of our time for money? Suppose, for example, we did paid work for 30 instead of 40 hours each week? Life would certainly be different. Perhaps it would be better – for people, for the planet and for our beleaguered post-industrial economy. If that were so, how could we change our habits of thought and practice, our regulations and institutions, to build a new consensus about what makes a 'normal' paid working week?

You will find these questions tackled in these pages by a range of authors offering a rich mix of expertise. They were brought together by the new economics foundation (**nef**), following the publication of our report *21 Hours*. In this we proposed a radical redistribution of paid and unpaid time, calling for a slow but steady move towards shorter and more flexible hours of paid work, with the provocative end-goal of a 21-hour week. We set out evidence-based arguments as to why such a shift would bring substantial social, environmental and economic benefits. The report received such a wide and enthusiastic response that we were encouraged to convene a major conference at the London School of Economics in 2012, followed by an expert seminar where we discussed early drafts of the essays in this book.

Why time matters

The economist John Maynard Keynes famously predicted in 1930 that rates of productivity, driven by technological change, would rise so rapidly that by the twenty-first century no one would need to work more than 15 hours a week. He was right about a lot of things, but spectacularly wrong about that. Certainly, productivity rates have risen dramatically since the 1930s. But in the last three decades, workers' share of the surplus has not grown at the same rate. Meanwhile, markets have developed – globally – by encouraging people to buy and consume more and more. Faster cars, bigger houses, more furniture, 'convenience' foods and labour saving devices, gadgets galore, copious clothing and cosmetics, toys for children, toys for adults, flights and foreign holidays. All these things have become 'normal' accoutrements of everyday life in the rich world, and aspirational goods for many in the developing world.

To afford rising levels of consumption (from our diminished share of productivity growth), we have had to keep on working long hours. By 2011, on average, all people of working age in the UK were putting in 36.3 hours' paid work a week, while those working 'full-time' were clocking up 42.7 hours.[1] In the United States, people work much longer.[2] Even so, many have found their wages too low to meet the costs of all the shopping required of them to stoke and service the capitalist economy. So they've been encouraged to borrow money, shedloads of it. The need to service their debts locked them even more tightly into long hours of employment, while the banks turned their high-risk credit into dodgy 'derivatives' and gambled them away on the global markets.

We all know what happened in 2008. By this time, people on lower wages had accumulated debts they could not repay, however many hours they worked; and the banks ran out of ways to hide their losses. The global economy plunged into an unprecedented crisis, from which it has yet to 'recover'. Millions lost their jobs in the wake of the crash and now have no paid work at all. The wealthier elites emerged unscathed. The widening gap between the rich and the poor, the powerful and powerless, is one of the dirtiest scandals of the twenty-first century.

Running alongside this economic drama, hand-in-hand, has been the rapid rise of greenhouse gas (GHG) emissions, accelerating climate change and the steady depletion of the earth's natural resources – mainly a consequence of the high-rolling consumerism of the rich world. In a nutshell, people have been working long hours to earn money to buy stuff that's made and used in ways that inflict profound and irreversible damage on the ecosystem on which all life depends.

It's clear that time, money, consumer goods and planetary boundaries are interdependent. The lines on the graphs are heading in the wrong direction. That's a very good reason to think again about time and to change the way we value and use it, whether it is traded or not. Time is not just money. It is far more precious than that.

Time beyond growth

In her opening essay, Juliet Schor argues that countries in the rich world cannot continue to grow their economies if they are to reduce greenhouse gas emissions to sustainable levels. We must face up to a future with little or no economic growth. One of the worst effects of a flat-lining economy is usually high unemployment – but this can be offset, to an extent, if people work fewer hours. Schor proposes that workers, especially above-average earners, should start negotiating annual increments due from increased productivity (where this occurs) in terms of more time rather than more money. This, she argues, will help to keep more people in employment and to erode the prevailing ethos that attaches higher pay and status to those who work longer hours. It will also help to reduce greenhouse gas emissions. People who work shorter hours tend to have a smaller ecological footprint. This is not just because they are earning less *pro rata* and therefore have less money to buy energy intensive stuff. It is also because they have more disposable time, which makes it possible to live at a different pace and to think again about what life is for and how much money is enough to live a good life.

Robert Skidelsky picks up this theme. He argues that we must develop a shared understanding of what constitutes a 'good life' and suggests seven elements: health, security, respect or dignity, personality, friendship, harmony with nature and leisure. There are two political requirements, he says, for moving towards a good life: first, to create a 'market in hours' so that workers have more control over how much labour to supply, and, secondly, to remove the pressures to consume that currently distort people's decisions about how much time to spend in paid employment. He suggests legislation to support a progressive reduction in paid working hours, combined with further curbs on advertising, and a consumption tax that falls heavily on luxury items. Only by pursuing the goals of a good life, says Skidelsky, can we escape from today's rat race, where accumulating money and stuff has become an end in itself and where much of our consumption is pathological.

Tim Jackson points to another, related pathology: 'squeezing time though the frame of productivity growth to increase output in the economy'. He suggests we relinquish our 'fetish for labour productivity'. There are some jobs and professions where working faster and faster makes no sense at all. Think of teachers, doctors, nurses, carers, actors, musicians. The quality of their work depends not on producing more per hour of human labour, but on irreducible inputs of time. In conventional economics they count for little because they can't sensibly increase their productivity. This, says Jackson, comes 'perilously close to the lunacy at the heart of our growth obsessed, resource intensive, consumer economy': a whole set of activities that could provide meaningful work and contribute valuable services are written off as worthless. Yet an economy built around the exchange of human services rather than the relentless throughput of materials would be far more sustainable. Questioning how we experience and value time would help us think differently about productivity, Jackson observes. Time has malleable qualities: 'More things can happen in a very short space of time doing absolutely nothing, than can happen in a very full working day, working as hard as you possibly can.'

Time beyond 'efficiency'

Beyond our 'common sense' understandings, time has a multitude of meanings, functions and effects. As Barbara Adam argues, long before time became associated with the fixed regimes of clocks and money, it was – and remains – associated with 'life, change and difference'. All times are *not equal*; context matters, including season, place and infinitely varying circumstances. Crucially, social relations are not characterised simply 'by time as abstract exchange value, but also by time as gift in the context dependent interactions between spouses, lovers and friends, carers and the cared for'. When people give time to one another, they do so according to a very different set of principles from those involved when they sell time for money. They have a different take on past and future: think of parents and children, or friendships based on years of shared experience. There are, says Adam, two equally unquestioned sets of assumptions about time: one is time measured in discrete units by clocks and calendars; the other is time subject to the multiple rhythms of nature, evolution and human relations. The first is a relatively recent construction; the second predates the first, underpinning, interweaving and surrounding it. But in modern economics, politics and employment practices, the first entirely blots out the second – because 'only as an abstract, standardised unit can time become a medium for exchange and a neutral value in the calculation of efficiency and profit'.

When time is money, speed matters a lot. The more work that is squeezed into a unit of time, the greater the efficiency and profit. This conflicts sharply with other realms of experience, such as caring for children or practising a musical instrument, where using more time rather than less can yield far more valuable results.

The idea of speed as a means to efficiency has come to dominate our lives in ways that were unimaginable only a few decades ago. Mark Davies considers how new mobile technologies, online consumerism and social media are transforming everyday experience. In our 'curiously hurried lives', our perception of time has become 'so acutely accelerated that we live in a series of fleeting episodic moments… characterised by a series of seemingly disconnected intensities'. We are under growing pressure, as individuals, to consume, to be efficient and productive, and to connect and communicate. This is apparently made easier for us by increasingly speedy and sophisticated technologies. But the pace of technological 'progress' simply piles on the pressure. We are online for much of our waking hours – to work, to buy or to interact with others at any time, anywhere, often 'multi-tasking' to squeeze more into the same passage of time. It gets quicker and easier to buy stuff, so we buy more and more. We can mass-produce social relations on a global scale with minimal investment of time, physical exertion or emotional engagement. So we have more and more 'friends', with whom we communicate more and more. We can work not just in the office but in bars and cafes, in bedrooms, kitchens and bathrooms, on trains and planes, day and night. So we work more and more. Almost imperceptibly (no one has made much fuss about this) the digital revolution has crashed open the barriers between work time and home time, and hugely increased the scale of activity that can be accomplished in a single moment.

In other words, while we count out units of time according to the old industrial clock, which still ticks away in our heads, most of us in the rich world and growing numbers in the developing world live by a very different set of time rules: much faster, much less compartmentalised, much more intense. Perhaps we have the impression of more control, flexibility and choice. But that's illusory and the price is high. Not only do we all seem much busier, lacking time to do things we want to do, but busy-ness attracts higher status: a desirable condition to which we should all aspire. Not only are we beset by more and more information, but we are also more easily bored; we are losing the capability to ponder slowly and think deeply. As Davies observes, knowledge has become 'a commodity to be consumed just like any other'. Not only do we have flimsier relations with friends we contact via social media, but this can mean we have less in the way of meaningful face-to-face contact, which is 'fundamental to an ethical life lived in the company of others'; more of us feel lonely and isolated, in spite of – or more likely because of – the amount of time we spend surfing the web and 'facebooking' other people.

Our hurried lives aren't making us any happier; rather the reverse. New technologies may be churning up the conventional boundaries between paid and unpaid time, but moving to a shorter standard working week could nonetheless open an escape route, by challenging contemporary values, and helping to change habits and expectations. As Davies says, it might help 'each of us to become citizens, carers and creators within our own communities, through reconnecting with other human beings in their physical (and thus moral) proximity'.

Economies of time and care

Time devoted to intimate personal relationships that develop through love, kinship, care and physical proximity has a different character from time exchanged for money. Valerie Bryson observes that it is fluid and open ended, revolving around being, doing and interacting, rather than simply getting things done. She argues that moving to shorter hours of paid work could help make significant strides towards gender equality. It would validate patterns of time use that are typically female. It would help to distribute caring and workplace responsibilities more equally between women and men. It would 'challenge the dominant temporal mind set of society, encouraging a relationship that is more appropriate to giving and receiving care'.

Without care, as Bryson says, society would collapse. Most of it is done by women, unpaid and invisible (or overlooked) by elites, who base notions of importance, normality and success on male paradigms and give lower status and reward to the 'roles, attributes and patterns of behaviour traditionally associated with women'. The time that women devote to caring and housework locks them into patterns of employment that are low paid, marginal, insecure and predominantly part time. But what if 'part time' became the new 'full time', with – say – 30 hours as the new standard? Think of all the time this would free up for men to share caring and housework. It could transform the distribution of choice and opportunity between women and men. Bryson is under no illusion that all men will readily accept such a 'radical inversion of dominant thinking', especially when it threatens their 'inherently fragile' masculine identity. But she argues that attitudes are changing: there is evidence that fathers are now more inclined to favour a more equal division of paid and unpaid labour. A shorter working week could overturn conventional ideas about which abilities are natural and which skills are valuable, as well as what's important, normal and successful. It might stimulate fresh thinking about how to value and organise work (such as caring) where success depends on quality of relationships and on processes that are inherently slow, rather than on speedy throughput. It could also ease the growing pressures on time poor families, as paid work becomes less secure and more intense.

People can be described as 'time poor' when their time is so thoroughly absorbed by earning a living, caring and other responsibilities that little or none is left to their discretion. Tania Burchardt demonstrates that how much 'discretionary' time an individual has depends on a combination of resources and responsibilities. Notably, levels of income and obligations to care for others have a strong influence. Discretionary time is an important measure of an individual's 'substantive freedom' – that is, what you are capable of doing with the resources available to you, in order to pursue your personal goals. Burchardt develops a model to investigate the balance of resources and responsibilities available to people in different circumstances. She finds several factors that – singly and combined – may diminish discretionary time. These include having low educational qualifications, having many and/or young children, being single and being disabled. The crucial point here is that moving towards a shorter paid working week will not alleviate time poverty on anything like an equal basis, because people have different degrees of control over their time, depending not just on the number of hours they are expected to work in a particular job, but also on their income and responsibilities. Typically, a lone mother with a low wage job would not necessarily have more 'freedom' if her hours of paid work were reduced. How far the potential benefits are realised – and by whom – 'depends critically on what other policies are put in place'. Affordable child care and a higher hourly minimum wage could help to ensure that the benefits are more evenly distributed.

Economies of time use and climate change

Efforts to reduce paid working hours have, until now, focused mainly on achieving social goals, such as a better 'work–life' balance, and economic goals such as avoiding redundancies and retaining skills in the workforce in recessionary times. They have less often focused on environmental goals. But, as Juliet Schor has noted, it is becoming increasingly urgent to fend off global warming and there is some evidence that a shorter working week could help to reduce GHG emissions – by helping to change energy intensive patterns of behaviour by individuals and businesses. Martin Pullinger asks whether policy can 'reconcile diverse environmental, social and economic goals whilst being tailored to respond to the needs, preferences and capabilities of different demographic groups and different employment sectors'. Comparing the UK and the Netherlands, he models the effects of work time reduction on GHG emissions, showing the differences between income groups in three scenarios: a 20 per cent reduction in hours equivalent to a four-day week; a number of new career breaks for care, study and other purposes, and a combination of the two. The effect on emissions is greater in the first and third scenarios and, in all three, it is far greater for higher earners.

The estimated cuts are significant, but the contribution of lower income groups is negligible. It may therefore be tempting to focus on reducing hours for those at the upper end of the income scale, as this would cut more carbon and would also help to reduce the pay gradient between lower and higher earners. On the downside, however, it would intensify the time dimension of inequality identified by Burchardt: lower earners would still be poorer and they would also have less discretionary time. Pullinger reviews a range of policy options, combining rights to shorter hours and career breaks with increased support for lower earners in what he calls a 'green life course approach'. Above all, he points to the need for careful analysis and customisation, tailoring policies specifically for environmental gains as well as for fairness and accessibility.

If spending less time in paid work appears to reduce GHG emissions, can we safely conclude that using time instead for unpaid work and leisure will be more environmentally friendly? Well, up to a point. Angela Druckman and her co-authors analyse emissions related to different activities and find (not surprisingly) that 'a simple transfer of time from paid work to the household may be employed in more or less carbon intensive ways'. A significant proportion of carbon is 'locked up' in basic household provisioning, such as how we cook, shop, care and commute. Some household activities, such as reading, playing games, or simply spending time with friends and family, have relatively low emissions, while some pastimes – particularly those involving travel – are carbon heavy. Strategies to encourage low carbon activities would 'have to navigate the subtle and sometimes not so subtle differences that characterise people's use of leisure time', which are closely bound up with gender and identity. Druckman *et al* agree about the danger of deepening inequalities and the need to make 'appropriate changes in underlying and supporting physical and social structures'.

Learning from other countries

Working hours have been reduced in different ways in different countries, with various motivations and effects. Over the last two centuries, as Anders Hayden points out, reductions have reflected a wide range of objectives:'higher quality of life for employees, creating and saving jobs, gender equality, reducing work-family conflicts, ecological sustainability, and workplace modernisation. 'There are often tensions between these goals. For example, where business interests predominate, work time reduction may lead to the same amount of work being compressed into fewer hours, or to people having less choice over when they put in their hours. Such arrangements may reduce 'time poverty' but they would be unlikely to improve quality of life or to reduce work-family conflicts.

What is striking from Hayden's review of working time across Europe is the wide variety of arrangements and trade-offs, responding to different pressures and interests. Some enhance workers' own needs for flexibility, choice and security; others give the advantage to employers. Some privilege particular groups of employees at the expense of others. Some are negotiated, others imposed by law. Some are more likely than others to reduce GHG emissions, or to retain skilled employees in the workforce, or to improve gender equality. In short, social justice, environmental sustainability and a flourishing economy are possible consequences of shorter paid working hours, but *not* inevitable. It all depends on how it's done. And there are plenty of real-life examples – of good and bad practice – from which we can learn.

The French experience of a 35-hour week is a case in point. This was introduced by the two 'Aubry' laws (named after the then Minister for Employment, Martine Aubry) in 1998 and 2000. Dominique Méda traces the political manoeuvring behind the legislation, the different goals and effects of the two laws, and public responses to them. The first, says Méda, aimed to reduce unemployment and share out jobs, while the second 'did less to reduce the working hours of individuals, than to make their hours more flexible, largely to the advantage of employers'. Workers responded differently according to their experience: when and how their employers introduced and managed shorter hours; their personal circumstances (parents with young children and in managerial roles reported much more favourable effects); how far their work had been intensified; whether they felt they had been consulted; and how much control they retained over their time. There is no evidence, says Meda, to support the claim that the innovation undermined the 'work ethic' in France or reduced productivity. A substantial proportion of employees reported better working conditions as a result of the 35-hour week, which survived efforts by Nicolas Sarkozy to abolish it during his term as president. Méda's findings confirm that the devil is in the detail – and the politics – of a shorter working week.

Cutting to the chase

So far we have learned, from these essays and from **nef**'s earlier work, that there are no simple equations between shorter paid working hours and social, environmental and economic gains. It is complicated by a vast range of variables – including income, gender, culture – and the complex ways in which different policies and habits, role and responsibilities, and interests and institutions interact.

But some certainties can be pulled from the tangle of ifs, buts and maybes. Here are just four. One: moving to shorter hours of paid work across the labour force would be more likely than not to encourage slower and more sustainable patterns of living. Two: it would be more likely than not to release more time for men and women to fulfil caring responsibilities. Three: some countries have demonstrated that it is possible to have significantly shorter average hours than, say, the UK and US. Four: there is no correlation between shorter average paid working hours and the strength of a country's economy.

Andrew Simms and Molly Conisbee offer a provocation to challenge conventional assumptions about time. They propose a four-day week coupled with rapid expansion of green spaces for cultivation in urban areas. They call it 'National Gardening Leave' and argue that using time differently, for purposes other than earning money, can bring manifold benefits. Of course not everyone has a garden, but it would nevertheless help to 'resolve the paradox of overwork and unemployment'; it would give people more time to be better parents, carers, friends and neighbours (as well as gardeners) and – crucially – it would help to safeguard the environment. They argue that it could help us all to get off the treadmill of energy intensive consumerism that drives us, as Tim Jackson puts it, 'to spend money we don't have on things we don't need to create impressions that won't last on people we don't care about'. More urban greenery, more local food production and more community-based gardening would all contribute, say Simms and Connisbee, to the well-being of people and the planet. They point to the state of Utah, USA, where all public service employees worked a four-day week in a brief but popular experiment, and to a city analyst who found that cutting down to four days greatly improved his quality of life: 'You may get 20 per cent less pay but you get 50 per cent more free time.' Whether the extra free time is for gardening or not, the nub of their argument is that, with all the caveats, the call for a shorter paid working week deserves serious attention and bold imagination.

A *zeitgeist* issue

It is an argument that will not go away. Judging by the huge volume of response it generates whenever it is aired through the media (as it is increasingly), nearly everyone has an interest in time. Some feel they have too much of it on their hands; others that they are impossibly busy. Many wish they had more hours to call their own, or to spend with their children or elderly parents. Some can see retirement bearing down on them and wonder how to cope with 'doing nothing' (which is how not working for money is routinely understood). As these essays have demonstrated, we are interested in time as not just a matter of seconds, minutes and hours – or even just as something associated with paid work – but as something that we experience, value and utilise in various ways that are largely unnoticed and unexplained. And, as Barbara Adam says: 'all times are not equal'.

If there is now a gathering momentum behind the idea of moving to shorter hours, it is for at least three reasons. One is the fading lure of consumerism. There's good evidence that, beyond the point of meeting life's necessities (albeit a changeable concept), buying more stuff doesn't enhance our well-being and it's increasingly apparent that needless consumption is taking an impossible toll on finite natural resources. Another reason is that more and more people are aware of being caught in a profound and prolonged crisis: we have a global economy that is damned if it grows (because of the likely negative impact on climate change) and damned if it doesn't grow (because of the likely negative impact on jobs and income). Crisis provides a strong incentive to think afresh and seek out alternatives.

A third reason is this. The 'problem that has no name', as Betty Friedan called it, is ready to be named again. The phrase was used by Friedan in 1963, to describe the way women felt obliterated by an unquestioned division of labour and purpose, which they had not chosen and could not control. Her book *The Feminine Mystique* has often been credited with launching the 'second wave' of feminism, which raged through the later 1960s and 1970s. Fifty years on, the problem is only marginally different. It is less about enforced joblessness and housework; more about the pressures of paid work and caring. It is still about the combined impact of under-valued responsibilities and stifled opportunities, locked in place by the gendered distribution of paid and unpaid time.

Nowadays women are expected to go out to work and bring home a wage, but they must do so in ways that interfere as little as possible with, first, caring for children and, later, caring for ailing parents – and often both at once. They are under-valued in the workplace when they do so-called 'part-time' jobs, which attract lower wages and status because they are not seen as proper (that is, 'full-time') employment. The formal economy could not survive for a moment without the work women do at home. Yet in the terms of the formal economy, this work is un-valued and largely unnoticed: a problem that has no name. It is an absurd situation that is ethically indefensible and politically unsustainable. Moreover, it is avoidable.

Making the transition
Reducing hours of paid work for men as well as women would loosen the bolts that hold up the edifice of gendered inequalities. It would make it possible to manage an economy that isn't growing without widening income inequalities, by sharing out the work and keeping more people in paid jobs. It would challenge accepted notions of 'normality', changing aspirations and patterns of behaviour that are wrecking the planet and failing to improve human well-being. Looked at this way, time offers a powerful lever for change, with huge scope for helping to build a sustainable future.

No one here is suggesting that it will be easy to shift to, say, 30 hours as the new standard working week, or that there are no bear traps along the way. The most important next step, in our view, is to address the problem of low pay. There is no point trying to cut hours of paid work if the poor suffer first and most. This is an issue that **nef** is beginning to address, but it needs to be tackled from several angles: what is 'fair' pay and what's a reasonable ratio between high and low pay in any organisation? What is a reasonable minimum wage or 'living wage' for workers who put in 30 rather than 40 or 50 hours a week? What must governments, employers, trade unions and political campaigners do to achieve levels of pay that are compatible with social justice and sustainability?

Another important goal is to explore ways of improving incentives for employers. Many of them currently assume that shorter hours would threaten their capacity to manage staff effectively, to increase productivity and to remain competitive. This is partly a matter of learning from successful economies where employers routinely manage workers on shorter hours. It also requires parallel strategies for training (so that work can be shared among people with the requisite skills), while managers learn to deal effectively with job-sharing, shift patterns and other arrangements for combining larger numbers of workers that are each doing fewer hours per week.

As I was writing this introduction I received an unsolicited email from Qaiss Dashti, who works with the UN Development Programme in Kuwait. He had read about **nef**'s case for a shorter working week and wanted to tell us this: 'In the month of Ramadan in the Middle East all companies reduce the working hours from eight hours to five hours for

30 days, and surprisingly we all finish our work like it's an eight hour work day. We even discuss this between ourselves as employees: how a shorter day is much better and makes us more positive and willing to use the rest of the time for sports or family, and I guess it reflects back on our performance at work.' His account suggests that shorter hours can be uncontentious, productive and popular, once a pattern of working time is established as 'normal' and culturally acceptable.

A third challenge is to find ways of achieving incremental change while building popular support. We have always maintained that a reduction in paid working time is something to be pursued gradually over a decade or so. We have seen that there's a wide variety of policies adopted by different countries for reducing working hours. Several of the authors here make suggestions about how to get started in the right direction. Overall, there would seem to be three entirely plausible and promising strategies, which could be mutually reinforcing. The first is to trade productivity gains for a bit more time each year rather than just for money, as Juliet Schor suggests. This will work better for some kinds of employment than for others where (as several authors note) increasing productivity is neither possible nor desirable.

A second strategy is to follow Belgium and the Netherlands by enshrining in law the right to request shorter working hours and the right to fair treatment regardless of hours worked. Accordingly, employees would be able to apply for shorter hours, within agreed parameters, while employers would be obliged not to withhold permission unreasonably. It would be unlawful to discriminate unfairly against individuals because they do shorter hours. This would help to improve flexibility for workers and to establish shorter hours working as an entitlement rather than a deviation from the norm.

A third strategy is to initiate hours reduction at both ends of the age scale. At one end, following the Netherlands, young people entering the labour market for the first time could be offered a four-day week (or its equivalent). That way, each successive cohort adds to the numbers working a shorter week, but no one has to cut their hours. Before long, there would be a critical mass of workers on shorter hours and others may want to do the same. At the other end of the age scale (following an idea suggested by **nef**'s earlier work) incremental reductions of working time could be introduced for older workers. For example, those aged 55 and over could reduce their working week by one hour each year. Someone on 40 hours a week at 55 would thus be working 30 hours a week by 65 and – if they continue in paid employment – 20 hours by 75. The shift would be gradual and universal, enabling people to carry on working for more years without undue stress and strain, adjusting slowly but steadily to shorter hours and then to retirement. Over time, the cohorts of youngsters who enter the workforce on a four-day week will reach 55. Thirty hours will be the new standard. Gradual reductions could continue for older workers: deciding how exactly this is done can be left to future generations.

These essays offer a range of evidence, analysis, insights and ideas. Together, they make a powerful contribution to the debate about time, work and moving towards a sustainable economy. They are a beginning, not an end: we welcome responses, critiques and additions from all who read the book. We cannot say at this stage whether – or how fast – this growing body of knowledge will inspire widespread practical action. We think it should be soon. Time will tell.

Essay summaries

Why we need a shorter working week

The triple dividend
Juliet Schor

How people divide their time between paid work and other activities can make a big difference to their ecological footprint, to rates of unemployment, and to the quality of individual and community life. Current policies on work and time, based on the relentless pursuit of economic growth, are failing to avert catastrophic damage to the environment. Juliet Schor examines the structural connections between hours of work and ecological impact, paying attention to the effects of both scale (size of economy) and composition (mix of products produced and consumed). She presents new findings on the impact of working hours on ecological footprints and CO_2 emissions across OECD countries, showing how working hours are a powerful lever for reducing eco-impact. She then suggests how to make the transition to a shorter-hours economy, trading productivity growth for time not just money, as people's preferences adapt to changing circumstances.

Two commentaries

In search of the 'good life'
Robert Skidelsky

Why did Keynes' 1930s prediction that people today would be richer and work far fewer hours fail to materialise? Robert Skidelsky suggests it's because more people find work enjoyable and satisfying than in the past, because many are afraid of unstructured leisure time, and because wages are low and too few think they can afford to work shorter hours. The promise of consumption and of good things to come keeps people striving for more. If we get off this treadmill to consume, we might reconsider what we mean by the good life. We could then work out how to structure our institutions to make it easier to live such a life. The basic components of the 'good life' include health, security and dignity. The political means of achieving this goal include job sharing, a reduction in working hours, wealth distribution, changes in taxation and basic income. Overall, there is such a thing as a good life, it can be achieved, but it is not the life that is currently on offer.

The trouble with productivity
Tim Jackson

Tim Jackson challenges the argument that more labour productivity inevitably leads to more growth and more jobs. What happens if we let go of our fetish for labour productivity? How can we make an economy work when it isn't chasing continual growth? We might rely less on technological developments and more on building an economy around care and culture. These are areas where it seldom makes sense to apply conventional productivity goals. . Once we understand that human labour is at the heart of society, we can think again about how we experience and value time. It's a slippery commodity. More things can happen in a few minutes of doing absolutely nothing, than in a very full day of hard-pressed paid employment. . Thinking differently about time helps us to reassess the value of what we do and to challenge assumptions about productivity and growth.

Challenging assumptions

Clock time: tyrannies and alternatives
Barbara Adam

Time is not what most of us think it is. Our assumptions are taken for granted and rarely explored. We think of time measured by clocks and calendars: standardised units applied uniformly across the world. This is how we've come to think of time as money. It's a resource that can be priced and traded. Barbara Adam shows how time has become a commodity in capitalist economies, with speed highly valued as a route to greater productivity and profit. In fact, time is much more complex and flexible, experienced variously, depending on context. All times are not equal. Season, hour, place and condition all make a difference. If we unearth and challenge our assumptions about time, we can shed new light on gender, age, sustainability and social justice – and this will help us to develop alternatives to current working practices.

Hurried and alone: time and technology in the consumer society
Mark Davis

The idea that we are 'saving time' through digital communications is deeply flawed and ultimately self-defeating. In fact we just get busier, cramming more and more into our increasingly hurried lives. And, paradoxically, the more we communicate via digital technologies, the more likely we are to become isolated and lonely. Our rapidly intensifying relationship with new technologies triggers two significant questions. How can we live an ethical life in relation to others if we communicate with them in ways that are more virtual than real? And how can principles of equality, democracy and self-determination survive if we live our lives primarily as individual consumers, rather than as citizens, carers, or creators? What's required, argues Mark Davies, is fundamental change to the way in which we use and distribute our time. As we go on trying to living faster, in pursuit of more money to fund more consumption, we are living not just on borrowed money, but also on borrowed time.

Redistributing paid and unpaid time

Time, care and gender inequalities
Valerie Bryson
A radical reduction in 'normal' paid working hours could help to redistribute responsibilities between women and men. It would leave more time for giving and receiving care. Care work, whether paid or unpaid, is time-consuming and mainly provided by women. The time involved in caring for others tends to go unnoticed and be under-valued. Carers are economically penalised, entrenching gender inequalities. Bryson contrasts the temporal logic of the workplace with the interpersonal flow of time in caring relationships. She argues that this flow of open-ended and contingent time is very different from the time-is-money logic of the capitalist workplace. A redistribution of paid and unpaid time would benefit men by enabling them to live in a less pressurised, more care-oriented society with a broader understanding of masculine identity. Women would benefit from a new 'standard' paid working week that better supports and rewards their existing patterns of life.

Time, income and freedom
Tania Burchardt
People should have enough free time to pursue their own goals and interests, while securing an adequate standard of living and caring for those who depend on them. The number of hours of paid and unpaid work required to secure a standard of living and to provide for the care of family members, varies significantly between individuals, depending on their resources and circumstances. This essay offers a conceptual model of how resources interact with responsibilities to produce a range of feasible time allocations, which in turn generate combinations of disposable income and discretionary free time. Some groups need much greater support than others – in terms of public policy interventions – to ensure that a shorter working week helps to narrow, rather than widen, inequalities.

Shorter hours, smaller footprint

The 'green life course' approach to designing working time policy
Martin Pullinger

What level of environmental benefits could arise from reductions in paid working time? Martin Pullinger proposes a 'green life course' approach that supports and encourages working time reduction to benefit people and the environment. He models the impact on greenhouse gas emissions and household incomes of different scenarios in the UK and the Netherlands, involving a 20 per cent reduction in the weekly working hours of full time workers. He assesses the impact on incomes, expenditure and carbon footprints of households, estimating the total change in national greenhouse gas emissions. He then looks at the implications for the design of working time policy, drawing lessons from the Netherlands and Belgium.

Time, gender and carbon: how British adults use their leisure time
Angela Druckman, Ian Buck, Bronwyn Hayward and Tim Jackson

To meet the UK's challenging targets for cutting greenhouse gas emissions, we will need to change the way we do things in our daily lives. One way is to focus on the goods people buy and on shifting to alternatives with a lower impact. But it is just as important to change the way people use their time. This essay explores the greenhouse gas emissions per unit of time spent on different types of unpaid activity, such as household chores and leisure pursuits, by an average British adult. How does time use vary within households, and how does this affect carbon emissions? The authors find that leisure activities are more closely associated with lower carbon emissions than non-leisure activities, and that a higher proportion of an average man's carbon footprint is due to leisure than an average woman's. They consider the implications for the varying roles carried out in different types of household, with carbon as a potential marker for social justice, along with the implications for policies to reduce working time.

Learning from other countries

Patterns and purpose of work-time reduction: a cross-national comparison
Anders Hayden

A range of goals have driven recent reductions in paid working time: the pursuit of better quality of life, creating and saving jobs, gender equality and ecological sustainability. There are tensions and synergies between these goals. For example, a shorter working week can help to reduce carbon intensive consumption and to generate more employment. Anders Hayden provides an overview of work-time reduction in different countries, mainly in Europe. He outlines the main ways to pay for shorter working hours, and examines the pros and cons of different work time options, along with barriers and opportunities for change.

The French experience
Dominique Méda
What happened when the French government introduced a 35-hour week? Dominique Méda considers the impact of the two 'Aubry laws' to reduce working hours in France in 1998 and 2001. The first aimed primarily to create more jobs, but triggered opposition from employers. The second worked more in employers' interests, giving them more flexibility to decide when workers would put in their hours. The laws were generally popular with parents of young children but popular support for them eroded as workers found, after the second law, that they had less control over their time, with tasks compressed and labour intensified. Méda argues that changing individualised assumptions about working time would make it easier to share work and to open up space for public deliberation. A serious reduction in working hours would also challenge gender norms, as men and women rebalance their time investment across public and private spheres, leading to an increase in men's responsibility for household and family tasks and thus to an improvement in the public status and financial independence of women.

A provocation

National Gardening Leave
Andrew Simms and Molly Conisbee
Britain would be better off if we all spent less time at the office. Andrew Simms and Molly Conisbee make the case for a new, voluntary scheme to introduce a shorter working week, called *National Gardening Leave*. The authors propose giving people entering new jobs (and, where possible, those in existing jobs) the option of working a four-day week, while adapting a wide range of available spaces for the rapid expansion of gardening, both productive and aesthetic, in Britain's towns and cities. They argue that these changes would make people happier and healthier, the economy more resilient, and communities stronger and more convivial places to live. It would create the space to cultivate a society where individuals and communities could flourish, grow together and plant the seeds of a better Britain.

Why we need a shorter working week

The triple dividend

Juliet Schor[1]

The failure of conventional approaches: technology, efficiency and marketisation

In recent years, the conversation about what is necessary to achieve sustainability has expanded substantially around the globe, including in the rich countries of the global North. In the political mainstream, the emphasis has been on technology, efficiency, and the expansion of markets to put prices on nature and on the pollution from using natural resources. There is a variety of reasons for this approach, but an important one is that addressing these variables does not challenge the central economic logic embraced by these nations: market-driven capitalism in a context of continual growth. Technological changes hold out the promise of future profitability, as new technological paradigms are typically associated with higher profit rates and expanded market opportunities. Efficiency gains are effectively reductions in price, which in turn raise profits. And focusing on technology, efficiency and markets keeps the conventional mechanisms for job creation in place, thereby obviating major transformations in how populations gain access to work and income.

In the case of climate change, the debate on how to reduce emissions focuses on policy instruments such as carbon taxes and carbon markets, public investments in alternative energy sources, and green financing for renewable energy projects or forest preservation in the global South. In terms of eco-systems, the pricing of their 'services' is designed to place nature more firmly inside the market nexus. To the extent that growing demand for energy or resources is addressed, it is mainly through the mechanism of reductions in derived demand for energy through efficiencies that do not reduce demand for the final good associated with that energy (e.g. a warm home being produced with less energy loss) or through reductions in waste (e.g. DEFRA's campaign against food waste)

Governments especially have been loath to attempt to achieve reductions in environmental impact by shifting the preferences of households or firms, although there have been some tentative steps in this direction. They have been even less willing to constrain national purchasing power. Among academics, policy analysts, and governments, technology, efficiency and market-oriented policy innovations have been the preferred path.

However, the farther we go down this road the more its shortcomings have emerged. In Europe, the carbon market has nearly collapsed, and in the United States it has not begun. Emissions continue to increase, and while China is blamed for its recent surge in fossil fuel use, the conversation has failed to take into account the fact that a significant part of Chinese emissions should be accounted for in the consumption totals of importing countries.[2]

Rebound effects are another factor that cast doubt on the ability of the technology/efficiency/market approach to achieve necessary reductions in emissions or pressure on ecological resources. York et al[3] have found that in the US, China, Japan, and Indonesia, higher ecological efficiency – measured as ecological footprint per dollar of gross domestic product (GDP) – has been associated with higher consumption. Studies of trends in energy use across a variety of countries also find that energy consumption tends to rise even as efficiency improves.[4]

Both the science and the ethics of climate change imply that high carbon legacy countries such as the US and the UK should reduce their emissions to near zero by 2050.[5] As the daunting arithmetic of this trajectory becomes more transparent, the failure to address demand for energy and other natural resources is less and less justifiable. Indeed, as countries begin to grapple with real targets for emission reduction, the evidence shows that technological and efficiency gains have not been keeping up with increases in demand. This is a point that has been made by numerous analysts, among them **nef** (the new economics foundation) itself.[6] A compelling case study of the UK by Anders Hayden shows that once carbon targets were legislated in 2007, the realisation that growth as usual was not compatible with them became much more widespread. Indeed, under business-as-usual (BAU) growth assumptions, the entire carbon budget for the UK would eventually be needed by one sector (aviation) alone.[7]

The debate about growth

The failure of wealthy countries to make enough progress in reducing emissions has begun to create cracks in the consensus around the necessity of economic growth in a number of countries. This conversation has been most active in Western Europe, and especially in those countries that are taking climate targets most seriously. Hayden's work on the UK during the Labour years has described a 'dance' in which policymakers and campaigners approach the possibility that growth may not be possible but also back away at the enormous implications of that view.

And yet in the last six years, mainstream voices have begun to question the feasibility of continued growth. These include Lord Stern himself, who has raised the question of whether wealthy countries can continue to grow and still keep humanity at safe atmospheric concentrations of GHGs, as well as Lord Giddens. The widespread attention paid to Tim Jackson's report for the UK Sustainable Development Commission, 'Prosperity without Growth?',[8] was indicative of the growing legitimacy of this conversation, as is the success of a number of **nef** publications and initiatives. In France, former President Sarkozy enlisted two Nobel Laureates in economics (Joseph Stiglitz and Amartya Sen) to report on the shortcomings of GDP as a measure of national progress. In Germany, a three-year commission on alternatives to GDP is an indication that a process of de-centering growth is now underway. In Austria, government conferences on 'growth in transition' have shown that new paradigms for economic security and well-being are being discussed across the continent.

Not surprisingly, the global financial crisis and its aftermath have pushed the climate conversation to the sidelines and changed the nature of the conversation. But austerity policies are failing repeatedly and economic and political turmoil is increasing. This troubling trajectory also undermines the case for growth, on grounds of its feasibility rather than desirability. As the years since the 2008 collapse go by without a solution other than fiscal pain, high unemployment and austerity, faith in the possibility of growth is on the wane. Perhaps de-growth is asserting itself willy-nilly.

Among environmentally-oriented scholars in the social sciences, the critique of growth has followed a different trajectory, beginning in the 1970s with the publication of the Dennis and Donella Meadows' *Limits to Growth*[9] bestseller. While there were relatively few adherents to this position after the economists' critique, interest in slow or no-growth economies expanded by the mid-1990s and has developed more rapidly in the 2000s. There is now a considerable literature advocating the rejection of a growth-centric society and economy.[10] In general the argument is that global North countries should reduce their carbon emissions and materials footprints by a combination of technological change and constraining or reducing demand. The global North is assumed to be wealthy enough to absorb the costs of slow or zero growth, in contrast to poor countries, which need to expand output to raise living standards for large populations living in poverty. This approach goes by a number of names, such as steady-state economics, sufficiency, new economics, *de-croissance* or de-growth. Increasingly, shorter hours are at the core of this conversation.

The controversy about working hours reductions in a struggling economy

The idea of reductions in working hours may be a hard sell at the moment. After all, the conventional wisdom is that hard times should lead us to work longer and more intensively. On the face of it, the work intensification approach makes sense. The downturn has reduced incomes and growth. For the individual, trying to work more is rational. Future conditions in the labour market are more uncertain. Expected future returns on financial assets are lower. Housing prices are deflating. At the national level, if a country is in decline, putting its nose to the grindstone makes intuitive sense.

But doing so risks triggering forces that operate in the other direction. At the moment, Organisation for Economic Co-operation and Development (OECD) countries and many other parts of the world are experiencing glutted labour markets. Labour economist Richard Freeman estimates that over the last decade, the effective global labour supply has about doubled, from 1.46 to 2.93 billion.[11] If people offer more hours to the market, wages fall and unemployment rises. Excess supply of labour also undermines investment and innovation, which decelerate when labour is plentiful relative to capital.

Orthodox critics reply that this argument – that unemployment should be solved by reducing hours – suffers from a mistake of logic, which has been called the 'lump of labour fallacy'. They think the market can always provide enough work for whoever wants it.

Under current conditions, that type of reasoning makes little sense. Most of the OECD now finds itself in a Keynesian trap of weak aggregate demand, ineffectual monetary policy and investor pessimism. And reducing budget deficits makes these problems worse, as the last few years' experience has shown. In a number of countries, such as the US, corporations are sitting on enormous cash reserves unwilling to invest them, which means that falling wages won't clear the labour market and lead to more employment. In the UK, which has taken the austerity path, GDP is far below what is predicted for a recovery at this stage.

In the models of neo-classical economics, times like the present are assumed away. But when we're actually living through them, we need to recognise that measures that result in higher hours can be counterproductive. That's because they create more unemployment and in turn spur investor pessimism. Similarly, responding to shortfalls in pension programmes by asking people to stay in the labour force more years further dis-equilibrates the market by creating more demand for a limited number of jobs. Proponents of the 'lump of labour fallacy' view miss the fact that sometimes there are impediments to job creation. We happen to be living through one of those painful periods.

For most of the last 150 years, the nations of the global North have kept their labour markets in balance partly by continuous reductions in hours of work.[12] These increases in leisure time have been funded by higher labour productivity. But recently, the US, Japan and the UK have done far less of this than other wealthy countries. In the US hours have actually risen, which is part of why unemployment and underemployment are so high there. Work time reduction has become another causality of the wrong-headed economics of austerity.

The need to dramatically decelerate greenhouse gas emissions and to equilibrate the labour market are goals that can be achieved in part through reducing hours of work. To see why, I turn to a thought experiment: what if wealthy countries fail to grow, either because they can't manage it or because they choose not to in order to meet carbon targets? What does this imply for hours of work?

Some possible ways forward

Let us now consider the case of a country that can only meet its carbon targets by reducing its growth in output to low levels or even to zero. (Assuming that technological improvements are ongoing, but they are insufficient to meet carbon targets without controlling demand.) In this case, reduced work time becomes an imperative. To see why, consider the alternative: a path of low growth without changes in working hours. Productivity would be rising, but domestic consumption and investment would be more or less fixed. Companies would take their profits, and rather than invest them domestically to expand production, they could shift them to global South countries whose carbon budgets allow increased investment. This could stabilise consumption-related emissions of global North countries. It would also result in a rising share of ecological space being allocated to the South, an outcome that most justice-based solutions to shortages of global ecological space would agree is a fair outcome.[13] In such a scenario, the economies of the global North would remain more or less intact, but the benefits from their productivity growth would be transferred to the global South. Thus, northern populations would not receive higher wages despite working more productively. While there is certainly a moral argument that this would be a fair trajectory based on the historical transfers of wealth from south to north as a result of colonialism and neo-colonialism, it will be politically difficult to sell to northern populations.

While this scenario may sound dystopian, it may be a reasonable description of what has already been happening in the US, where wages have stagnated or fallen for many workers, living standards are in decline, and investment is shifting to low-wage countries. This is not happening for ethical or ecological reasons, but because the power to dispose of the economic surplus has become concentrated in the hands of a small group of powerful corporations and individuals. It is possible that Western European workers may suffer a similar fate, particularly if the economics of austerity continue to dominate the European debate. However, this trajectory will prove to be one that generates discontent and backlash and is hardly a democratic response to ecological overshoot. It is not a direction of choice.

Therefore, let us consider the alternative preferred by most ecologically-oriented economists, which is to stabilise GDP growth and use productivity gains to reduce annual hours of work and/or the length of working lives. To see why shorter hours are necessary under this scenario, let's begin with the assumption of a constant labour force (i.e. no population growth or immigration) and annual increases in labour productivity growth. If GDP growth is zero, then the normal workings of the economy will lead to progressive reductions in the demand for labour. Each year a given level of output can be produced with fewer hours of work, on account of productivity growth. Firms can lay off workers, because they are no longer necessary to produce the (stable) level of production that is required in the no-growth economy. If productivity rises by three per cent annually, three per cent of workers will be made redundant under this scenario. Each year the pool of unemployed will grow, and the labour market will become increasingly disequilibrated. Clearly, this is not a feasible scenario. Peter Victor's macro-model of the Canadian economy[14] yields this type of outcome, under a plausible set of conditions.

And yet, if a nation cannot grow because it needs to meet its carbon targets, this is what is likely to happen unless the labour market is regulated. That is because firms face a variety of incentives to hire fewer people and have them work longer hours rather than have a bigger workforce with shorter schedules.[15] Because many labour costs are paid on a per person basis or do not vary with hours, longer hours are more profitable for employers. Many labour costs are per person, such as health insurance (in countries such as the US), hiring and training costs, and employer taxes for pensions, unemployment insurance funds or worker disability. In many countries, these so-called 'hours-invariant' costs have grown substantially and comprise a rising fraction of total compensation. And there are other reasons employers prefer long hours of work. They can be a way for employees to signal their commitment and loyalty. Employees who work more hours have more income loss if they are fired, so they tend to be easier to discipline. Indeed, a variety of explanations suggest that employers dislike hours reductions. Perhaps the strongest piece of evidence for this claim is that to be offered short hours jobs, employees typically have to accept severe penalties in wages, benefits and career mobility, which are common characteristics of part-time work.

Let us now return to our hypothetical no-growth economy. The alternative to an expanding pool of unemployed is to reduce hours of work for all employees, by an amount equivalent to the rise in productivity growth. This will avoid increases in unemployment, and provide the benefit of more free time across the labour force. However, to achieve this outcome there must be countervailing factors to firms' preferences for longer schedules. In the past, the most important countervailing factors have been strong labour unions and government commitments to use hours reductions to avoid unemployment.[16] Going forward, policy interventions that restructure the incentives facing firms will be necessary. There are also tax and subsidy policies that can provide positive incentives for firms to reduce hours, such as tax credits for avoiding layoffs, and use of the unemployment insurance system to facilitate shorter hours of work.

Another option is to shift workers into earlier retirement, and thereby concentrate hours reductions among the most senior members of the labour force. This circumvents the financial disincentives associated with work sharing for firms, and avoids the problem of rising unemployment. However, a reduction of the retirement age poses other challenges. One is that public pension plans in many countries are facing actuarial shortfalls. There must be a funding mechanism to protect the solvency of pension systems if their liabilities are to rise. Furthermore, unless earlier retirements are voluntary or pension benefits are generous, this path means that senior employees are forced to take on a disproportionate share of the adjustment burden. While this may be fair, given the high consumption of the current senior generation and its attendant contribution to emissions and eco-degradation, adding generational differentiation to a shorter hours programme must be done with care.

Thinking from the other direction: how hours reductions affect ecological outcomes

So far I have considered the question of hours from an assumption that ecological considerations have created a consensus for slow or zero growth, and argued that hours reductions are likely to be a necessary component of a successful steady-state economy. We can also explore the question from the other direction. If a country is able to achieve a path of progressively shorter hours of work, what are the likely ecological impacts?

To date, there is relatively little research on this question. However, there are at least two reasons to believe that shorter hours are conducive to reductions in ecological and carbon footprints and eco-impacts more generally. The first is the 'scale effect'. It is best illustrated by considering how the economy behaves over time. Assume that the economy is experiencing annual increases in productivity as well as yearly improvements in the carbon and eco-intensity of GDP. If productivity growth is used to produce extra output and incomes, then the rates of decarbonisation and de-materialisation are reduced by the extent to which production is increasing. On the other hand, if productivity growth is used to reduce hours of work, and output is stabilised, then carbon and materials reductions will all go to reducing footprints, without being 'erased' by rising output. The key issue here is controlling aggregate demand, and through it, the volume of production. Because shorter hours are an alternative to higher incomes, they affect the scale of production. Therefore, we expect that countries which take a higher fraction of their productivity growth in the form of hours reductions will have lower ecological and carbon footprints, all other factors being equal.

In addition to their connection to household incomes, hours are also an economic resource in themselves, because time is always an input into all forms of consumption and domestic production. As Gary Becker and Kelvin Lancaster noted more than 50 years ago[17] households consider both their income and time budgets when they make choices and engage in activities. This is a point that is typically left out of economics teaching, and is often neglected in research, perhaps because it complicates simple welfare conclusions. However, it is widely accepted in theory. Households who are richer in money and poorer in time will opt for time-saving activities and products, such as faster transportation. We call this the 'compositional effect'. Activities with low eco and carbon intensity seem to be more time consuming, although there is relatively little research on this question.[18] However, transport is a clear case in which speed is associated with higher energy costs. Food preparation is likely another.[19] An expected effect of shorter hours of market work is that households will opt for more sustainable activities, products and practices, and thereby have lower ecological footprint (EF) and carbon footprint (CF), holding income and other factors constant. We anticipate that the scale effect will be considerably larger than the compositional effect, but that both should be operating over time.

There are relatively few studies of the relationship between hours of work and EF and CF. At the micro level, this is likely to be due to the absence of datasets that combine time use, expenditure and environmental impact. One study of Swedish households that put together disparate datasets[20] finds that a one per cent decline in hours of work results in a decline in energy consumption and GHG emissions of 0.8 per cent. Their analysis of what we have termed scale and composition effects finds that the former is much larger. The compositional effect is significant, but its size is small. A French study finds that households who work longer hours have more eco-impact, in particular via larger houses, higher transport expenditures and restaurants and hotels.[21]

At the macro level, there are only a few studies. David Rosnick and Mark Weisbrot focus on the relation between overall energy consumption and productivity. They find larger effects than the Swedish study (1.3 per cent reduction in energy use for every 1 per cent decline in hours).[22] Anders Hayden and John Shandra[23] use the ecological footprint as a dependent variable in a cross-national regression of 45 countries and find that higher average hours per person are associated with a higher national footprint, controlling for income, GDP, productivity and other standard variables. Ideally, however, one would look at both data over time and across countries, i.e. a pooled time-series, cross-sectional model.

I have recently completed a study using such a pooled model for high-income OECD countries from 1970 to 2007 with co-authors Kyle Knight and Eugene Rosa. The results reported here are from our joint work.[24] Our full model, technical discussions and details can be found in our paper.

We estimated three dependent variables – ecological footprint, carbon footprint (which is just the carbon portion of the EF), and national CO_2 emissions.[25] Our independent variables are average annual hours of work, as reported by the Conference Board in the Total Economy Database, which is a harmonised international dataset that includes annual hours, GDP, labour productivity, and population. Hours of work are intended to measure actual hours worked, including overtime and excluding holidays, vacation and sick days.

Table 1 below is derived from our results and displays the size of the scale and compositional effects for the three ecological measures. The main finding is that there are large and significant impacts of working hours on carbon footprints, emissions and eco-footprints. Countries with longer hours have more emissions and environmental pressures. Countries that have reduced their hours of work also reduce pollution and ecological degradation. Take for example, the carbon footprint. If a country were to reduce its annual working hours by four per cent (roughly half a day's work per week), its carbon footprint would fall from two effects. The scale effect yields nearly a 15 per cent reduction (14.6 per cent to be exact). The composition effect adds another 8.6 per cent. A much more substantial 25 per cent reduction in hours of work yields about 2.5 more pollution reduction. The impacts for eco-footprint and carbon emissions are a bit smaller, but still important.

The one case that diverges is the composition effect of CO_2 emissions, which is not statistically significant. This is likely due to the fact that the CO_2 measure includes emissions caused by production in a country, including exports, but excludes the emissions associated with imported goods. This is in contrast to the eco and carbon footprints, which are consumption measures. Because OECD countries have been outsourcing their emissions to countries in the global South and to Eastern Europe, the footprint and CO_2 measures diverge. We believe this is why the results vary between the two models. (See our paper for more discussion of this issue.)

It is also worth noting the impacts of some of our control variables, which are not reported here. While many analysts believe that ongoing structural changes in economies, such as the shift away from manufacturing towards services, are an environmental panacea, our findings suggest this is not the case. These variables have relatively small impacts, and in the case of urbanisation they are not significant. Theories such as ecological modernisation or the environmental Kuznets curve, which contend that the process of growth and development causes counter-trends that reduce environmental degradation, are not supported by our analysis. By contrast, de-growth is supported, because higher GDP is associated with higher eco-impact. Countries that hope to reduce emissions and impact need to introduce structural reforms. Labour market policies that reduce average hours will be among, if not the most effective, they can institute. In contrast to policies that deliberately slow productivity growth, shorter hours of work yield high benefits to populations.

Preferences and pathways to hours reductions

If reductions in working hours are an environmental *desideratum*, but there is no national consensus for slow or zero-growth, how can countries get onto a shorter hours path? To answer this question, it may first be useful to consider what the trajectory of hours has been over the last half century. In Table 2, I present the estimates of annual work hours for seven countries from the Conference Board data – France, Germany, Italy, Japan, the Netherlands, the UK and the US, and the total change over the period 1950–2010. A number of observations stand out. First, all countries have experienced declining hours of work, but the magnitude of reduction ranges from about 40 per cent in Germany to 11 per cent in the US. Continental Europe especially has been able to achieve large and sustained reductions in hours of work over this 60-year period.

The US is an historical exception in that its early role as a leader in work time reduction has ended and it is now a laggard nation. In fact, according to data from household surveys rather than employers, hours of work have actually risen in the US, in contrast to the small decline recorded here. The difference is likely due to multiple-job-holding and unpaid hours worked, which are counted in the household surveys, but not in the employer data.[26]

The failure of US hours to fall more is especially surprising given the country's high productivity, which is ordinarily a major predictor of trends in hours. Part of the difference is likely to be due to the fact that in the US hours reductions happened earlier, so that by 1950 US hours were considerably below the other six countries. Today the US ranks as a high hours nation with Japan and Italy, countries that are 50 per cent less productive on an hourly basis. But in the US, the structure of costs, particularly high health care costs, mitigates against work time reduction, as does the weakness of unions.

By contrast, Germany and the Netherlands experienced very significant declines in work time over the 1950–2010 period – 41 and 40 per cent, respectively. The magnitude of reduction was somewhat lower, but still large for France, Italy, and the UK, at 26–31 per cent. Looking just at the 1975–2010 period, the uniqueness of the US is even more pronounced, given its small decline of 3.4 per cent, in comparison to roughly ten per cent in Italy and the UK, and 20 per cent in France, Germany, Japan, and the Netherlands.

Table 3 shows annual changes in productivity growth and hours. Productivity growth is central to the dynamics of work time on both the firm and the worker side. For firms, unless reductions are financed by increased productivity (or lower wages), they will raise costs. For workers, the role of productivity is also key and is discussed below. As we see, only in unusual cases does work time reduction occur in the absence of productivity growth, such as Italy since 2000.

GDP per hour increased more in the early period than during the last decade in all countries but the US. And as we would expect, the extent of hours reduction also slowed, in some cases to about half its previous annual rate. However, everywhere but in the Netherlands, the fraction of productivity growth taken as hours reduction actually increased during this period, perhaps because policies to reduce hours are characterised by inertia. The uniqueness of the Dutch results may be due to their already having reduced hours considerably before 2000 and to their status as the lowest hours country. Again, the US is an outlier. The fraction of productivity it used to reduce hours was small (15 per cent) in comparison to other countries' shares of 25–43 per cent. US workers realised small, or if household data is correct, no gains in free time despite the country's relatively high productivity growth. Italy is also an outlier case, because it failed to stem the momentum toward shorter hours even as its productivity growth collapsed in the decade from 2000–10. This is bound to result in rising costs, declining profitability, an investment slowdown and poor economic performance.

While the importance of productivity-financed work time reductions is perhaps obvious from the employer side, it is also central to a politically viable path for employees. To see why, let us consider some basic findings about employees' preferences and attitudes towards work and income. There are two kinds of questions that researchers ask employees about work time. The first is a generic question which does not tie hours preferences to money, and merely asks whether hours are too high, too low, or just about right. A second standard question asks whether the respondent would prefer more hours/more income, same hours/same income, or fewer hours/less income.

We now have data on work time preferences for a large number of countries from the International Social Survey Programme (ISSP). A useful survey is from Reynolds[27] who focuses on the first kind of question (i.e. no explicit discussion of changes in income). He argues that tying preferences to monetary considerations in survey questions is the wrong way to understand how people feel about their working hours, because those connections are not straightforward for many workers, including those who are paid by salary, and because money is only one aspect of work. On the other hand, this question formulation leaves unspecified the extent to which respondents themselves are attaching monetary outcomes to the options. Using the 1997 survey, Reynolds analyses data from the US, Japan, West Germany and Sweden. His basic findings are that the fraction of workers who desire more work is small, and ranges from a high of 21 in the US, to 6, 10 and 7 per cent in Japan, West Germany and Sweden, respectively. By contrast, a large percentage indicate that their preference is the status quo, with 42, 49, 52, and 32 per cent respectively, in the US, Japan, West Germany and Sweden choosing this option. That leaves 37, 46, 38, and 61 per cent preferring to work less. I have had similar findings with my own surveys of US workers. The National Survey of the Changing Workforce, which last asked about this issue in 2002, found that a majority of US workers preferred to work less, and the median amount of money they would be willing to give up was ten per cent.[28] Reynolds' analysis of demographic difference in preferences finds that high education is a strong predictor of the desire to work less across all countries. Preferences by age and family structure differ by country. Similarly, Stier and Lewin-Epstein,[29] using 27 countries included in the International Social Survey Programme (ISSP) data, find that people with higher education and income prefer to work less, as do older people. Conversely, those with less education and lower income prefer longer hours.[30]

By contrast, questions that specify income losses find that shorter hours are far less popular. Otterbach, using ISSP data from 1985 through 2010 finds that large majorities of workers prefer their existing hours/income choice.[31] In the UK, for example, 70 per cent of respondents expressed satisfaction with their status quo in 2005, while 20 per cent wanted more hours and 10 per cent preferred fewer. In the US, 63 per cent preferred the status quo, while 30 per cent wanted more hours and only 7 per cent wanted fewer. Similar findings are longstanding, and can be interpreted in at least two ways.[32] On the one hand, the mainstream economic explanation is that people have fixed hours/income preferences and the market mainly delivers what they prefer. The alternative explanation is that preferences are adaptive and adjust over time to the structure of hours and income that the market delivers. The two views can be roughly described as workers getting what they want, or wanting what they get. In the early 1990s, when Schor proposed the endogenous preference model for work time, there was relatively little data to support it. However, since then the findings of behavioural economics as well as work done by the MacArthur Network on Endogenous Preferences suggests the relevance of this line of argument.[33]

This brief survey of the pattern of preferences suggests a feasible path for work time reductions and also some directions to avoid. First, involuntary reductions in work time that are accompanied by reductions in income will be resisted by large majorities, and will be almost impossible to sustain politically. They will not be popular with workers, nor will employers have a vested interest in this path. This path lacks a viable politics.

Second, reductions in work time that are income neutral will likely be popular, but they will have more complex economic consequences, because they are associated with increases in real hourly wages. To some extent the cost increases can be offset by higher per hour productivity, which seems to be a common consequence of work time reductions, although there is little research on this issue. However, over time progressive reductions may lead real wages to rise in excess of the productivity increase. That in turn, may lead firms to relocate production to lower-wage areas or substitute capital for labour, and in the long run to a negative employment effect. The extent to which this will happen is an empirical question on which we need more research.

A more promising path is to use productivity growth to finance reductions in hours of work. This is a gradual strategy that can be compatible with the needs of firms and the preferences of workers. With respect to the former, productivity-financed hours reductions are broadly cost-neutral, particularly once hours-invariant costs are transformed into hours-variant ones. If firms do not raise wages, but instead offer productivity-financed shorter schedules, their competitive position will not be adversely affected, a result that is supported by the strong competitive position of Germany and Netherlands, two low-hours countries. For competitiveness, hourly labour costs are the relevant variable, not the number of hours per worker.

For employees, keeping incomes steady and progressively reducing hours allows policymakers to exploit a key asymmetry in preferences found in behavioural economics and first noted by Schor for hours of work in *The Overworked American*. People value income they have already received much more strongly than the option of future income. The path of stable income and rising time off the job allows the strong preferences for more free time found in the studies cited above to be satisfied without income loss. Furthermore, because income is a positional good and free time is not, on average workers will experience a higher utility gain with a path of rising free time than rising income.[34] In the first instance it may be useful to concentrate on reducing hours among high income/high educated employees. Their preferences for free time tend to be stronger, and their lifestyles are more ecologically intensive. Policies such as job sharing and four-day workweeks will be most useful among this group, rather than shorter working days. Finally, evidence that income inequality leads to higher working hours suggests that equality-enhancing measures of all sorts will facilitate the shift to a shorter hours regime.[35]

Conclusion
Evidence of the failure of standard approaches to achieve emissions and footprint reductions is mounting. The next phase of approach must therefore be policies that maintain or reduce aggregate demand, given its paramount role in driving environmental impacts. Hours reductions are a necessary mechanism for successfully achieving a stabilisation of demand, because they allow the labour market to remain in equilibrium during the process. Furthermore, time off the job is a benefit to individuals, so that employees are able to reap gains from the policy, a political necessity in a democratic society. In this paper I have surveyed recent trends in hours, analysed their relation to ecological outcomes, and briefly discussed the nature of preferences for work and income. The conclusion of that discussion is that a path of taking productivity growth in the form of shorter hours is the most economically and politically feasible path to follow. Concentrating at first on those demographic groups with the highest value for free time, namely older workers with higher educations and incomes, may be a good initial strategy.

Table 1: Predicted change in dependent variables for 10% and 25% reductions in work hours with all other variables held constant

	Scale effect[a]		Compositional effect[b]	
Reduction in work hours:	10%	25%	10%	25%
Ecological footprint	-12.1%	-30.2%	-4.9%	-12.2%
Carbon footprint	-14.6%	-36.6%	-8.6%	-21.5%
Carbon dioxide emissions	-4.2%	-10.5%	ns[c]	ns

[a] Scale effect refers to estimates based on models that control for population, urbanisation, manufacturing as a percentage of GDP, services as a percentage of GDP, labour productivity, and the labour participation rate.

[b] Compositional effect refers to estimates based on models that control for population, urbanisation, manufacturing as a percentage of GDP, services as a percentage of GDP, and GDP per capita.

[c] Ns indicates that the estimated effect of work hours on carbon dioxide emissions in this model was not statistically significant at the 0.10 level and is therefore not reported here.

Source: Knight, Rosa and Schor 2012b

Table 2: Annual hours of work per worker: A 1950–2010 cross-national comparison

	France	Germany	Italy	Japan	Netherlands	U.K.	U.S.
1950	2,241	2,387	2,469	2,076	2,299	2,218	1,909
1975	1,953	1,808	1,934	2,076	1,740	1,928	1,755
1990	1,705	1,576	1,867	2,031	1,508	1,783	1,724
2000	1,591	1,471	1,861	1,838	1,435	1,712	1,739
2010	1,552	1,408	1,778	1,735	1,377	1,650	1,695
Change '50-'10	-689	-979	-691	-341	-922	-568	-214
	/ 31%	/ 41%	/ 28%	/ 16%	/ 40%	/ 26%	/ 11%

Table 3: Average annual rate of change in productivity and work hours: 1975–2000, 2000–10, and 1975–2010

	Average annual growth of labour productivity, %			Average annual change in working hours, %			Decrease in hours as % of productivity gains		
Years	1975–2000	2000–2010	1975–2010	1975–2000	2000–2010	1975–2010	1975–2000	2000–2010	1975–2010
France	2.70	1.12	2.20	-0.86	-0.44	-0.69	31.9	39.3	31.4
Germany	2.74	1.20	2.26	-0.87	-0.52	-0.75	31.8	43.3	33.2
Italy	1.99	0.02	1.43	-0.18	-0.48	-0.25	9.0	24.0	17.5
Japan	2.84	1.77	2.52	-0.52	-0.45	-0.53	18.3	25.4	21.0
Netherlands	1.95	1.27	1.74	-0.82	-0.38	-0.70	42.1	29.9	40.2
UK	2.81	1.43	2.38	-0.52	-0.39	-0.48	18.5	27.3	20.2
US	1.61	1.79	1.63	-0.08	-0.27	-0.13	5.0	15.1	8.0

Two commentaries

In search of the 'good life'

Robert Skidelsky

I am a no day a week professor, having retired. In economics, work has always been regarded as painful. It's the cost you pay to get the products you want. That's why in standard economic analysis people prefer leisure to work. They only work up to the point where the marginal utility of one extra hour of income is worth no more than one extra hour of leisure. That's the way the problem is approached. You can draw the conclusion that as productivity improves, people will work less as it takes less effort to obtain the same basket of goods. This is indeed what Keynes wrote in his 1930 essay – *Economic Possibilities for Our Grand Children* – that today people would be 4 or 5 times richer and would work on average 15 hours a week. In fact they work 40 hours a week.

What's happened is that an inverse relationship has developed between income and work: the richer you are, the more hours you work. There are few rich who are idle and few who are idle are rich. Why has the trade-off between income and leisure that Keynes predicted not occurred? There are several possible explanations.

The first explanation is the joys of work. Work has become much more agreeable, not so much a pain as a pleasure. It involves much less physical toil, there's more variety and workplaces are more agreeable: work is fun. That's why people don't give it up. Google, for example, operates by facilitating a fun environment for its workforce.

The second explanation is fear of leisure. Workaholics dread the weekend. For some, a vacation is a four-weekend reminder of what a loser they are. While not the main explanation, there is a sort of compulsory sociability about work that some people treasure and they wonder what to do if it's removed.

The third explanation lies beneath the averages. It's true that average per capita of income has grown, but inequality of income has also grown with the richest gaining most from the growth of the economy. This suggests that a large number of workers are not receiving salaries consistent with the marginal product of their labour. The structure of the labour market is such that many workers are not in a position to determine their own real wage; they are off their supply curve – which is straightforward Marxist theory of exploitation – and not as rich as the average implies. Indeed, median income has been repressed.

The fourth explanation relates to the labour market. In a number of books Juliet Schor argues that competitive pressures force employers to work their existing workforces harder, rather than spread the work around. She also makes a very important point: that the inability of workers to realise their desire for less work and more leisure is compensated by the illusive promise of more consumption. The power of capital in the labour market has its exact counterpart in the growth in the pressures of consumerism.

The final explanation has more to do with the rather reprehensible feature of human nature: we tend to be insatiable. In any society there seems to be some relational aspect of consumption, which is what causes people to want more and more. Economists have identified three forms of this. First there are 'bandwagon' goods, desired because others already have them: all my friends have iPods so I must have one too. Then there are 'snob' goods, desired because others don't have them. Such goods cater to the desire to be different, exclusive, to stand apart from the crowd. They're not necessarily expensive but mark their possessors out as having exceptionally good taste. Bandwagon and snob goods are not mutually exclusive. Many snob goods mutate into bandwagon goods, leading to their abandonment by true snobs.

Overlapping with both snob and bandwagon goods are 'Veblen' goods, so called in honour of the great theorist of conspicuous consumption. Veblen goods are desired because they're expensive, known to be expensive and in fact function as advertisements of wealth. Some houses in Chelsea cannot do without underground swimming pools.

In sum, if you are trying to analyse reasons why productivity has not been translated into more leisure time, the most important are the structure of power in the economy and this fact of human nature: relational competition in consumption.

How do we escape from the rat race? The problem has two aspects. The first, an intellectual problem, is to work out what one might mean by the good life: a life desirable in and of itself, regardless of whether it is actually desired. This is important for it is only in relation to such an idea that the notion of having enough can be given a fixed meaning; without it we have nothing but the shifting fortunes of the Jones' to direct our wants. The second, a political problem, is to structure our institutions to make it easier for people to actually lead a good life.

It's not as difficult to reach agreement on the nature of the good life as one might imagine. The intellectual and religious leaders of the pre-modern world all had similar ideas on the subject. While these varied to some extent – some stressed political participation, others communion with nature, civic debate, family happiness, etc. – they all shared the common idea that there was something such as the good life and that money was only a means towards it. To want more than enough was considered a vice: the vice of avarice. To accumulate without end, like Mrs Marcos and her shoes, is plainly pathological.

A lot of our consumption is pathological. Money is for something so that to mindlessly pursue it – to get more and more of it in order to buy more and more stuff – is rather like saying that the purpose of eating is just to get fatter and fatter. One should regard that as a pathological condition. Keynes certainly did, writing that 'there will come a time when the love of money as a possession as distinguished from the love of money as a means to the enjoyments and realities of life will be recognised for what it is, as a somewhat disgusting morbidity – one of those semi-criminal, semi-pathological propensities that one hands over with a shudder to specialists in mental disease'. He thought that by this time, 100 years hence, the mindless pursuit of wealth would indeed be regarded as pathological. But far from it, it is regarded as one of the great signs of our progressive, dynamic, competitive civilisation. And so one has to try to recapture the idea that there is something called a good life, to which wealth is a means, and to orient our social institutions towards it.

I am writing a book with my son that identifies seven basic goods which an individual must possess in order to be said to lead a good life. These include health, security, respect or dignity, personality, friendship, harmony with nature and leisure. Notice that happiness does not appear on this list. For happiness in the standard modern sense of a pleasant state of mind is not necessarily a good at all. It all depends on what one is happy about. Oscar Wilde once wrote, 'To sweep a slushy crossing for eight hours on a day when the east wind is blowing is a disgusting occupation...To sweep it with joy would be appalling.' So the idea of making everyone joyful as an aim of social policy must be rubbish.

What are the political requirements for moving to a good life? Firstly, there is a need to alter the labour market and create a market in hours so that workers have greater choice over how much labour to supply. Secondly, there is a need to remove the pressures to consume which distort people's decision to supply labour. So in technical terms, we should (a) try to get workers back on to their labour supply curves and (b) to shift those supply curves downwards on a permanent basis.

There are different sets of policies that one can imagine doing these things. The simplest would be to promote work-sharing by legislating for a progressive reduction in the hours of work, for example by limiting weekly hours and/or increasing statutory vacation times. There is a long history of such initiatives from the Factory Acts of the nineteenth century to the European work-time directive, which our government opted out of. That is why the British work more than most Europeans (as do the Americans) without any apparent gain. Such a framework is not totalitarian but would allow employers and workers to work out their own bargains in a flexible way.

An alternative would be to have a basic income, which could be financed by a tax on wealth. The rich have always lived off unearned wealth, so why shouldn't more people? And as society gets richer, there is more wealth to redistribute.

Now we turn to the other side of the story: pressures on consumption. A progressive tax system, in particular a progressive consumption tax, would deal with the distribution question and the consumption question at the same time. This is a very old idea and shouldn't be too difficult to administer, no more so than an income tax. A consumption tax that falls very heavily on luxury items would reduce the pressure to escalate competitive consumption upwards, which the luxury consumption of the rich now does.

Finally, advertising should be limited. People often say this is an unacceptable infringement of liberty but in fact the state already forbids many kinds of advertising, particularly of 'sin goods' like tobacco. And a lot of other goods are 'sin goods' but aren't defined as such. Advertising is a big problem, however, as it has migrated to the internet and if restricted in one area it will spread in others. Our society is organised on that principle. And unless there is an intellectual acceptance or – if you like – a spiritual acceptance that there is a good life and it is not the life that we are being offered, none of these reforms will be implemented, or they will be in such an emasculated form that they won't do any good.

The trouble with productivity

Tim Jackson

Society is faced with a profound dilemma. To refrain from growth is to risk economic and social collapse. To pursue it relentlessly is to endanger the ecological systems on which we depend for survival.

For the most part, this dilemma goes unrecognised in mainstream policy. It's only marginally more visible as a public debate. When reality starts to impinge on the collective consciousness, the best suggestion to hand is that we can somehow 'decouple' growth from its material impacts. Green growth – as this idea is called – will be all the rage at the 'Rio plus 20' conference this June.

The sheer scale of action implied here is daunting. In a world of nine billion people all aspiring to US lifestyles, the carbon intensity of every dollar of output must be at least 130 times lower in 2050 than it is today to have a hope in hell of meeting internationally agreed carbon targets. By the end of the century, economic activity would need to be taking carbon out of the atmosphere instead of adding relentlessly to it.

Never mind that no-one knows what such an economy looks like. The dilemma of growth, once recognised, looms so dangerously over our future that we are desperate to believe in miracles. Technology will save us. Capitalism is good at technology. So let's just keep the show on the road and hope for the best.

The reasons for this blind utopianism are easy enough to find. The modern economy is structurally reliant on growth for its stability. When growth falters, as it has done recently, politicians panic. Businesses struggle to survive. People lose their jobs and sometimes their homes. A spiral of recession looms. Questioning growth is deemed to be the act of lunatics, idealists and revolutionaries.

But shooting the messenger won't evade the dilemma. With oil prices clinging tenaciously to the once inconceivable $100 a barrel mark and carbon emissions rising faster than ever before, we need something more than wishful thinking to avert the calamities ahead. The policy mantra 'growth equals jobs' is frankly unhelpful when growth itself is not just unlikely but sometimes positively unpalatable.

More to the point, this mantra turns out to be false in general. The relationship between growth and jobs isn't direct at all; it's mediated by something called labour productivity: the amount of output delivered (on average) by each hour of work in the economy. So if labour productivity doesn't move, then sure, an increase in output leads to an increase in employment. But if labour productivity increases faster than output does, then unemployment can rise even with a rise in the GDP: hence jobless growth. Conversely of course if labour productivity stabilises or declines then it's possible for employment to rise even without a rise in the GDP.

At first sight this doesn't seem very comforting either. We've become so accustomed to see labour productivity as the engine of progress in modern capitalist economies. It's our ability to generate more output with fewer people that's lifted our lives out of drudgery and delivered us the cornucopia of material wealth – iPhones, hybrid cars, cheap holiday flights and plasma screen TVs – to which we would all very much like to become accustomed.

Let's leave aside here momentarily that one of the ways we've achieved this remarkable feat is by substituting capital (lots of clever technology) and material resources (fuel and other minerals) for people's time. And that in the process we've created a lot of the ecological problems we now have to solve. My point here is rather to draw attention to the structural demands imposed by ever rising labour productivity.

Put simply, the obsession with labour productivity means that if our economies don't grow, we risk putting people out of work, even without increases in the population. Higher unemployment generates rising welfare costs. Higher public spending leads to unwieldy levels of sovereign debt. Higher debts can only be serviced by increasing tax revenues from future income. We're literally hooked on growth.

This unhappy dynamic has recently prompted the revival of an old idea. If there's less work to be had in the economy, for whatever reason, then perhaps we should all just work less and enjoy it. As it happens, we've always taken some of the labour productivity gains in the form of increased leisure time. Working hours in the UK declined by 15 per cent between 1970 and 2005.

Reducing working hours further is the simplest and most often cited solution to the challenge of maintaining full employment with declining output. And it has a surprising pedigree. In an essay called simply *Economic possibilities for our grandchildren* published in 1932, John Maynard Keynes foresaw a time when we would all work less and spend more time with our family, our friends and our community. Every cloud has a silver lining? It's certainly a strategy worth thinking about, when growth is hard to come by.

But simple arithmetic suggests one further option for keeping people in work when demand stagnates. What happens if we relinquish our fetish for labour productivity? Sounds crazy at first. We've become so conditioned by the language of efficiency. Output is everything. Time is money. The drive for increased labour productivity occupies reams of academic literature and haunts the waking hours of chief executive officers and treasury ministers across the world.

In some places, this still makes sense. Who would rather keep their accounts in longhand? Wash hotel sheets by hand? Or mix concrete with a spade? Between the backbreaking, the demeaning and the downright boring, labour productivity has a lot to commend itself.

But there are places too where chasing labour productivity doesn't stack up at all. What sense does it make to ask our teachers to teach ever bigger classes? Our doctors to treat more and more patients per hour? Our nurses to rush from bed to bed no longer able to feel empathy and offer comfort. Compassion fatigue is a rising scourge in the caring professions, hounded by meaningless productivity targets.

Or to take another example, what is to be gained by asking the New York Philharmonic to play Beethoven's 9th Symphony faster and faster each year? Trivial though this example seems, it has its roots in another famous economic essay by the nonagenarian economist William Baumol. Analysing the dynamics of the cultural sector, he identified a general trend in modern service-based economies to slow down over time. Why? Because services require irreducible inputs of people's time. The phenomenon has come to be called 'Baumol's cost disease'. Low productivity growth sectors are the scourge of modern economies. In formal terms these enterprises barely count. They represent a kind of Cinderella economy that sits neglected at the margins of consumer society.

We're getting perilously close here to the lunacy at the heart of the growth-obsessed, resource-intensive, consumer economy. A whole set of activities which could provide meaningful work and contribute valuable services to the community are denigrated as worthless because they are actually employing people.

People often achieve a greater sense of well-being and fulfilment, both as producers and as consumers of these activities, than they ever do from the time-poor, materialistic, supermarket economy in which most of our lives are spent. And here perhaps is the most remarkable thing of all: because these activities are built around the exchange of human services rather than the relentless throughput of material stuff, there's a half decent chance of making the economy more sustainable.

Finally it is worth considering the quality of the work experience itself. Time is a strange commodity. The speed with which it passes depends on the quality of experience. This is as true of work as it is of leisure.

It certainly isn't just about work being bad and leisure being good (as economists generally suppose). Nor is it simply about the nightmare of vacation when you have built all your social standing and credibility around yourself as a working person. Both work and leisure can be either heaven or hell. At the root of the declining quality of working time is the pressure to create a continually growing economy in which productivity is squeezed, our working hours are more intense and our leisure lives are full of more carbon intensive shopping activities. This pathology – squeezing time though the frame of productivity growth to increase output in the economy – is at the root of these issues.

Once upon a time I even remembered this myself. When I started my working life it was up to me whether I went to work or not. Occasionally, I would choose not to go. Every now and then I would ask myself, what is the purpose of my working day? My purpose, broadly speaking, was to help reduce carbon emissions across the world. Sometimes then, particularly when it was sunny, I would weigh up the costs in terms of carbon emissions of travelling across London to work and instead go to the common, lie in the sun and read a book.

That's not an entirely trivial analogy. It's not naïve to ask ourselves what is the value of our time; and what is the quality of our experience in that time? When you begin to ask these questions you discover that time itself has some rather malleable qualities. It isn't always a simple division between work and leisure, good and bad, pleasure and un-pleasure: time itself is a slippery commodity. More things can happen in a very short space of time doing absolutely nothing, than can happen in a very full working day working has hard as you possibly can. Those kinds of questions enable us to think differently about time. And about productivity.

The one big remaining task is how to make an economy work when it isn't chasing productivity and continual growth. That's a task – fortunately for those of us working on it – that is almost insatiable in its appetite for working time. The bottom line is this: escaping the dilemma of growth may be less to do with technological utopianism and more to do with building an economy of care and culture. And in doing so, restoring the value of human labour to its rightful place at the heart of the society.

Challenging Assumptions

Clock time: tyrannies and alternatives[1]

Barbara Adam

Time forms a largely unreflected aspect of our daily working lives in the public and private sphere. To understand the politics of working time therefore demands that we render explicit what is currently implicit. To this end I first seek some answers to the question 'What is time?' before I address the issue of 'work time'. There is a vast literature on the subject of working time, spanning the entire range of the social sciences,[2] which I cannot review here. Instead, I select for attention some key aspects, which facilitate thinking about work through an explicitly temporal lens. These include the commodification of time, the valorisation of speed, and work in the shadows of the time economy. Such conceptual work on time is important as it forms a foundation on which alternatives to current working practices can be developed. Moreover, understanding the complexity of social time raises practical issues for the agenda of shortening working hours. It identifies previously hidden barriers and opportunities. It provides an enhanced anchorage for gender, age and environmentally sensitive approaches to work. And, finally, it sheds new light on sustainability and social justice.

What is time?

This question is rarely asked in Western industrial societies because our knowledge of time is largely implicit. When we focus explicitly on matter, space and time as key dimensions of thought and practice, we quickly realise that we know them in different ways. Matter is the stuff our world is made of: nature's and society's products. Space is the domain we operate in. It defines nations and wars are fought over their territories. For time, in contrast, there is no such equivalent: it is quite unlike matter and the 'wars over time' are far more subtle. That is to say, whilst the social relations of matter and space are negotiated explicitly in the realm of politics and policy, the social relations of time are left implicit, thus operate in a less accessible realm. Debates and disputes over working time form an exception to this rule. Yet, even here, the time involved remains largely taken for granted.

What then is taken for granted about time in a Western industrial society like Britain at the beginning of the twenty-first century?

- It is common sense that clocks and calendars measure time, which means that time is a quantity that can be given a number value.
- It is equally obvious that clocks and calendars divide time and that these divisions function as boundaries, such as years, days and hours, which structure our activities.
- Furthermore, we know that time is standardised into the 24-hour clock, which, in turn, is divided into equal hours where one hour is the same irrespective of season and place, that is, whether it is summer or winter in Italy, Ireland or Iceland.
- In addition, time is rationalised across the globe and divided into equal time zones.
- We do not question that time is a personal and public resource with a use value on the one hand and economic resource with an exchange value on the other, where employees sell their time and employers calculate their profit with reference to time as an economic resource.
- Daily experience teaches us that time is money and, associated with this socio-economic fact, that speed means progress, efficiency and cost effectiveness. The more work that can be produced in a given period, the higher will be the profit.

This cluster of implicit assumptions works together as an integrated, mutually implicating whole.

Simultaneously, however, there exists another set of equally unquestioned assumptions about time, which pertains largely to the natural environment, to embodied experience and to the private domain of social life. Moreover, this second set of assumptions is not necessarily compatible with the first set. And, because assumptions are implicit, these two sets tend not to be placed in relation to each other, which means the inherent conflicts and contradictions remain unchallenged.

Long before time came to be associated with the invariable time of clocks and money, time was, and still is, associated with life, change and difference.

- Without giving much explicit thought to the matter, we know that time has something to do with development and evolution, birth and death, growth and decay.
- Equally, we appreciate that time is tied to the movement of earth, moon and sun, which affects all life on earth and we take for granted that this movement is the silent pulse that structures our

being and makes us who we are: time-based and rhythmically constituted earthlings that are governed by patterns of activity and rest, work and play.

- Moreover, we experience daily that there is a direction to time – people age, cars rust, burning logs turn to ashes – and that these processes are not reversible.
- Finally it is obvious that nature is suffused not with one but a multitude of times, each appropriate to the plant, animal or ecosystem in question: the life time, metabolism and life world of an earthworm, for example, is irreducibly different from the life time, metabolism and life world of an oak tree or a polar bear. Each plant or mammal has a typical life span and a characteristic reproduction cycle.[3]

This second implicit knowledge base leaves us with very different assumptions from the first one. It tells us that all times are *not equal* and that context matters, which means that season, time, place and condition make a difference. It points to the fact that there is a *right* time for in/action and an in/opportune time to intervene. Importantly, when placed next to each other it becomes apparent that social relations are not just characterised by time as abstract exchange value but also by time as gift in the context-dependent interactions between spouses, lovers and friends, carers and the cared for. Equally, it becomes clear that time giving works to principles that differ significantly from those involved when time that is exchanged between people and/or for money in remunerated work or service relations. Finally, it becomes noticeable that both sets of assumptions include past and future as fundamental extensions to our present, but are played out differently depending on which set of assumptions is foregrounded at the time. In our daily lives we weave our way through these different sets of assumptions and live the inherent contradictions without giving much thought to the issues.

Matters are complicated further by our taking for granted that the first cluster of assumptions is primary and takes priority over the second set. It means that policies and employment relations are structured around a particular one-sided set of unquestioned assumptions, which disadvantage all those groups of people and activities whose primary time deviates from the dominant model. Not the variable time of life and death, growth and decay, of seasons and opportune moments, of hopes and visions for the future, but the abstract time of the clock where one hour is the same irrespective of context and emotion, is the dominant time that enters public policy and underpins the economic relations of work. Locally and globally, it is the invariable time, that goes round and round in a circle, which is imposed on the variable cycles of nature and social life. Moreover, only the quantitative, invariable, divisible time of the clock can serve as an economic exchange value. Only as an abstract, standardised unit can time become a neutral value in the remuneration of work and the calculation of efficiency and profit. As I demonstrate below, a whole raft of economic and social consequences arise from this skewed relation to time.

What are today taken-for-granted assumptions about time, however, are fairly recent historical developments, which are shared neither across the globe nor by all sectors and individual members of industrial societies. Rather, assumptions about time are historically, contextually and biographically unique, while being influenced by dominant public conceptions that become so normalised that they are considered a 'natural fact'. Naturalised, these assumptions are no longer recognised as historical constructions. What is currently implicit, therefore, needs to be lifted to an explicit level of understanding, so that negotiations over working time may be effective and achieve the stated goal of sustainability. Sustainability demands that we bring together what is currently separate and incompatible, using the opposing tendencies for common goals. In temporal terms this means looking explicitly at the times embedded in both sets of assumptions and consider them in relation to each other. From these very different sets of assumptions time emerges not as a single time but a 'time complex' that would best be described a 'timescape'.[4]

This timescape comprises the following elements:

- From life, seasonal, diurnal and clock-time cycles we get 'timeframes' that set boundaries within which events unfold and duration can be measured.
- While the natural cycles are fundamentally contextual and include directional change, the clock repeats the same unchangeable hours and minutes. For clock time, change would mean that the clock is telling the wrong time. 'Temporality', the changing aspect of cyclical repetition, is an aspect of time that belongs to the second set of assumptions associated with lived and experienced time. In nature everything is embedded in seasonal change: Spring returns but never exactly the same as in previous years. In addition to this repetition with change temporality encompasses unidirectional change processes: children grow into adults; adults grow old and die; cars rust.
- Change, in turn, is linked to the 'tempo', speed and intensity of processes and to the 'timing' of interactions. While tempo and timing are crucial and contextually unique in living processes, the tempo and timing of clock-time are pre-set by the designer. Here, variation in tempo and timing would mean a malfunction of the clock.

- Finally, human beings and fellow species are embedded in a 'past-present-future' continuum. For clock time, in contrast, past, future and the unique present are irrelevant.

From a timescape perspective, therefore, we can recognise that in their daily lives people *are* time; they live, use, know and create time in interaction. Embedded in their socio-natural environment, they are past and future oriented. They remember and anticipate, learn in the context of past experience and live their lives with purpose and motivation, hope and trepidation. Time for them is characterised by personal, social and historical timeframes, by the directional change of temporality and by contextual timing. The tempi and intensities of their activities can enhance or reduce their well-being. In their working lives, in contrast, people's lived temporal complexity is anchored in the time world of clocks where contextual uniqueness, change and variation have been abandoned for the abstracted simplicity of sameness. Only on the basis of this invariable, decontextualized clock time can time be translated into money and traded as an abstract exchange value. The distinction between the two sets of assumptions and the hegemony of clock time in public life have implications for work time practices and the proposed changes, which require further attention.

Work time

In the world of remunerated work, clock time is the precondition to paid for time. Only as an abstract, standardised unit can time become a medium for exchange and a neutral value in the calculation of efficiency and profit. Absolute decontextualisation is the prerequisite for time to be translated into and equated with money.

Karl Marx theorised this relation some 150 years ago. His analysis still stands and forms the basis for most of contemporary work on the 'commodification of time'.[5] His argument was as follows: for workers to be paid for their time rather than the goods and services they provide, time had first to become an abstract exchange value which needed to be differentiated from the use value of such goods and services. All the different products of work have use values that are always context and situation specific, as is clearly the case with, for example, the use value of a table, a coat, an operation and a pension scheme. However, when we want to exchange something for money, a third neutral value has to be introduced to mediate between the two. Unlike the use value, which is context and situation specific, this mediating exchange value has to be context independent. Time is the common, decontextualised value by which products, tasks and services can be evaluated, exchanged, traded and remunerated. Not the variable time of seasons, ageing, growth and decay, joy and pain, but the invariable, abstract time of the clock where one hour is the same irrespective of context and emotion, allows work to be translated into money and traded as a commodity on the labour market. Only in this decontextualised form can time become commodified on the one hand and an integral component of production on the other. The resulting equation of time with money has far-reaching consequences for the world of paid employment, which differ significantly for business and workers.

For business it means the faster something moves through the system the better it is for profit. Accordingly, efficiency and profitability are tied to speed. There is pressure to produce ever more in ever shorter time spans. Again, it was Karl Marx[6] who first theorised this process as time compression. He pointed out that governments have the power to limit working hours but have no jurisdiction over the intensity of work that is extracted from labour. Thus he argued, when laws are put in place to restrict or reduce working hours, capital tends to compensate for this with the compression and intensification of work, both of which are beyond legislative reach. Furthermore, when time is money any unused time is money wasted, hence the development of the 24–7 system with its demand for non-stop activity and availability at all times where, for example, computer operators in India respond to queries that have arisen for workers in the UK, which eliminates some of the time-and-money-wasting elements of sleep. This system requires flexibility not only to provide round-the-clock cover but also to respond to peaks and troughs in demand, which all too easily transforms promises of flexibility *for* the worker into flexibility *of* the worker. In addition, when time is money it makes sense to take business where the cost of work time is lowest, as this will yield the greatest profit. For corporations global mobility in search of profitability is a workable proposition because employees are replaceable in their various functions. That is to say, within the corporate system workers are interchangeable like functional parts of a machine. Importantly, when time is money, any working time that does not easily fit the commodified time of industrial employment is defined as 'other' and finds itself operating in the shadow of the dominant time economy of money.

For workers the situation is clearly very different. They constantly have to synchronise the two time systems and guard the socio-environmental limits of their lived time within the commodified time of work. For them time and place are contextual: when and where they work matters. All hours are not the same to them. It makes a significant difference whether they work during the day or at night, whether or not their non-working time can be networked and co-ordinated with the activities of relevant others and whether the 'free time' arises from paid work or is enforced through unemployment. Their capacity for flexibility is tied to their commitments to significant others and likely to vary over their working lives. Patterns of work and leisure, activity and rest matter to them, and so do the distances between their work, home, children's schools and public facilities. As contextual social beings rather than abstract entities, employees learn from the past and are motivated by their future. They build up loyalties and commitments, nurture relationships and develop specialist knowledge and skills over time. Past and future, therefore, are of significant relevance. Crucially, as members of communities and families, people are not exchangeable or interchangeable but are unique and irreplaceable in the contextual network of relations that make up families, work places and communities.

From this brief account of the different time systems that govern our working and private lives, we can see that the social times of workers are lived and negotiated in conflict because the different sets of incompatible times co-exist in friction and a hierarchy of status. Tensions arise in the interstices of the different temporal spheres, that is, between nature, society, home, work, production, employer, employee, economic exchange and the money economy, for example. When one looks across these domains of social life, it quickly becomes obvious that not all time is money. Not all human relations are exclusively governed by the rationalised time of the clock. Not all times are equal whether this is within the domain of paid work or between remunerated and unpaid work.

Conflicting temporal values

The difference becomes most visible when contrasting work contexts are placed next to each other or when the focus is on practices that are not easily quantifiable. One of these contexts is the world of parenting. Here, the conflict of perspective and values becomes obvious when economic efficiency criteria are applied to this particular 'work'. What is considered efficient in the one work system is recognised as inefficient and even harmful in the other.

For example, parents know that feeding their baby takes the time it takes. Speeding up rarely works and certainly does not increase efficiency. Moreover, in such a context, parents are not *exchanging* their time for money but *giving* their time. Unconditional, non-quantified time giving is their investment in the child's future. Furthermore, from an economic perspective of working time, the longer a task takes the less efficient and profitable it is thought to be. From the parent-child perspective, in contrast, the opposite is the case: time spent together creates a bond in the present and a store of psychological well-being and security for the child's future.

Different conflicts of interest arise when we look at the issue of wealth in relation to the dictum that time is money. Here, the issue of equity between social groups is intimately tied to temporal matters. This is the case because the poorest members of our society – the unemployed, pensioners, non-earning parents/carers, people with disabilities, and children – tend to be poor in financial terms but rich in time. The wealthy, in contrast, have money but tend to be short on time, that is, time poor (the aristocracy being an exception to this general rule). Clearly, the time-is-money equation does not apply equally here. While the wealthy are able to use money to buy the time of others to work for them, the time-rich groups, identified above, rarely have the opportunity to exchange their time for money. Time banks are beginning to partially address this problem. However, as long as time banks are organised with an implicitly economic model of time as clock-time, conflicts over incompatible timescapes will remain and the inherent social inequities persist.[7]

Closely related is the issue of 'free time', as it illuminates from a different angle the distinction between work time in employment and work in the shadows of commodified time. From a historical perspective, the steady shortening of working time – from around 80 hours per week without holidays during the middle part of the eighteenth century to below 40 hours plus weekends and holidays at the beginning of the twenty-first century – created an appearance of ever-increasing free time, even of 'time wealth'. However, this has been misleading since `free time' and its correlate leisure time are *produced time*, a *not-work time* that exists only in relation to the time of markets and employment. This means that outside the framework of economic time – for periods of childhood, education, unemployment and retirement, for example – the idea of `free time' must remain relatively meaningless since its very definition is tied to the history of labour and paid employment.

In these examples the difference between time systems with their attendant values is brought into stark relief; inherent contradictions are highlighted and their previously invisible inequality becomes tangible.

Concluding reflections on sustainable work

In the context of working time and the challenge of work time reduction, sustainability takes on a particular meaning. It encompasses not just the quantity but also the quality of working time, not just the commodity but also the lived complexity. It involves combining into a coherent whole the incompatible time systems that currently stress and stretch our lives beyond endurance. A precondition to sustainable work would be that we render explicit what is currently known implicitly and that time was understood in its complexity as timescape. Different practices would need to be appreciated in terms of their temporal logics, which are not necessarily compatible with the logics of other work time systems. Working time understood in its economic, social and environmental complexity would therefore be the starting point from which we could begin to take account of the temporal needs at all these levels and address current inequalities embedded therein. As such it would be an essential first step on the long path to sustainable work.

Hurried and alone: time and technology in the consumer society

Mark Davis

During his Commencement Address at Hampton University on 11 May 2010, President Obama remarked that the class before him were graduating at a time of great difficulty for America and for the wider world. Beyond the more obvious remarks about economic and environmental crises, and the continuing challenges of American foreign policy, Obama also chose to reflect on the role of new technology in reshaping the socio-cultural landscape of the new century. He said to the Graduating Class of 2010.[1]

> *'You're coming of age in a 24/7 media environment that bombards us with all kinds of content and exposes us to all kinds of arguments, some of which don't always rank that high on the truth meter. And with iPods and iPads; and Xboxes and PlayStations ... information becomes a distraction, a diversion, a form of entertainment, rather than a tool of empowerment, rather than the means of emancipation.'*

He went on to add that new technology was 'putting new pressure on [the] country and on [its] democracy'. Chief amongst Obama's complaints was that 'With so many voices clamouring for attention on blogs, and on cable, on talk radio, it can be difficult, at times, to sift through it all; to know what to believe; to figure out who's telling the truth and who's not.'

Obama was surely right to note the growing prevalence of new technology within our consumer societies. On 28 May 2010 – the day on which Apple launched the first version of its (then brand new) iPad device in the UK, amidst reported 'carnivalesque' scenes outside its stores – the company's net worth overtook its main competitor, with Apple estimated at $222 billion against Microsoft's $219 billion. The mobile phone industry sold 1.2 billion units in 2008 and is estimated to sell 1.3 billion units by the end of this year, leading to an estimated industry value of $200 billion. In 2010, Facebook claimed more than 400 million active members. 132 million unique visitors dropped-by in March 2010 alone, not far behind the mighty Google (147 million) and well ahead of MySpace (48 million). In comparison, Twitter currently enjoys some 100 million active users worldwide. So, how might we seek to understand the dramatic socio-cultural changes that are occurring in relation to the increasing prevalence of new technology in our lives? And what implications does this prevalence have for our understanding and use of time?

Living our lives primarily as consumers – rather than as citizens, carers, or creators – poses a number of difficult questions. Chief amongst these, it seems to me, is the question recently posed by the internationally acclaimed sociologist, Zygmunt Bauman: Can such notions as equality, democracy and self-determination survive when society is seen less as a product of shared labour and common values and far more as a container of goods and services to be grabbed by competing individual hands?[2]

The enduring decline of welfare provision and the retreat of the democratic state in favour of evermore deregulation and privatisation, and the growing preference for 'online' rather than 'offline' life, can each be seen as a consequence of a super-individualised form of life politics that champions consumer freedom over and above hard won human rights and civil liberties.

In what follows, I argue that as consumers of new communications technology we now live a curiously 'hurried life' in which the perception of time has become so acutely accelerated that we live in a series of fleeting episodic moments, or 'pointillist' time,[3] a lived experience characterised by a series of seemingly disconnected intensities. In desperately trying to cope, let alone to 'get ahead', the preferred strategy of contemporary men and women has been to embrace new communications technologies because of their basic marketing promise: namely, to allow us to do things more swiftly, and to allow us to circumnavigate the allegedly tedious, awkward and time-consuming business of having to encounter other human beings in their physical proximity.[4] In so doing, however, we are each increasingly devoid of meaningful human face-to-face contact in our daily lives, instead spending much of our time staring at the multifarious screens that now seem to dominate our every waking moment, including televisions, mobile phones, internet forums, emails, blog posts, and all those vast digital screens that have ever so quietly taken up residence in our shared public spaces to offer us a cocktail of news headlines, advertisements, and state of emergency warnings. As any readers familiar with Bauman's[5] wider work will know only too well, meaningful human face-to-face contact is fundamental to an ethical life lived in the company of others and its growing absence from our everyday lives presents a moral problem that is unique to our technological times.

Offered below are two snapshots of this contemporary landscape, through which I will focus in particular on the relationship between time and new communications technologies, in order to locate the urgent debate about the need for a shorter working week within a wider social panorama. The connection between current time use and increasing consumption of such technologies has recently received much attention. The *Communications Market Report* by Ofcom, published in August 2010, stated that the average person spends about 15 hours and 45 minutes every day awake. Of this time, the report found, the average person spends seven hours and five minutes 'engaging in media and communications activities'.[6] Although perhaps startling enough that half of our waking lives is spent with new communications technology, the report also found that most people are able to cram in even more by 'multi-tasking', effectively using two or more technological devices at once. For example, although adults aged between 16 and 24 appeared to consume the least, spending just 6 hours and 35 minutes a day on the phone, laptop, radio or television, by multi-tasking the survey found that young adults were able to squeeze the equivalent of 9 hours 30 minutes worth of consumption into that same time period.

My argument here is thus motivated by a desire to show that the current strategy of looking to new communications technologies as the solution to our increasingly 'hurried lives' is in fact self-defeating. I claim that greater reliance on such technology is actually playing a fundamental role in further accelerating the experience of everyday life in the twenty-first century. What is required is fundamental social structural change to the way we use and distribute our time in contemporary society and, in this context, the call by **nef** (new economics foundation) for a 21-hour week could not be timelier.

Connecting people in a lonely society

The first snapshot I wish to offer begins with a curious problem that struck me whilst in the underground station in London, around this time last year. Facing the enormous advertising hoardings that seem to line the far wall of every tube station, there was an advert for a well known mobile phone company that displayed the slogan: 'Connecting People'. Moments later, on entering the tube and opening my newspaper, I was met with a then recent report by the Mental Health Foundation entitled *The Lonely Society?*[7] How is it possible to be simultaneously more connected to others and yet feel lonelier?

According to the report, social relationships that are vital to health and well-being are under threat by the various ways and means of modern life that serve to isolate people from one another and thus lead to a greater sense of loneliness. Forty-eight per cent of the people included in the study believed that people are getting lonelier. There were many reasons given for this. One of the more thought-provoking reasons put forward was that, for some, investing time in social activities is seen as being far less important than work. With people feeling an ever-growing pressure to be 'productive' and busy, one of the central consequences of this was neglecting vital social relationships with friends and family. In this context, the claim by Jonathan Gershuny[8] that it is now 'busy-ness', rather than leisure, that has become the new badge of honour for many in contemporary society appears to be evermore convincing. The report continued by proclaiming that individuals, pursuing aspirations in a market-driven world, may be doing so at their own expense, often neglecting the basic human need to spend time with others. Polling for the report revealed that 42 per cent have felt depressed specifically because they felt alone.

What struck me most about the report however, and what I wish to explore further here, was that 18 per cent of people said they spend far too much time communicating with family and friends online when they felt they should be seeing them in person. Perhaps surprisingly, the report indicated that these feelings of isolation, loneliness and depression were most prevalent amongst the young, the age group that are most involved in the consumption and heavy use of new communications technologies marketed specifically because of their professed ability to 'connect people'.[9] Nearly 60 per cent of those questioned who were aged between 18 to 34 spoke of feeling lonely 'often' or 'sometimes', compared to 35 per cent of those aged over 55. A recent study by the Institute of Psychological Sciences at the University of Leeds lends further weight to this claim, concluding that people who spend a lot of time browsing the net are more likely to show depressive symptoms.[10] In the very first large-scale study of young people in the West to consider the relationship between internet addiction and depression, researchers at Leeds found striking evidence that some 'heavy users' had developed a compulsive internet habit, replacing 'real-life' social interaction with online chat rooms and social networking sites. The results of the study suggest that this type of addictive surfing can have a serious impact on mental health.

With the arrival of the internet and mobile phones, the void of meaningful human contact can certainly be covered up and momen-tarily forgotten about, the pain of isolation temporarily assuaged. For those growing up in this world of virtual connectivity, perhaps the skills of human face-to-face interaction are no longer deemed necessary, or at the most are seen as a cumbersome form of communication full of shortcomings compared to their online, 'virtual' alternative. One can see these preferences in action on any given day in any given public space. Surrounded by the immediate physical proximity of others, individuals frequently make themselves 'socially absent' by losing themselves in the flow of electronic signals from their technological devices, opting for the virtual connections of online life and thus sending a very clear social signal to all around them that they wish to be 'on their own'.

This has potentially significant consequences for our shared under-standing of public space and civic life and, it seems to me, can be use-fully understood through the frame of Erving Goffman's[11] sociological concept of 'civil inattention'. In the consumer societies of today, social-ity seems always to be occurring elsewhere via new communications technologies, with our attention firmly housed in a virtual world of connections to physically absent others, rather than concerned in any meaningful way with those who are physically around us in the offline communities of the here and now. With new technologies in hand, if so wished it is seemingly possible to become entirely alone on a tube train or on a crowded shopping street. Indeed, the sight of people send-ing text messages in bustling passageways of underground stations is incredibly common, as is their furious reaction to anyone in that crowd who accidently nudges them physically back to reality, forcing them to shift without warning from the virtual to the material world, and thus momentarily reminding them that there are other people in the social world entitled to share public space, each with their own competing desires, wishes and wills. To recall Bauman's question in this context: 'Can such notions as equality, democracy and self-determination survive when society is seen less as a product of shared labour and common values and far more as a container of goods and services to be grabbed by competing individual hands?'

To borrow again from Goffman,[12] at least a part of the appeal of the virtual world seems to be the way it limits the risk of an awkward social 'encounter', the subtle art of the presentation of self having moved online whereby it is now possible to nano-manage the self so that individuals increasingly come to resemble online commodities: thousands of carefully posed for or subsequently airbrushed Facebook photographs; delicate product placement within a never-ending web of consumer tastes and preferences that we 'like' and invite others to 'like' also; the visual display of personal consumer satisfaction surveys, communicated by pointing out how many people 'like' the self that we are now promoting in the hope that they too may join the growing ranks of our online 'friends'.

What this suggests, it seems to me, is that in seeking to overcome existential feelings of loneliness by embracing greater levels of virtual con-nectivity with other human beings we are – to borrow a phrase employed in a different context by Slavoj Žižek[13] – perhaps taking 'a right step in the wrong direction'. We rightly seek greater connections with people to reaffirm increasingly fragmenting social bonds. But in seeking to achieve this through new communications technologies we step in the wrong direction, because online networks lack proximity to the human other. They lack the face-to-face contact that is the basis of a form of human sociality that can overcome feelings of isolation and loneliness. In short, one may be in the virtual company of millions whilst online, but one is invariably alone in front of a screen whilst doing so. Such a dominant part of the knowledge economy in our consumer societies, these new communications technologies are frequently cited by politicians and business leaders as a major global industry capable of providing much sought after growth that will drive our economies out of recession and beyond the age of austerity into a new age of abundance. Or so, yet again, we are told. At the same time, that a central trigger for the current global crisis – i.e. greater levels of consumer spending – is also offered as a solution to the worldwide malady appears (perhaps at best) to be an acute case of cognitive dissonance amongst key international decision-makers. Perhaps, however, the willing embrace of new communications technologies comes at a cost many of us are hitherto unaware of, namely that in increasing the quantity of our online social networks we are sacrificing the time needed to enjoy the quality of human togetherness.

'Interactivity' versus 'interpassivity'

The second snapshot I wish to offer begins with the observations of Sullivan and Gershuny[14] in relation to their 'cash rich/time-poor' complex that stands behind their sociological concept of 'inconspicuous consumption'. Crudely summarised, the idea here is that as rapacious consumers we continue to buy evermore things in spite of lacking the time to use them, instead simply storing products away in garages, attics, or paid-for storage facilities for an imagined future of increased leisure time.[15] Skis, fishing rods, mountain bikes, cooking equipment and even small boats are piling up in households around the country, reflecting a new and growing class of consumers who have fallen in love with the idea of a leisured lifestyle, but who lack the time to lead it. Related research, conducted by Datamonitor in 2004, also found that the typical UK shopper spent an average £1,725 a year on luxury items, gadgets, accessories and memberships which are 'under-utilised', and food which is thrown away, suggesting that contemporary Britons 'waste a staggering £80 billion a year' on goods that are either never used or used so rarely as to have not been worth buying.[16]

There are many ways one could interpret these developments. My own reading of this, in the light of the wider concerns of this paper, is that consumer goods – especially new communications technologies – have in some sense cheated us of the their basic marketing promise. That is to say: consumer goods have not, to employ Marxian terminology, served to reduce 'socially necessary labour time' and thus create a world of leisure. In spite of the advertising imagery that accompanies such products, with happy families or young professionals leisurely reclining with their feet up on expensive sofas, the rise of our consumer societies has resulted in the majority of men and women in the Western world now working longer hours. In the UK we work an average of 42 hours per week, more hours than any other nation in the European Union.[17] A clinical study in the same year found that people who work 41 hours or more a week are significantly more likely to have high blood pressure than those who work for less.[18] A survey presented to the European Parliament in 2007 predicted that the stress of over-scheduled lives means that 60 per cent of middle-aged adults will suffer from high-blood pressure by 2027.[19] One of the principal drivers of this trend is the emergence of a culture of over-working whereby status is increasingly attached to being 'over-worked' and busy as a sign of success, as was mentioned earlier in relation to Jonathan Gershuny's work in this area. And the consumer object of choice for the stressed and over-worked employee is of course new communications technologies because, so we are told, they will allow us to accomplish far more in the amount of available time. In one way, this is undoubtedly true, for many modern institutions would cease to function today without the constant flow of digital signals that have become the necessary circulatory system of global capitalism. But a crucial point appears to have been overlooked: the capacity to 'do more, more quickly' has not created a world in which 'socially necessary labour time' has been reduced. Instead it has fostered a culture of over-working, especially in the UK, and I suggest that this is connected to the proliferation of new communications technologies in our everyday lives.

By way of illustration, let us greatly simplify matters and propose that new communications technologies allow us all to do things only twice as quickly (even though in reality it is of course many more times that). In this hypothetical example, in a standard eight-hour working day, technology allowing us to do things twice as quickly does not mean – as we may rightly have assumed – that we work half of the time by accomplishing our daily working tasks in four hours. Rather, it seems, being able to do things twice as quickly simply means that we accomplish twice as many tasks in 8 hours, in effect producing 16 hours' worth of labour time in the same standard working day. One explanation for this is that, because of an awareness of the role of new communications technologies in the modern workplace (and their increasing prevalence in our wider 'non-working' lives), other people's expectations of what is possible have also shifted in line with the advent of such technologies. 'Why haven't they responded to my email, I sent it nearly 60 seconds ago?' has fast become the frustrated cry of contemporary men and women plugged into the circulation of digital media to such an extent that time is frequently experienced in intervals of the second. And not having received a response within this dramatically truncated time-frame affects our emotional state and our well-being. We can become cross, frustrated, sometimes furious, because our increasingly heavy use of new communications technology is not in fact making our lives simpler, happier, or anything else that we were promised that it would. And to find some evidence for this, we can look to the fascinating work of Philip Zimbardo.

Zimbardo's research *The Secret Powers of Time* [20] claims that we are fundamentally under-estimating the emotional costs to our well-being wrought by the increased prevalence of new technologies in our daily lives, in particular how new technologies have profound effects on what he and Robert Levine call 'the pace of life'. Zimbardo proposes that we are under-estimating the power of new technology in rewiring people's brains, specifically the shift from analogue to digital time perspectives whereby everything is measured by the second. For example, when studying people's 'time duration responses' to the boot-up times for their personal computers, Zimbardo found that the average limit was around 60 seconds, before people exhibited advanced emotional states of anger. New technologies have led to a world in which any form of waiting, even for pleasurable experiences, is now understood simply as 'a waste of time', 'a waste of valuable seconds' that could (perhaps should) otherwise have been used to provide pleasure.

For Zimbardo, there is a fundamental change occurring within our culture whereby new technologies are shifting our time perspectives with disastrous consequences for our emotional health and well-being. A study with *USA Today* about how busy contemporary Americans believe themselves to be revealed that over 50 per cent thought they were busier now than they were one year ago and that as a consequence they frequently sacrifice friends, family and sleep for their success in the workplace. So, Zimbardo and his team proposed the hypothetical possibility of an 'eighth day' in the week and asked respondents what they would do with it. All respondents said that this would be a great initiative, because with an eighth day they could work harder, get more done at work and so 'get further ahead' of their colleagues and peers. In other words, in spite of their own statements earlier in the research process, they would not spend any such eighth day catching up with friends, family or sleep.

What this suggests, it seems to me, is that – just as with the global financial crisis – a fundamental cause of the problem is being seen as a primary solution. That is to say: new technologies are now seen as the cure for an accelerated social reality that their very introduction and growing use has helped to create. In exploring this apparent contradiction, it is instructive to recall Slavoj Žižek's remarks in *How to Read Lacan*,[21] where he states that the advent of the VCR as a consumer good ensured (rather counter-intuitively) that one actually watches fewer and fewer films. The logic of Žižek's analysis is that, in recording more and more films and TV programmes with the VCR, it is as if the consumer is no longer required actually to watch the films themselves. In other words, it is as if the VCR is watching them for us. This process has been exacerbated amongst heavy users of digital recording boxes that can now store several weeks' worth of television and movie content that one is never likely ever to find the leisure time to watch and so is simply deleted at a future date. All of this taken together seems to raise an interesting question about our relationship with new technology: namely, is what we so often refer to and champion as 'interactivity' in the world of Web 2.0 in fact leading to an acute form of 'interpassivity'?

Viewed from one perspective, the increasing consumption of new technologies suggests that we have ceded more and more of our skills and capabilities to various forms of machines. The prevalence of new technologies in everyday life means that we expect more and more of our daily activities to be done for us, often becoming frustrated when we suddenly realise that we may have to do things for ourselves. As Žižek's analysis of the VCR implies, we appear to want new technologies to labour for us. And so we watch increasing numbers of television programmes about the art of cooking fine food, whilst simultaneously avoiding the art of cooking for ourselves by regularly eating-out or consuming ready-meals. We watch seemingly endless television programmes about improving our homes and gardens, whilst seldom feeling like we have the time, energy or resources actually to do these things ourselves. We buy personal gym equipment for our homes, but seldom use them, perhaps preferring to use these vast contraptions for the rather more quotidian task of drying laundry.

A further consequence of such 'interpassive' behaviour to emerge from Žižek's work is that we are now very easily distracted, struggling to retain ever-dwindling attention spans. In his recent book, *The Shallows: What the internet is doing to our brains*,[22] Nicholas Carr seeks to account for these developments by suggesting that new technology is fundamentally changing the way in which our brains operate. Encouraged by the frenetic, hyper-linked web, Carr argues that we are losing the capability to process information at 'less-than-internet' speeds. We are easily distracted, he argues, and increasingly incapable of paying attention to books or articles of any sustained length. We are no longer knowledge seekers, but information data processors, simply roaming from one fact to another. The internet assumes that our minds should operate as high-speed data-processing machines and thus our capability for 'deep thinking' is limited because we frequently lack the time that is essential for digesting information, developing knowledge and then drawing our own reasoned conclusions. Knowledge has seemingly moved from the Platonic realm of 'justified true belief', that once sound epistemological claim that knowledge is based on reason, experience, and perception, and has instead become a commodity to be consumed just like any other.

By way of example, Mark Fisher's recent book *Capitalist Realism* reflects on the absence of 'deep thinking' amongst heavy users of new communications technology. Based on his experiences as a teacher in a Further Education college, Fisher states:

> '*Ask students to read for more than a couple of sentences and many – and these are A' level students mind you – will protest that they can't do it. The most frequent complaint teachers hear is that it's boring. It is not so much the content of the written material that is at issue here; it is the act of reading itself that is deemed to be 'boring'.*'[23]

Fisher proposes that in this context 'to be bored' simply means to be removed from the communicative sensation-stimulus matrix of new communications technologies, the constant text messaging, blog writing/reading, Facebook status updating, online profile managing, and the sharing of and commenting on YouTube clips. In other words, 'to be bored' is to be momentarily forced out of the flow of communication that has become the lifeblood of lives assimilated into the virtual world that new technologies have made possible.

Conclusion

The outcome of these profound socio-cultural changes is that we seem to have more information of what is going on in the world, but seemingly less awareness of what we could or should do about it. As President Obama suggested in his Commencement Address at Hampton, perhaps information has indeed become 'a distraction, a diversion, a form of entertainment, rather than a tool of empowerment, rather than the means of emancipation'. To rephrase his concerns for the present discussion, perhaps for all the interactivity offered by new communications technology, Obama is fearful that it is a growing 'interpassivity' that now reigns in our consumer societies. Having bequeathed many of our most vital social relationships and social capabilities to those machines offered by the advent of new communications technologies, it is more vital than ever before that the dangers inherent in these processes are recognised and addressed. The invitation to reflect on the need for a transition to a 21-hour working week is exceptionally timely because it has the potential to start the 'great transition' from our over-worked lives as consumers and perhaps allow each one of us to become citizens, carers and creators within our own communities by reconnecting with other human beings in their physical (and thus moral) proximity, rather than being limited to a virtual online existence that may lead to greater unhappiness and even depression.

Yet there is a desire to escape the perceived inevitability of this shift to a primarily online life: Transition Towns [24] and various forms of 'community supported agriculture' [25] are established examples, as are 'Buy-cott' and 'No Phone' days. Perhaps less well known, and specifically resisting the accelerated experience of time, is the 'Cittaslow' [26] movement, started in Italy in 1999 following Carlo Petrini's 'slow food' revolution and now here in the UK. On the same theme, but with a dramatically different strategy, is the Long Now Foundation. [27] Established in 01996 (the additional zero intended to counteract the 'deca-millenium bug', anticipated to arrive in around 8000 years), they state on their website:

> '*Civilisation is revving itself into a pathologically short attention span. The trend might be coming from the acceleration of technology, the short-horizon perspective of market-driven economics, the next-election perspective of democracies, or the distractions of personal multi-tasking. All are on the increase. Some sort of balancing corrective to the short-sightedness is needed – some mechanism or myth which encourages the long view and the taking of long-term responsibility, where 'long-term' is measured at least in centuries.*' [28]

This kind of radical proposition is needed to awaken us once again to our true interests. I see the call for a 21-hour working week as a vital part of this wider mission. From the brief snapshots I have presented throughout this paper, I hope to have shown that there are two key resources that are inequitably distributed around the world and which are in urgent need of being rebalanced in a post-crisis context: time and money. Living life at such incessant speed in the pursuit of greater financial resources to fund our excessive consumer lifestyles, we are seldom aware of the seriousness with which we need urgently to address the fact that we are now living on borrowed money, for sure, but also on borrowed time. Snatching what we can of both, social life appears to have adopted as its guiding principle the Red Queen's advice to Alice in Wonderland, in that we know it takes all the running we can do just to keep in the same place, and that if we want to get to somewhere else, we must run at least twice as fast as that. The debate on 21 hours is our chance to decide if we wish to keep running at such speed and, if we choose not, then where it is that we ought to be walking to.

Redistributing paid and unpaid time

Time, care and gender inequalities[1]

Valerie Bryson

As other papers in this volume make clear, a radical reduction in 'normal' working hours could have major beneficial effects on the environment, the economy and social well-being. This paper argues that shorter hours could also provide an important step towards greater gender equality by validating patterns of behaviour typically associated with women rather than men and facilitating a redistribution of caring and workplace responsibilities between the sexes. Reducing working hours could also help challenge the dominant temporal mind set of society, encouraging a relationship with time that is more appropriate to giving and receiving care.

The first section identifies the importance and time-consuming nature of care, and shows that care, both paid and unpaid, is mainly provided by women. It argues that, because the time costs of care are often unrecognised and carers are economically penalised, this gender difference in time use plays a key role in perpetuating gender inequalities.

The second section digs deeper into our human relationship with time, arguing that interpersonal relationships and caring work require a fluid, open-ended and process-oriented sense of time that is very different from the time-is-money logic of the capitalist workplace. It finds that this temporal logic of the workplace is increasingly being extended into caring relationships with damaging effects, and it argues that a reduction in working hours could help counter this trend.

Because women on average already work relatively short hours, many would find that a shift in expectations around working hours would support and reward their existing patterns of behaviour. The gains for men are, however, less clear cut. Men are therefore the focus of the third section, which suggests that many men will feel threatened by the challenge to the 'normality' of their current work patterns and their masculine identity that is bound up with this. Many may also have difficulties with a shift to greater gender equality and the loss of power and status that this would entail. Nevertheless, men could benefit in many ways, and some current trends provide grounds for optimism.

The fourth section provides a brief outline of some practical steps that could lead the way to a shortening of the working week. The paper concludes that these changes can contribute to the development of a more equal and caring society and that all citizens will ultimately benefit.

Care and the exploitation of women

The social and economic importance of care

The need for care is part of the human condition. We were all once totally dependent babies, most of us will need the care of others when we become sick or old, and many who assert their self-sufficient independence are in fact dependent on the care of others – whether it is a secretary who reminds them of appointments or a partner who cooks their meals. Without care, society would collapse; if care is only minimal, human relationships and well-being are impoverished. Care is sometimes provided as a form of paid employment, sometimes as an expression of love or through a sense of obligation, and it usually involves both practical activities and the development or maintenance of interpersonal relationships.

Although the outcomes of caring activity are often intangible and highly subjective, time-use studies can help demonstrate their economic value. It is now generally agreed that the most accurate form of study is based on time-use diaries, which require respondents to report on their activities at 15-minute intervals over a 24-hour period, and that these diaries should also ask if the respondent is doing anything else at the same time, and if someone else is with them. The last national government studies in the UK in 2001 and 2005 took this form. These clearly demonstrated that unpaid work is a major and growing part of the economy: in 1961, 41 per cent of all work done in the UK was unpaid; by 2001 this had risen to 52 per cent.[2]

Time-use studies highlight the obvious, but often forgotten, nature of time as a finite scarce resource: there are only 24 hours in a day and there are limits to how many things we can do at any one time. This zero-sum nature of time means that when people are looking after family members, or engaged in domestic tasks associated with this care, or helping friends and neighbours, they cannot simultaneously be in the workplace. However, their unpaid roles represent an economic and social contribution that is often at least as important as many forms of paid employment.

The invisibility of care

In practice, however, unpaid work is all too often invisible. Politicians of all parties may be happy to pay rhetorical tribute to parents, carers and volunteers, but they also stress the duty of all citizens to seek paid employment, and their language often seems to support those who equate welfare claimants with scroungers. Thus for example when David Cameron asserts the need to end 'welfare dependency' and ensure that 'work pays', or when Ed Miliband declared in his 2011 conference speech that 'The wealth of our nation is built by the hands not just of the elite few but every man and woman who goes out and does a day's work',[3] they seem to forget that not all work is paid for, and that the important unpaid domestic and caring work that some claimants are doing already would have to be done by someone else if they became part of the paid workforce.

As indicated above, time-use studies can provide a useful corrective by measuring the time spent on unpaid work. However, they still tend to understate the sometimes all-encompassing nature of caring responsibilities and the time constraints that these involve.[4] Particular problems arise because most analyses of time-use study data draw only on the 'main activity' diary information, although this captures only a fraction of caring responsibilities. To take an obvious example, if someone records their main activity as 'watching television', they will be identified as at leisure rather than as providing childcare, even if there is a small child in the room, no other adult in the house, and the television programme is chosen for the child. Their activities are, however, clearly constrained by their responsibilities; even if the person then watches a programme of their own choice when the child has gone to bed, they are still unable to leave the house. The inclusion of secondary and 'with whom' data would provide a clearer picture, but even this only covers waking hours, losing sight of the extent to which sleeping hours 'on call' can prevent people from working away from home or curtail their leisure activities. The studies also assume that time unfolds and can be recorded as a series of discrete activities. As discussed later in this paper, this assumption reflects a particular view of time that is often alien to caring responsibilities. The studies are also unable to fully capture the stresses involved in trying to juggle the competing demands of family life and employment, with complex chains of responsibility thrown into disarray if one child is sick or another has to be taken to the dentist, or the child minder goes on holiday, or the school closes because of snow, or an elderly parent has a fall. It is therefore important to recognise both that the findings of time-use studies are significant, and that they can provide only a partial picture of the 'time costs' of care.

The gendered nature of care: from gender difference to gender inequalities

The invisibility of unpaid care is bound up with the gendered nature of caring responsibilities in a society in which notions of 'importance', 'normality' and 'success' are based on male paradigms, and in which the roles, attributes and patterns of behaviour traditionally associated with women are given lower status and reward.

Although men's contribution has increased in recent years, time-use studies indicate that women still do nearly twice as much unpaid domestic and caring work as men.[5] As we have seen, the impact of these responsibilities on carers' lives may be much greater – sometimes over-whelmingly greater – than these studies indicate. Family responsibili-ties are of course experienced differently by different groups of women, varying with age, health and family situation as well as with class and ethnicity, and some women are able to 'buy time' by paying others to clean their house, look after their children or care for their elderly parents, while a minority fully share caring responsibilities with a male part-ner. However, gendered social expectations mean that women may be criticised and feel guilty about 'outsourcing' care, while men's 'domestic absenteeism' remains largely unremarked. For example, while a 'good son' is one who ensures that his elderly mother is well looked after, a 'good daughter' may be expected to provide this care herself. Similarly, a man who collects his children from school twice a week is likely to be seen as a highly involved father, while a woman who collects them three times is seen as an absentee mother.

Unpaid responsibilities have major effects on women's employment prospects. There is a particularly clear 'motherhood penalty', whereby initial decisions become self-perpetuating, as mothers' 'traditional caring roles lead them to leave paid work or to work part time, which leads to lower remuneration, which reinforces domestic gender roles so that it makes financial sense for fathers rather than mothers to work full time'.[6] This cycle is not inevitable, but reflects the long hours expected of many full time employees[7] and the lower hourly wages and career prospects of part time workers, with mothers who return to work part time often finding that they have to accept a less-well graded post or a job in a low-pay sector.[8] As discussed in the penultimate section of this paper, it is also difficult for fathers to challenge gender stereotypes that expect them to be the main wage earner, while 'the development and implementation of policies supporting fathers in their role as parents lags far behind that of mothers'.[9] If there is to be greater equality in the home, employment policies must start with the assumption that it is not only women but 'normal' employees who have responsibilities and a life outside their workplace; this assumption points firmly in the direction of a much shorter and more flexible standard working week for all.

The domestic division of labour is reflected in the paid workforce where, as a recent report for the TUC shows, women workers are concen-trated in poorly paid sectors, including paid care work.[10] This gendered specialisation and the attached 'caring penalty' in employment are not simply a reflection of the limited workplace options open to mothers (although this is a factor), but begin at an earlier age. They are dramatically obvious in the pay and career choice of apprentices: the most recently available figures show that 97 per cent of childcare apprentices are female and earn an average of £142 a week, compared to £170 for automotive apprentices (100 per cent male) and £174 for construction apprentices (99 per cent male).[11] Such figures show the interconnected persistence of traditional gender norms, the devaluation of 'women's work', and the low importance attached to time spent caring for others. In general, care work is often treated both as unskilled and as an expression of women's 'natural' caring abilities, which should not be sullied by too much thought of financial reward. In accordance with this dominant perspective, attempts to improve young women's career prospects involve encouraging them to enter male sectors of employment[12] – begging the question of how society's caring needs are to be met if competent young women are told that such work is beneath them.

Women's lower earnings mean that many are at least partly dependent on the earnings of a male partner; women without such a partner are disproportionately reliant on state benefits. Women's caring responsibilities also mean that they generally have less 'usable' free time than men: although the hours women spend on unpaid work are largely balanced by men's longer hours in paid employment, men's leisure time is more likely to be in predictable and clearly demarcated blocks, while women's leisure time is less predictable, more fragmented and more likely to be interrupted and/or combined with caring responsibilities.[13] All this also means that women have significantly less access than men to the key resources of time, money and contacts that facilitate a political career and that the voices of carers are under-represented in political processes.

This first section has shown that, even when care is motivated by love, it involves significant time costs. These (often unacknowledged) costs make it difficult for carers to do other things, whether this be earning money, playing an active part in local politics, or enjoying uninterrupted leisure. The unequal distribution of unpaid care in the home is therefore a major source of cumulative, interconnected and ongoing inequalities between women and men in the public sphere. While the low pay and status attached to paid care work reflect this gendered invisibility. As Lynch and Walsh have argued, there is therefore 'a very real case for claiming that women's exploitation as carers is the main form of exploitation that applies specifically to women'.[14] As the next section shows, these inequalities extend to our relationship with time itself, as the kind of time that good caring relationships involve is increasingly subject to the temporal imperatives of the workplace, derived from typically male needs and experiences.

Different kinds of time

Barbara Adam's chapter in this volume discusses the complex nature of our human relationships with time in more detail. As she says, our society is dominated by commodified clock time. In this section I argue that this dominance is having damaging effects on our ability to give and receive care and that a reduction in working hours would help counter this.

Time for work, time for care

The capitalist workplace depends upon a commodified, forward-looking, clock-time culture, which treats time as an abstract, quantifiable entity that can be objectively measured and costed. It also sees time as a scarce resource that can be owned, spent, wasted or saved, and that should be used as efficiently as possible to achieve maximum outputs in the minimum amount of time. However, while this time-is-money rationality dominates our experience of time today, it does not exhaust it, and it is frequently at odds with the temporal rhythms involved in caring relationships.

Caring for other people is an inherently relational and often open-ended activity. Rather than a series of tasks interspersed with identifiable periods of leisure, caring for family members can feel more like a confused jumble of simultaneous activities, emotions and processes, and a constant attentiveness to risk or need. While it also involves identifiable tasks, the timing of these is determined partly by need rather than by the clock (a child's nappy has to be changed when it is dirty, not because it is four o'clock; you comfort a friend because they phone you in distress, not because you have a free half hour). Many caring tasks are very much focused on the here and now, and attempting to speed them up can often be counter-productive (trying to rush a child through dressing and breakfast may provoke a temper tantrum that makes them even later for school; bundling a confused and frightened old lady into a car without carefully explaining where she is going may ruin an outing that was planned to give her pleasure). Caring tasks are also often repetitive rather than with an identifiable end product (however clean and well-fed a child, it will soon need washing and feeding again; the old lady will need reassuring time after time).

Increasing pressures

All this makes it problematic to subject caring activities to rigid considerations of time management and cost-effectiveness. However, as competition and the pursuit of short-term profit are becoming ever more important in all sectors of the economy, this inappropriate temporal logic is strengthening its grip on paid care work, while the impact of cuts and efficiency savings is spilling over into family life.

The long-hours work culture, exacerbated by job insecurity, creates huge pressures on caring relationships within many homes, with 'quality time' for children, parents or partners to be scheduled, and tick-lists (or even spread sheets) of domestic tasks and activities to be co-ordinated. Although a report from the Future Foundation in the UK commended the increasingly 'professionalised' approach that parents bring to the raising of their children and the organisation of their time,[15] the attempt to apply principles of time management to the emotional and practical needs of family members can feel like the 'McDonaldisation of love'.[16] Because women do most of the work of domestic time management, it is they who have to 'straddle multiple temporalities',[17] and it is women who experience most stress and guilt in attempting to reconcile the need for efficiency with the open-ended nature of loving care. Here the problem is not simply that women do not have 'enough' time, but that the ticking of the clock intrudes into the more fluid and 'natural' time of family life, and usually has priority.

The pressures on paid care workers are also increasing, as much care provision has been privatised and driven ever more exclusively by the urge to maximise profit, and care users are regarded as 'consumers' in a competitive marketplace. Even when care remains publicly provided, the drive to cut spending means that it has become subject to an increasingly rigid culture of efficiency and accountability that focuses narrowly on measurable outputs and value for money. However, good paid care often involves the building up of reciprocal relationships, respect and affection, and this requires a more generous, open-ended approach to time than a cost-effective analysis of the practical tasks involved might suggest. For example, a care worker may be employed to call in at an old man's home to get him up and dressed in the morning. If she does this as speedily as possible, she is likely to leave her client confused and unhappy; if they are able to make this a leisurely process, involving a chat and a shared cup of tea, the man may be enabled to remain in his own home and out of residential care for longer (saving public money in the long run). Today, however, some councils are allocating fifteen minutes or even less for this: 'And what can you do in 15 minutes, bathe, feed and the run to the next client. It's totally undignified.'[18] Similarly, a study of community midwives shows an increasingly over-stretched service, with a stress on good time management and quantifiable efficiency that clashes with the open-ended needs of new mothers and the importance of building a relationship with them: 'You can't do eleven visits between 9 and 12 ... and give quality care to somebody.'[19] As with family care, the problem is not simply that paid workers do not have enough hours and minutes to do their caring work; it is also that they are expected to operate within an inappropriate, tightly managed time culture. Many care workers also face the added difficulty of combining this pressurised work with their own family responsibilities.

Reduced working hours and the defence of caring time
A radical reduction in the 'normal' paid working week would reduce 'time poverty' and ease the pressures on many households, making it possible to develop more relaxed and fluid forms of care, based on attention to human needs, processes and relationships rather than the demands of the clock. In recognising that time spent outside the workplace is socially important, it therefore validates the 'temporal logic' of care and counters the pervasiveness of the commodified, accountable time of the workplace.

However, if reduced working hours are to contribute to good quality care overall, it is also important that this recognition is extended to the time of paid care workers, and that these workers should not be required to use their time more intensively and 'efficiently' in their interactions with service users if they work shorter hours. As well as being enabled to spend more time outside the workplace, employees should be supported in developing working practices that respond to human needs rather than rigidly imposed timesheets.

As we have seen, women are disproportionately responsible for both paid and unpaid care, while men are much more likely both to work full time and to work very long hours. Some writers have therefore described the time culture associated with care and human relationships as 'women's time', and contrasted this with the 'men's time' of paid employment.[20] This distinction is problematic if it is taken as a simple dualism that deems all women or all men to share a temporal consciousness, and/or if these temporal differences are treated as somehow 'natural'. However, if it is carefully used, the distinction can help us to see that gendered experiences of time are bound up with other gender inequalities in a society in which typically female experiences and priorities are generally marginalised or subordinated to those more typical of men. In this context, a reduction of the working week that is intended to defend caring time also represents an assertion of the 'normality' of many women's time use that throws men's current relationship with time into question. Some of the implications of this are explored in the next section.

Men, time and care

Shorter working hours: a threat to masculinity?
This paper has argued that current temporal assumptions and patterns of time use reflect and maintain gender inequalities; in important respects, therefore, they appear to benefit men as a group. This means that, even though men might gain in many ways from shorter working hours, they also have much to lose.

While some men may welcome the possibility of living more rounded lives, others are likely to feel threatened by the prospect of losing their status as main household earner and the domestic bargaining power that this often confers. More generally, many men will be unwilling to see, let alone surrender, the privileges that their economic, social, political and cultural 'normality' bestows. Many will also be unable to accept the radical inversion of dominant thinking that would see current gender inequalities as a product not of women's failure to behave like 'proper' workers, but of men's domestic absenteeism, and not of women's irrational tendency to prefer childcare work to engineering, but of the low status and pay attached to traditionally female professions. There is of course also no guarantee that men who work shorter hours will spend more time with their families.

Even when men are willing to take on caring roles and responsibilities, they may find it difficult to transgress social expectations around appropriate masculine behaviour. It is now widely recognised that gender identity is not fixed and given, but variable, malleable and inherently fragile. From this perspective, gender is something that one 'does' rather than something one 'is'. Here gender time norms can play a key role in maintaining gender difference and a dualistic framework in which 'a male is worker/not carer and a female [is] carer/not worker'.[21] Because most people want to affirm their gender identity, these norms can have a disciplinary effect on their behaviour, deterring 'gender inappropriate' activities. This disciplinary effect can be heightened when traditional masculine roles are threatened by job insecurity or unemployment. Thus a study of North American men who were economically dependent on their wives found that they made a particularly low contribution to domestic work, even though they had plenty of time available, and concluded that: 'It appears that by doing less housework, economically dependent husbands also "do gender".'[22]

The potential for change
Gender time norms are however, much less rigid than in the past. This is particularly clear in relation to fatherhood. A good father is now no longer seen simply as a good provider, but also as someone actively involved in bringing up his children. Perhaps surprisingly, this shift in expectation appears stronger among men than women, with fewer fathers than mothers believing that it is a mother's job to look after children, and more fathers than mothers believing that the highest earner should work full time, regardless of gender.[23]

New attitudes to fathers' responsibilities may also represent a practical response to a rapidly changing employment market, in which the 'male breadwinner' or 'one and a half breadwinner' models of family life, which place all or most employment eggs in one career basket, appears an increasingly irrational deployment of domestic resources. While current economic insecurities can seem threatening to men who aspire to the traditional breadwinning model of masculinity, the destabilisation of conventional male assumptions around continuous employment and career trajectories could therefore also open up new possibilities.

Although fathers now provide more direct care for their children than they used to, men's attitudinal shifts are not fully reflected in changed behaviour, with most fathers still working full time, many working long hours and 45 per cent not taking their paternity leave entitlement[24] (introduced in 1997 as unpaid leave of two weeks at the time of birth, and with a low rate of pay from 2003). However, a large-scale survey for the Equality and Human Rights Commission found that two thirds of fathers who didn't take their leave would have liked to 'a lot', with most citing financial reasons as the main barrier.[25] A recent two-year study of fathers also found that they want to spend more time with their children, that they would like to work more flexibly in order to do so, but that opportunities for flexible working were restricted.[26] This suggests that fathers' wish for change is running ahead of working practices and legislation. At the same time, however, policy makers are increasingly aware that flexible working can be beneficial to employers as well as workers, and the needs of working fathers are recognised to a far greater extent than in the recent past. This reflects a new political and social consensus around the importance of involving fathers in the care of their children. This in turn means that boys are growing up in a society with a wider range of models of masculinity, opening up prospects for further change.

Time poverty and the inappropriate dominance of the time-is-money culture in contemporary Western societies, has damaging consequences for our ability to provide or receive good, loving care either among family, friends and community or as a form of paid employment. But women are not the only ones who suffer from this. As increasing numbers of people live into frail old age, more men will find themselves needing or providing care, while as traditional male employment opportunities decline, it is likely that some men will turn to traditionally female work, including care work.[27] Although at present low pay and status make it difficult to present this as a positive career choice, there is growing awareness that poor conditions of employment in the sector are contributing to neglect and poor care for vulnerable groups. If we want to live in a society in which elderly people and people with disabilities are supported with dignity, then care work will have to be recognised and rewarded as the skilled and demanding profession it is, and the temporal rhythms involved in caring for others will have to be respected.[28] While this would represent a shift to rewarding women's traditional role and relationship with time, it is clearly in the interest of men as well.

Policy implications and conclusions

The arguments in this paper have been underpinned by the belief that care is a public good that should not be left to the market or be seen simply as a private matter for individuals to sort out as best they can. Time spent providing unpaid care constitutes an important civic contribution that is often unrecognised. A shorter working week would both ease the pressure on carers, most of whom are women, and enable their responsibilities to be more widely shared with men. It could therefore help tackle the entrenched domestic bases of gender inequalities.

Paid care work too is currently undervalued. It should be delivered by appropriately paid professionals with workloads that recognise that good quality care cannot be delivered quickly, but involves the time-consuming development of human relationships. Such care is unlikely to be profitable so it should be provided as a public service. Improving the conditions of paid care workers might also make care work a more attractive employment option for men.

Some starting points for change

These general proposals contradict the neo-liberal belief that markets are more effective providers than the state, that regulation of employment should be reduced in order to stimulate growth and that caring responsibilities are generally a private matter, best left to individuals. As discussed in the previous section, challenging the 'normality' of men's current working hours may also be opposed by those who seek to defend their traditional role.

However, as we have also seen, there has been a recent shift in expectations and political rhetoric, particularly around the role of fathers, and there is a newly available language of 'work–life balance' and 'family-friendly employment' that enables new ideas to be articulated. There is also increased awareness of the damaging effects of stress in the workplace – estimated by the Confederation of British Industry (CBI) to cost the UK economy £12 billion a year[29] – and the link with long hours and tight deadlines. While the proposals outlined below are unlikely to be implemented in the short run, they are less far off the mainstream political agenda than in the relatively recent past.

Building on earlier changes, an obvious starting point would be to extend men's parental leave entitlements and to ensure that parental leave rights are enforced for all workers. Here, the coalition government has introduced the right to transfer the second six months of maternity leave to the father. However, lack of financial support means that few families will be able to take advantage of this.[30] In contrast, the Equality and Human Rights Commission recommends that both the initial two weeks of paternity leave and the additional six months should be at 90

65

per cent of the father's usual pay, with a further three months available for either. More robust encouragement of male take-up would also be provided if well paid parental leave were combined with a 'use it or lose it' model, as in Iceland, where three months' leave is reserved for each parent and cannot be transferred between them.

A related step would be the extension of the opportunity for flexible working hours to all groups of workers. Recent research on working fathers found that this makes it much easier for parents to request such leave,[31] and it can be seen as an important step towards normalising shorter working hours. Part time work too should be treated as a valid model of employment, without loss of workplace rights or career opportunities, rather than an as inferior 'mummy track' or last resort for those who really want full time work. In relation to part time work, the change to the working tax credit system from April 2012, which requires couples to work 24 rather than 15 hours (with one partner working at least 16 hours) to become eligible, is a highly retrograde step. While this step should be reversed, tax credits can be criticised as a way of subsidising low pay, and it would be more appropriate to raise the minimum wage so that workers do not have to work long hours to keep their families out of poverty. Flexible and part time employment are likely to be particularly appropriate for people as they near retirement, when many find the demands of full time employment difficult and many take on new caring responsibilities for their grandchildren, an ailing partner or their own elderly parents. This flexibility will become increasingly important as the age of retirement rises.

Such measures represent part of a shift to a less employment-centred model of economic and social life. They have been pushed for and prioritised more by female than by male politicians, and the real breakthrough in the development of 'family friendly' employment measures came with the near doubling in the number of women MPs in 1997.[32] While of course not all women share the same perspectives and experiences, ongoing differences in gender responsibilities mean that women MPs are more likely to see the value of unpaid work and the need to recognise the caring responsibilities of workers. This means that efforts to increase women's political representation can become an indirect part of the push for shorter working hours.

If policy makers are to be persuaded of the value of unpaid work, it is important to be able to demonstrate its time-consuming nature. It was for this reason that the *Platform for Action* resulting from the 1995 United Nations World Conference on Women in Beijing committed signatories to developing such studies and including their findings in national accounts.[33] Although as we have seen these studies may underestimate the demands of caring time, they do help document its value.

It is therefore unfortunate that, in response to the requirement to cut spending, the Office for National Statistics (ONS) is currently not planning any more time-use surveys. This position should be reconsidered.

Time, gender inequalities and care

Taken together, the above changes could support carers and reduce the economic motivation for men to conform to traditional gender roles, so that as old temporal patterns and identities become increasingly untenable, new ones can be encouraged to emerge. In contrast to current patterns of work and care, which reflect and maintain both gender inequalities and the often inappropriate dominance of commodified clock time, a general reduction in working hours would facilitate a redistribution of paid and unpaid work between women and men, and it would allow scope for a kind of time less dominated by considerations of cost-effectiveness and time management. It would also endorse the value of non-work activities, against the dominant assumption that it is only through paid work that citizens can contribute to society.

Women generally have little to lose from a shift to shorter working hours and they have much to gain. While the implications for men are more mixed, they too would benefit from living in a less pressurised, more care-oriented society in which masculine identity is not understood in narrowly economic terms. In the long run, a radical reduction in working hours would be in the interest of us all.

Time, income and freedom[1]

Tania Burchardt

The number of hours of paid and unpaid work required to secure a standard of living, and to provide for the care of family members, varies significantly across individuals according to their human and social capital and household circumstances. This essay offers a conceptual model of how resources interact with responsibilities to produce a range of feasible time allocations that people have, which in turn generate combinations of disposable income and free time – in other words a measure of an individual's substantive freedom. This approach is illustrated empirically with data and simulations based on the UK Time Use Survey 2000. The results show that having low educational qualifications, having more or younger children, being single and being disabled are each independently associated with having a limited level and range of possible combinations of disposable income and free time.

An important objective of public policy for liberal egalitarians should be to ensure that people have sufficient free time to pursue their own goals and interests, after having secured an adequate standard of living and having provided (directly or indirectly) for the care of those that depend on them. This essay contributes to the debate about the feasibility of moving towards a shorter working week in two ways. First, it allows a distinction to be drawn between necessary and discretionary activities. Discretionary activities are potentially suitable targets for public subsidy or taxation, or other forms of (dis)incentivisation, according to policy objectives such as reducing working hours, promoting gender equality or reducing carbon emissions. Second, it highlights groups in the population who have particularly limited combinations of income and time and who may therefore need special support in a period of transition to a shorter working week.

A capability approach to time and income

Both time and income are important means for individuals to be able to work towards their various goals. A central strand of liberal egalitarian thought holds that a 'good society' is one in which individuals are free to pursue their own conceptions of the good life, and providing citizens with the means to do so is therefore a key demand of social justice. For example, Rawls[2] identified income as one of the primary goods that are to be distributed according to his second principle of justice (any inequality is permissible only in so far as it is to the benefit of the worst-off). Bojer[3] argues that this should be extended to the idea of full income, that is the combination of income and free time that individuals have at their command. Sen[4] shifts the focus from the resources themselves to what people are able to be and do with the resources available to them – their substantive freedom, or capabilities. He observes that the rate at which given inputs (for example, an hour of free time or a unit of income) can be converted into valuable outcomes (pursuit of a person's goals and projects) varies according to the characteristics of the individual and their circumstances, including the commitments they may have to others. One 'unit' of income goes less far for a disabled person, or for someone with several children to look after, than the same unit for someone without impairments or caring responsibilities. One hour of time can be converted into a wide range of opportunities for a high-paid individual, and a much narrower range for someone who is low paid or who must at the same time pay for childcare.

This capability approach provides a particularly attractive theoretical framework for considering time and income. First because of its emphasis on the idea of substantive freedom, and second, because it recognises the significance of different rates by which inputs are converted into valuable outcomes.

The importance of discretionary time

Furthermore, the model presented in this paper is related to the work of Robert Goodin and colleagues on 'discretionary time'.[5] While free time is defined as the time that is left over after time spent on personal care, paid and unpaid work, discretionary time measures the time that is left over after the 'minimum necessary' time spent on these activities. The minimum necessary relates to a social standard, for example, the minimum number of hours of paid work necessary to generate an income above an agreed poverty line, while the minimum necessary unpaid work and personal care time are defined relative to population averages. Assessments based on discretionary time are more revealing than those based on free time, it is argued, because discretionary time represents 'temporal autonomy' – the degree of control a person has over the scarce resource of time – whereas free time represents merely the outcome of a chosen allocation.

The contrast can be illustrated by considering a single young professional working long hours in a high-powered occupation, and a lone parent juggling a low-paid job and looking after her children. While the two individuals may have equally little free time, the single professional has considerably greater discretionary time (she could increase her free time by reducing her paid work hours, without risking falling below an income poverty line). The lone parent may face a trade-off between time poverty and income poverty: if she reduces her paid work hours or pays for additional childcare to increase her free time, her disposable income is likely to fall below the poverty line.

This analysis seeks to build on the concept of discretionary time by offering a model of how resources (including time and human and social capital) interact with responsibilities (including personal care, childcare and other unpaid work) to produce a range of feasible time allocations, which in turn produce a set of combinations of disposable income and free time. It extends the existing applications of discretionary time by assessing the time-and-income consequences of a range of different time allocations available to a person, rather than focusing exclusively on the amount of time left over after the minimum necessary activities have been performed.

A conceptual framework for time and income capability

The time allocated by individuals to personal care, paid work and unpaid work is influenced by a wide range of constraints and choices. This is reflected in the model in Figure 1. The model is based on individuals within households but also a broader social context (for example, for many people the process of arriving at an allocation of time is under-taken more or less jointly by two or more members of the household, and will be determined in part by cultural and social norms including gender norms). This social context is also shaped by factors such as the physical environment (such as transport infrastructure which influences the feasible travel-to-work area), the economy and cost of living, entitle-ments, returns to different forms of capital (for example, the wage dif-ferential between low and high-skilled workers), the availability of part time and flexible work and the overall level of demand for labour. All of these can be affected by public policy, and so individuals' capabilities are subject to policy intervention. While they are treated as fixed in this analysis, they should by no means be regarded as fixed when consider-ing future policy options.

Individuals must decide how to allocate their time between four categories of activity: paid work, unpaid work, personal care and the residual, free time. Their decision about how to allocate time is con-strained in two ways: by the *resources* available and by the *responsibilities* for looking after themselves and others which they must meet.

Resources are defined to include time (24 hours per day), since individuals can use their time either directly to meet responsibilities (for example by looking after their own children) or indirectly to earn

Figure 1: Conceptual framework

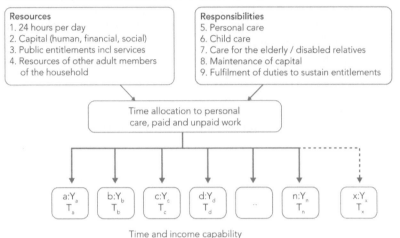

Environment: physical infrastructure; the economy; public policy; cultural and social norms

Resources
1. 24 hours per day
2. Capital (human, financial, social)
3. Public entitlements incl services
4. Resources of other adult members of the household

Responsibilities
5. Personal care
6. Child care
7. Care for the elderly / disabled relatives
8. Maintenance of capital
9. Fulfilment of duties to sustain entitlements

Time allocation to personal care, paid and unpaid work

| $a{:}Y_a$ T_a | $b{:}Y_b$ T_b | $c{:}Y_c$ T_c | $d{:}Y_d$ T_d | ... | $n{:}Y_n$ T_n | $x{:}Y_x$ T_x |

Time and income capability

Key:
a - n are feasible alternatives,
x is an unfeasible alternative,
Y is disposable income
T is free time

income to pay for goods and services which in turn meet responsibilities (for example, paying a childminder). In addition, the individual may be able to draw on the resources, including time, of other adult members of the household. Income is not treated as a basic resource since it is derived through the application of time and one or more forms of capital – financial, physical, human and social. The individual's stock of each of these forms of capital, especially human capital, is crucial in determining the 'exchange rate' between their own labour and that of others. In addition to these private resources, the individual may also have a number of public entitlements.

Turning to responsibilities, the first on the list is personal care, which includes sleeping, eating, washing and so on. These are distinct from unpaid work, since in most cases it is not possible to pay someone else to do them for you and still get the same benefit. Childcare and care for elderly or disabled relatives may be provided directly, by performing the care oneself or indirectly by paying someone else to do it. Looking after oneself and others requires material inputs as well as time – food, shelter, clothing and so on. Providing material necessities therefore also counts as part of the 'responsibilities' side of the equation, and this implies the need to generate an income. The level of income that should count as the minimum required is discussed below.

Also included in the list of responsibilities is the maintenance of capital. This is to ensure that the model represents a sustainable scenario: if individuals were running down their capital, that would imply that a narrower range of time allocations would be feasible in future. A more sophisticated version of the model presented here would incorporate the lifetime dynamics of time allocation. As it is, the future is assumed to be like the present. Equally, the past is taken as given. Previous constraints and decisions the individual has made about allocating their time between different activities, including the accumulation or decumulation of different forms of capital (for example investing in human capital through studying, running into debt which now needs to be serviced), are regarded as fixed constraints on the present situation.[6]

Thus the resources individuals command and the responsibilities they must meet define a range of feasible time allocations. Each allocation implies a different combination of free time (T) and disposable income (Y). This set of feasible time-income combinations represents the individual's 'time-income capability'. Some individuals enjoy a large capability set, with plenty of scope to pursue their own projects and goals, over and above what is required for just getting by and meeting responsibilities in a minimally acceptable way. Note that those projects and goals may well include doing more of the same activities that are required to meet basic responsibilities. People may be bored or lonely in their free time but stimulated during work time or have great fun looking after their children, and may consequently choose an allocation which involves more time on these activities than the minimum necessary. Other individuals have a much more restricted range of combinations of free time and disposable income available to them. Indeed it is possible that the capability set is empty. Someone with no feasible allocations will necessarily be unable to meet their responsibilities – for example, they may be short of sleep, leaving children unsupervised, and/or be in material poverty.

The model requires us to examine all feasible time allocations, not just the observed (actual) allocation (as in most studies of free time), or just the allocation which would maximise free time.[7] In order to determine what counts as 'feasible', we need a definition of the 'minimum' required to meet responsibilities of different kinds. In general there are two approaches: absolute (defined with reference to a fixed standard) and relative (defined with respect to the actual distribution in the population, for example the distribution of time spent on the activity, or the distribution of disposable income), each of which has advantages and disadvantages. The main definitions adopted here of minimum necessary time on personal care, caring responsibilities and other unpaid work, and of minimum income requirements, are absolute. Full details and justification of the thresholds chosen are given in Burchardt,[8] along with sensitivity analysis using a range of alternative, relative, definitions.

Data and methods

To put the model into effect and examine the characteristics of individuals with smaller and larger time-income capability sets, we turn to a large-scale representative survey, the UK Time-Use Survey (TUS) 2000. The achieved sample size is 6,414 households, a response rate of 61 per cent. The data are used as the basis for simulating the range of free time and disposable income combinations available to respondents. The simulations are carried out for adults of working age (16–59 for women, 16–64 for men). A further restriction on the sample is that the individual is a member of a household with a 'simple' structure, that is, a single adult or a couple with or without dependent children. This accounts for around three-quarters of all households.

The simulations reflect the model in Figure 1 fairly comprehensively. On the resources side, human capital is captured in the wage rate and social capital is reflected in the help available free from others. No measure of financial capital is included. Public entitlements are summarised in free services from the state and social security. On the responsibilities side, the equations include terms for personal care, childcare, care of other adults, and other domestic work. It does not include terms for maintenance of human or financial capital. Some recognition of the need to maintain social capital is included in the model in so far as help received from others is evaluated net of help 'provided' to others. However, this is a rough-and-ready approximation, since typically help may be provided at a different stage in the lifecycle than it is received. The simulations also do not include a term for time necessary to sustain state entitlements.

Results

For each adult we calculate the free time and income which would be generated by different allocations of time to paid and unpaid work, given their responsibilities and other resources. Two cases selected from the sample to represent contrasting cases are illustrated in Figures 2 and 3 – a high wage individual with degree-level qualifications, and a low wage individual with no educational qualifications (neither has any caring responsibilities).

The horizontal axis is free time in minutes per week and the vertical axis is income in pounds per week (year 2000 prices, using modified OECD equivalence scale). As shown in the key, each line segment is for a different value of paid work hours (P).

We can see that Figure 2 has a far greater range of time and income possibilities than does Figure 3. Even if Figure 3 works 60 hours a week, he generates an income of only around £389 a week (compared to £1,442 for Figure 2), and that leaves him with 2 hours 48 minutes free time per day for a 7-day week. In general, fewer hours of paid work means lower income and more free time, so the line segment at the bottom right is the one corresponding to no paid work. There is a disjunction between the line for 16 hours paid work and no paid work because for the latter, income comes from social security rather than from earnings. In general, purchasing 'replacement services' (for example, domestic help) increases free time and decreases income, so the point towards the top left of each line segment represents zero replacement hours purchased and the point towards the bottom right represents the maximum number of hours purchased. This difference is more significant for individuals with responsibility for young children.

Other cases selected from the simulated results illustrate the differences made by variations in responsibilities and in gender roles within the household. Lone parents, for example, are shown to have much less free time to start with, and their additional paid work hours increase their income only slowly, because of the need to pay for childcare (if they work outside school hours or have pre-school children). Surplus income can be generated by working full time, but this is in many cases at the cost of 'negative' free time, in other words, not having enough time for the minimum sleep and domestic tasks, as defined using the absolute definitions used in the simulations. By contrast, those without caring responsibilities can keep the financial returns to their additional hours of work, without incurring time poverty.

For individuals who are part of a couple, the range of possible time-and-income combinations depends also on their partner's time allocation. In some cases, the difference in outcomes resulting from varying the intra-household allocation for a given number of hours of paid work is large; indeed greater than the difference in outcomes between the individual not working at all and working 60 hours per week.

In order to summarise these results and make more systematic comparisons between people with different characteristics and circumstances, we calculate what we call a 'time-income capability index'. The index excludes unfeasible allocations, that is, those that leave the individual with less than zero free time, or with income less than the absolute income poverty line. The index can be thought of as a measure of the area of the capability set. In Figure 2 for example, it is equivalent to the area of the triangle bounded by the y-axis (0 free time), the income poverty line, and a continuous line joining the point of maximum disposable income (top left) with the point of maximum free time (bottom right).[9]

Figure 2

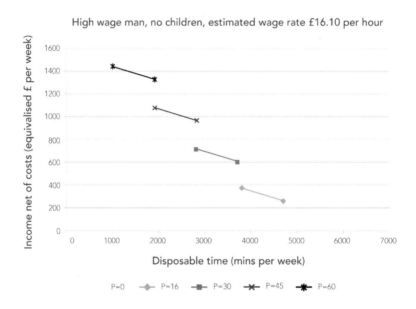

High wage man, no children, estimated wage rate £16.10 per hour

Figure 3

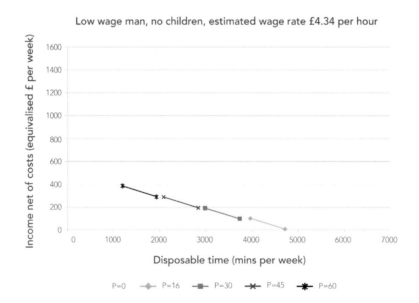

Low wage man, no children, estimated wage rate £4.34 per hour

Figure 4

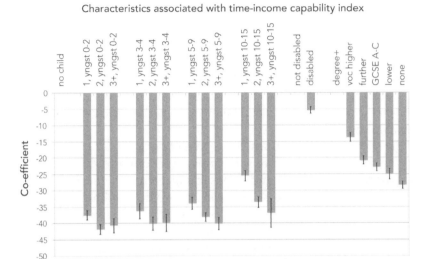

Characteristics associated with time-income capability index

(Note: Bars show point estimates; black lines indicate 95% confidence intervals.)

On this basis, 2.4 per cent of people of working age in the TUS sample have *no* feasible allocations in their capability set: however many hours they work and however much unpaid work they do or services they buy, they cannot secure an income above the absolute income poverty line and meet their minimum personal and care responsibilities. Households with children, and lone parents in particular, are strongly over-represented amongst this group. More broadly, multivariate analysis of the time-income capability index indicates that individuals without a partner, with more or younger children, who are disabled or who have lower educational qualifications, are likely to have smaller time-income capability (Figure 4). This fits with what we would expect from the model in Figure 1: those with lower human capital (low qualifications and disability), fewer household resources to draw on (no partner), and more responsibilities (more childcare, and more time-consuming personal care for disabled people) have a smaller range of feasible allocations available to them and less scope for pursuing their own goals and projects.

Discussion

The analysis presented here has a number of limitations. The simulations do not capture all aspects of the model in Figure 1, and the model itself is inevitably a simplification of the complex constraints and influences on individuals' lives. Perhaps the most important simplification is the implicit assumption that paid employment will be available at the individual's predicted part time wage rate for 16 hours per week, or at the predicted full time wage rate for 30, 45 or 60 hours, and that suitable childcare at average cost for the region can be found. Numerous studies attest to the fact that in practice choice over contracted hours is limited and childcare provision is patchy.[10] The results here thus represent the 'best case scenario' for all individuals. A more sophisticated version would take into account the differential effect on high- and low-skilled individuals, and on those with children of different ages, of the difficulties in finding suitable employment and childcare.

Despite these limitations, the model offers a way of conceptualising an important aspect of substantive freedom: the extent of your command over free time and disposable income with which to pursue your own projects and goals, over and above the minimum necessary to meet your socially determined responsibilities. Using the lens of the capability approach allows us to see that a person's substantive freedom is governed not only by her own characteristics (for example, human and social capital), but also by her commitments to others, by interactions at a household level, and, crucially, by the broader social and economic context within which decisions are taken, including the operation of the labour market. The rate at which a given time input can be converted into valuable outcomes thus differs significantly across individuals and depends on a wide range of 'conversion factors'.

It is difficult to anticipate the long-run macroeconomic effects of moving towards a shorter working week and the impact on those with currently limited time-income capability sets is likely to depend crucially on what remedial action is taken alongside changes in the maximum hours of paid work. Some of those with severely constrained time-income capability sets – especially those with low human capital and some caring responsibilities – currently work long hours, including in multiple jobs, in order to make ends meet. It would be disastrous for the household economies of some families to introduce a cap on working hours without improving the returns to each hour of paid work for the low-skilled (for example, by significantly raising the minimum wage, enhancing tax credits, or adding supplements to reflect the social benefits of some low-paid work) or tackling the underlying distribution of human capital in the population (through more effective training, access to re-training and genuinely comprehensive education from pre-school to university).

Others with severely constrained time-income capability sets are not in paid work or are working already under the 21-hour threshold; many of these are lone parents or others with substantial caring responsibilities. These families need different kinds of support, including better social care and childcare services (higher quality, more responsive to varying needs, and free at the point of use) and social security payments at a level that reflects the contribution these parents and carers are making – not only to the well-being of those they look after, but also society more widely.

A shorter maximum paid working week has the potential to improve gender equality and thereby enhance the capability sets of both men and women. However, while a reduction in women's paid work hours would reduce the demand for childcare, it would also, other things being equal, produce a reduction in the 'availability' of formal childcare and social care – since these services are in the main provided by women. It is unclear what the net effect would be. A reduction in men's working hours has the potential to increase their involvement in looking after their children, but again, whether this would actually occur depends on shifts in fairly deep-seated cultural norms. In the model developed for this paper, the most severe instances of time-income capability poverty induced by intra-household gender inequality are the result of decisions made within the household, rather than by purely external factors.

A reduction in paid work hours clearly has a wide range of possible benefits, including for those who currently experience severely limited time-income capability set. However, whether this potential is realised depends critically on what other policies are put in place to facilitate and support the desired outcomes.

Shorter hours, smaller footprint

The 'green life course' approach to designing working time policy

Martin Pullinger[1]

This essay discusses the effects of reducing paid working time on income, consumption and carbon footprints, and outlines an approach to designing policy to support and encourage working time reduction which benefits people and the environment. While it has been argued that working time reduction could, if carefully implemented, bring simultaneous environmental and well-being benefits,[2] little work has been done to measure the effects on environmental impacts,[3] or to work out how to manage the practical transition to shorter working hours equitably and fairly. In this essay, I focus on two key questions:

- What level of environmental benefits, specifically reductions in greenhouse gas emissions, could arise from reductions in paid working time?
- What are the implications for the design of working time (or work life balance) policy?

The first section of this essay deals with the effects of working time reduction. It starts with a brief summary of the environmental and well-being arguments for working time reduction, and then presents results from my own research, modelling the effects on greenhouse gas emissions[4] and household incomes of different scenarios of working time reduction in the UK and the Netherlands. The scenarios comprise a 20 per cent reduction in the weekly working hours of full time workers, and increasing use of career breaks for parental leave, early retirement, and other purposes over the working life, with corresponding reductions in earned income. I look at how these reductions would affect the incomes, expenditure and carbon footprints of households, and estimate the total change in national greenhouse gas emissions.

The second section looks at the implications of these results for the design of working time policy. Ideally, this design should be compatible with existing working time policy, to be acceptable and credible to policymakers and other stakeholders. To this end I focus on how working time policy is approached in the Netherlands and Belgium, where innovative policy for working time reduction is in place. The Dutch approach gives workers strong rights to reduce their working hours and take career breaks, and includes incentives to do so. This 'life course approach' focuses on enabling workers to alter their working time to suit their situation at different stages of their lives, with support to manage their incomes. However, it does not include environmental goals, and the incentives to reduce working time comprise just a few financial benefits. To design working time policy which incorporates environmental goals, I build on this model to develop a 'green life course approach', which emphasises diverse and innovative ways to encourage individuals to voluntarily reduce their working time. To account for inequalities of income, this approach gives due consideration to the different situations that people find themselves in, and considers ways to support low income groups to be able to reduce their working hours if they so wish.

The essay finishes with a brief look at future challenges for implementing working time reduction, including ways to achieve **nef**'s vision of a 21-hour working week,[5] and the barriers to working time reduction that need more consideration.

The effects of working time reduction in the UK and the Netherlands

Environmental and well-being benefits
The environmental benefits of reducing paid work, and hence income, seem intuitive as people would consume less and hence have smaller ecological footprints. It is also the case that, with different patterns of time use and levels of income, the relative amounts of different products that people buy would also probably change, independently of the total amount they spend. As different products have differing carbon footprints per pound or euro of their price, this too would alter carbon footprints, although in my research I find this to be a relatively minor effect compared to the changes in total expenditure. The well-being benefits of reducing working hours have also been studied. As Speth et al[6] put it, 'Scientists are discovering a convenient truth: our happiness does not depend on the consumption of conventional economic goods and services, but instead is enhanced when we have more time and space for socialising, for nature, for learning, and for really living instead of just consuming'. Certainly, a secure income and employment seem to be important to well-being,[7] but the link between increasing income

and increasing happiness reduces once a level of income is passed at which basic material needs for food, shelter, warmth, and physical safety can be securely met.[8] In short, time is a key resource for achieving well-being, happiness and other life goals, and the evidence suggests that for those with a secure and moderate level of income, spending less time in work earning money and more time outside paid work, engaging with family, community and nature, practicing creative hobbies and cultivating positive, mindful mental states, could be more conducive to increasing well-being and to flourishing.[9]

Scenarios of working time reduction

In my research I modelled the effect of three scenarios of change in the working patterns of the populations of the UK and the Netherlands. The scenarios are described in box 1 below: shorter working hours for full time workers, various new career breaks, and the two combined. The scenarios are intended to be achievable in the near term, and so

Box 1: Scenarios of working time reduction modelled in my research

Scenario 1

A 20% reduction in the working hours of all full time workers (those working over 35 hours per week). This is equivalent to a reduction to a four-day week, or three and a half compressed-hours days, which would offer scope for factories to have two workers per job for a seven-day operating week.

Scenario 2

Various new career breaks, namely:
- A total of one year of career break over the working life. This could be taken in various ways: as one year in one go, as two six-month blocks, or as four three-month blocks, for example.
- An additional three-month increase in the parental leave taken by both parents for each child they have (taken before the child's fifth birthday).
- Another three-month career break in the later years of the working life (for those aged 50+), taken by most of the working population before retirement. This could be for slightly earlier retirement, for care purposes, or for any other reason.

Scenario 3

Scenarios 1 and 2 combined.

they mirror existing policies in the Netherlands and Belgium (which are described in more detail later). For example, the types and lengths of career breaks in scenario 2, and their levels of use, are designed to be similar to those found in Belgium's Time Credit Scheme. This does mean that the reductions in working time in these scenarios are less than some authors propose. **nef** for example makes the case for a 21-hour working week.[10] Nevertheless, the scenarios still represent what the UK's Committee on Climate Change classify as a 'stretch ambition': that is, scenarios for reducing greenhouse gas emissions 'for which at the moment no policy commitment is in place, including … [for] more significant lifestyle adjustments'.[11]

I estimated the effects that these scenarios would have on working patterns, incomes, consumption levels and carbon footprints for different household types, and also for national carbon footprints. The modelling was based on the assumptions that everyone who was eligible to work shorter hours and take career break opportunities took them, and that doing so would be voluntary. The results are indicative of what could happen under one particular set of working time reduction options.

Methods
The effects of these scenarios of working time reduction were estimated in two stages. In the first stage, I developed statistical models which show how a household's carbon footprint, arising due to the amount and types of goods and services which it buys, varies with the working patterns and earned incomes of its household members. I combined data from household expenditure surveys, conducted annually in the UK and the Netherlands,[12] with data on the greenhouse gas emissions arising per pound/euro spent on these same categories of product.[13] Combined, the data allow estimates to be made of the carbon footprints for each household in the UK and Dutch datasets, and to calculate how this carbon footprint varies with the working hours, incomes and other characteristics of the household.

In the second stage, I drew on the same datasets to model the three scenarios of change in the working patterns of the UK and Dutch populations. The values of the working time variables in the datasets are altered for particular individuals in line with the scenarios being modelled, and the effects on household emissions are calculated based on the statistical model from the first stage, assuming that income falls in line with working time (so a 20 per cent reduction in a household member's working hours, for example, is assumed to lead to a 20 per cent reduction in his or her gross earned income). As these results relate to a nationally representative sample of the population, the total effect on national emissions can also be estimated. For accuracy, these national changes in emissions are calibrated against national carbon footprints calculated by Hertwich and Peters as part of the Carbon Footprint of Nations project (www.carbonfootprintofnations.com and see Hertwich and Peters 2009).[14]

Effects on the household
Table 1 and Table 2 below present the sizes of the reductions in average working hours in the two countries for the different scenarios, and their subsequent effects on income, expenditure and carbon footprints. The percentage reductions in working hours are averages for the whole working age population (i.e. including those not actually in paid work). Framed another way, they represent the percentage reduction in total working hours among the whole working age population. They are calculated assuming the take up rates for the different scenarios described above in Box 1. Reductions in income, expenditure and emissions follow from this, based on the observed relationship between these different variables in the household expenditure surveys. Note that the figures in scenario 3 are slightly less than the total of scenarios 1 and 2 combined because of the overlap in those two scenarios, i.e. some workers are taking career breaks and are also reducing their weekly hours when they are in work.

Table 1: Effects of the scenarios on working patterns and incomes for UK working age households

| | Scenario | | |
	1	2	3 - total of 1 & 2
Reduction in average work hours among working age households	17%	4%	20%
Percentage of workforce using policy	74%	16%	79%
Average reduction in gross income of working age households	13.3%	3.1%	15.9%
Average reduction in total expenditure of working age households	5.2%	1.2%	6.3%
Average reduction in carbon footprints of working age households	4.2%	1.0%	5.1%

Source: Pullinger (2011)[15]

Table 2: Effects of the scenarios on working patterns and incomes for Dutch working age households

	Scenario		
	1	2	3 - total of 1 & 2
Reduction in average work hours among working age households	15%	4%	19%
Percentage of workforce using policy	65%	17%	71%
Average reduction in gross income of working age households	10.2%	2.8%	12.5%
Average reduction in total expenditure of working age households	7.2%	2.0%	8.8%
Average reduction in carbon footprints of working age households	6.4%	1.7%	8.0%

Source: Pullinger (2011) [16]

The effects in the UK and the Netherlands on working hours are similar, with the shorter weekly hours in scenario 1 being the main source of the total reductions in working hours (in scenario 3), and the career breaks of scenario 2 contributing a relatively minor amount. The policies, especially for scenario 1, affect a large proportion of the population in both countries, the lower figures in the Netherlands for scenario 1 reflecting the already higher prevalence of part time work there compared to the UK. Scenario 2 has similar effects in both countries in terms of the proportions of the workforce affected by it, as both have similar demographics and labour market participation rates, and hence similar chances of taking career breaks under the assumptions of the model.

In the UK, the scenarios lead to a reduction in average household gross income in the working age population of 16 per cent for all the working time policies combined (scenario 3). In the Netherlands average gross income drops by a smaller 12.5 per cent. The effect of this on household expenditure is lower though, as it falls by a little over six per cent on average in the UK, and just under nine per cent in the Netherlands. The differences between the drop in income and expenditure reflect the fact that household savings rates typically vary by income too – the lower the income, the more of the money is spent rather than being saved for the future or used to pay past debts.

This drop in expenditure translates into an average reduction in carbon footprints of five per cent for working age households in the UK, and eight per cent in the Netherlands. These numbers are lower than the fall in expenditure because as a household's income varies, so does both its total expenditure and the relative amount it spends on different types of goods and services (so both the scale and composition of expenditure vary with income). At lower levels of income and expenditure, a larger share of a household's money tends to be spent on products which have comparatively high carbon footprints per pound or euro that they cost – things like gas and electricity for heating and lighting the home, and food, particularly meat. So a reduction in income tends to mean, on average, a larger reduction in expenditure on lower impact products, such as entertainment services, and a smaller reduction in expenditure on higher impact products, with the result that a household's carbon footprint falls a little less than its expenditure does in the scenarios.

Effects on national greenhouse gas emissions

My research indicates that a general reduction in full time working hours (as in scenario 1) would have a substantial effect in reducing greenhouse gas emissions, reducing the total carbon footprint of all working age households by 4.2 per cent in the UK, and 6.4 per cent in the Netherlands. The career breaks in scenario 2 meanwhile lead to a more modest but still significant reduction of 1 per cent of working age household emissions in the UK, and 1.7 per cent in the Netherlands. Combined, the two policies would lead to an estimated 5.1 per cent reduction in emissions from these households in the UK, and 8 per cent in the Netherlands. As emissions from these households represent just a proportion of both countries' total emissions, these total reductions are equivalent to 3.1 per cent and 4.5 per cent respectively of total national emissions. The annual tonnage reductions, 28.6 million tonnes CO_2e in the UK, 12.1 million in the Netherlands, are, to give an indication of scale, approximately equivalent to the total annual carbon footprints of Croatia and Cyprus respectively.[17]

The effect of the household's income band on its emissions reductions is also, as would be expected, significant. Figure 1 and Figure 2 present total emissions reductions from working age households split into five income bands (quintiles) based on their equivalised per capita income.[18] The disparity between income bands is marked, particularly in the UK, where the lowest income band accounts for just 1–3 per cent of emissions reductions in the different scenarios, whilst the highest income band accounts for 42–47 per cent of total reductions. In the Netherlands,

Total national reductions in UK greenhouse gas emissions for different scenarios of reduced working time, by per capita equivalised income band of household

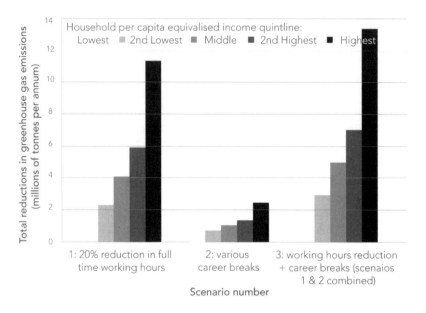

Source: Pullinger (2011)[19]

the results are slightly less divergent, but still highly unequal: the lowest income band contributes 5–8 per cent of total reductions, and the highest 25–37 per cent.

The results reflect the unequal distribution of jobs and wages in both countries. Within each scenario the take-up of working time reduction opportunities, and the fall in income and hence expenditure and carbon footprints which result, increase with household income band. Those who are not in work, even if receiving unemployment benefits (such as Jobseeker's Allowance) or other benefits, are likely to be in the lowest income bands so that a much larger share of low income households cannot reduce their working hours or take career breaks in the scenarios simply because they are not in work. At the same time, those individuals in lower income bands who are in paid work and who do reduce working time in the scenarios will typically have much lower hourly wage rates, so that their reductions in income, and hence expenditure and emissions, will also be much lower than for the higher bands.

This inequality between income bands is important: with the incomes of the low paid already low, how likely are people in this group to be

Total national reductions in Dutch greenhouse gas emissions for different scenarios of reduced working time, by per capita equivalised income band of household

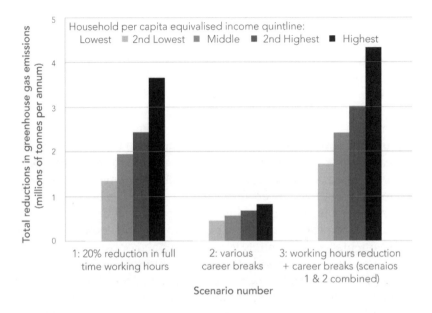

Source: Pullinger (2011)[20]

able or willing to reduce their hours if it means reducing their incomes still further? Wage inequality raises real issues for designing working time reduction policy that is fair and accessible to everyone in work, and the next section on policy design includes a look at possibilities for doing this.

Working time reduction policy – a 'green life course approach'

The results indicate that working time reduction could indeed contribute to greenhouse gas reduction goals. The total size of the reduction in the carbon footprints of the two countries in these scenarios also supports the argument that environmental impacts should be explicitly considered in the design of working time policy. However, when it comes to promoting working time reduction, how can policy reconcile diverse environmental, social and economic goals whilst being tailored to respond to the needs, preferences and capabilities of different demographic groups and different employment sectors?

The current situation

Existing working time policy, in the UK and the Netherlands as well as elsewhere, focuses primarily on instruments designed to influence people's working time choices through a mixture of time rights and financial (dis)incentives, so that people are either individually or collectively influenced to adopt particular working patterns at particular stages of the life course. Common examples are maternity and paternity leave rights, which may include pay; rights to reduce working hours (e.g. for childcare, or sickness); (pre)retirement policies; limits on the maximum number of working hours per week and the minimum number of holiday days per year; etc. These attempt to balance social goals – such as providing opportunities (for those who are able) to work and earn a living, ensuring adequate childcare, allowing time for rest and leisure and for recuperation after illness, and providing retirement rights – with economic goals, such as ensuring there is a high level of participation in the labour market and high levels of skills in the workforce to support economic competitiveness and provide an adequate tax base. Environmental goals are rarely if ever mentioned or considered.

The assumption behind modern working time policy is that all adults should be in paid work,[21] except when there are specific accepted reasons why the state should support them (such as in retirement, due to illness or disability, or for briefer periods of parental leave or involuntary unemployment). This is in keeping with the idea that 'paid labour plays an important part in the modern ideal of citizenship and makes up a vital element of any viable welfare state'.[22] At the same time however, other authors support the view that a person's life course is 'an individual project, one in which employment may not necessarily be dominant',[23] and there is recognition that people should be supported to lead increasingly diversified life courses as they wish (although this is usually taken as being within the constraints of being in paid work for much of the working-age life).

In the Netherlands, the life course approach to working time policy has been developed to balance an individual's freedom to live as they wish with the interests and needs of both the economy overall and different business sectors.[24] This approach aims to provide individuals with the freedom to manage their time, with support to save and borrow so that they can afford to have periods of shorter weekly working hours and career breaks. In this way, they have greater opportunities meet the varying demands on their time and income at different stages of their lives. The approach provides opportunities to exit and (re)enter the labour market in ways that suit individual circumstances, while tailoring these rights and the relative financial costs and benefits of different working patterns to also meet diverse economic and employer goals.

The Netherlands is an interesting case for working time policy. As well as drawing on this life course approach to design it, they go further than most countries in providing individuals opportunities for working time control and reduction. Weekly working hours (and wage rates) are moderated collectively, and are tailored to the needs of different sectors of the economy.[25] Individuals have the right to request further reductions in their weekly working hours for any reason, which employers can only refuse under exceptional circumstances. Part time work is commonplace, part time workers have equal rights (pro rata) to full timers, and average working hours are among the lowest of the Organisation for Economic Co-operation and Development (OECD) countries.[26] This combination of rights means that macro, meso and micro goals can all be pursued at once – that is, the overall total level of labour supply in the economy, the amount available for different sectors of the economy, and the working preferences of individuals, can all be balanced. In terms of career break rights, employees can use the Life Course Savings Scheme to request an (unpaid) career break of up to three years. However, this right is rather limited as the employer can refuse any requests, except where they involve statutory rights to a break (such as for maternity leave), for pre-retirement or for long-term care purposes.[27] This and the requirement to save in advance into a special Life Course account over a period of many years to fund any career break has severely limited its popularity among workers, with only about 3.5 per cent of the workforce saving for a future break.[28]

Belgium has a similar career break scheme, the Time Credit Scheme, through which individuals can take a break at any stage of their career, up to a year off work full time, two years part time (with a 50 per cent reduction in hours), or up to five years with a 20 per cent reduction in hours, in one or more blocks.[29] There are additional three-month, one-off 'thematic' career breaks for childcare, medical and palliative care purposes.[30] These are supported by a payment of around €600 per month,[31] representing stronger rights and incentives than those found in the Dutch policy. In Belguim, the employer cannot prevent an employee from taking a career break, except under specific circumstances, and must give the employee their post back at the end of a break. This scheme is popular with workers – use of the scheme is close to the maximum it can be within the rules, and it is increasingly used for part time breaks, that is, shortening weekly working hours.[32] However, there are problems with the policy too. Take-up has been 'limited to a rather privileged group of persons': mostly of relatively high income, two earner families,[33] who tend to have more financial resources to be able to afford a career break. By gender, take-up is primarily by women among younger workers, probably for childcare, although the balance is quite equal among older workers.[34] Despite, or because of, the scheme's popularity among employees, it also faces some pressures. Government expenditure on the benefits it provides during breaks and on the administration of the scheme is substantial, and growing.[35] Employer approval of the form of the policy meanwhile is rather low, particularly the limited ability to refuse take-up by employees, with employers reporting that the 80 per cent of full time option in particular is problematic for them to accommodate.

The Dutch policy arrangements also have their limitations. While the rights to reduce working hours are there, even with the constraints on the career break options, support to use these rights is fairly limited, so that the ability to use them is in practice also generally restricted to those with fairly high incomes.[36] Incentives to reduce hours and take career breaks are limited too, comprising just a few benefits for specific uses (such as maternity leave) and small tax breaks. In addition, due to rising government concern that in future labour supply will be too low rather than too high,[37] they are even rolling back some of the life course policies (the Life Course Savings Scheme is no longer available to new users, as of 1 January 2012). This in part reflects the lack of consideration of the environmental implications of such policies.

The green life course approach

In my work, I drew on the Dutch life course approach and developed and extended it in several ways to create a 'green life course approach' to thinking about and designing working time policy. Box 2 presents the main elements of this approach, and I describe some of these in more detail below.

Among its aims, the green life course approach gives explicit consideration to achieving environmental sustainability goals, as well as the social and economic goals normally considered in working time policy design. It also considers how to improve people's well-being in ways other than increasing material consumption, drawing on the growing evidence discussed earlier about the factors which are conducive to well-being, happiness and flourishing – factors which often require more time outside of paid work to cultivate.

For both environmental and well-being reasons, the policy instruments in the green life course approach aim to achieve a general and significant reduction in people's average working time through a mix of shorter hours and more and longer career breaks, with corresponding reductions in their total income and hence levels of consumption and carbon footprints over the life course. They are based on voluntary working time reduction and, through a range of financial and other support mechanisms, are designed to make working time reduction accessible to all workers, not just those on higher incomes, while diverse incentives aim to make it an attractive option for more people too.

Box 2: A green life course approach to the design of working time reduction policy

Aims

- To balance and meet:
  - » (macro) government environmental, social and economic policy goals;
  - » (meso) industrial sector labour needs, and goals for particular demographic groups, and;
  - » (micro) individual well-being and flourishing.

Policy instruments

Opportunities and capabilities:
- Provide individuals real freedom to control their own time:
  - » Time rights to alter working patterns at different scales: hours per week, days per year, periods of career break, retirement age, etc;
  - » Protection against impacts on future employability and career of reducing working time (job and employment security);
  - » Financial facilities: periods in paid work and in receipt of income decoupled, via saving and borrowing facilities – workers can take a career break and fund it either by saving in advance or through borrowing a loan and paying it back later;
  - » Other services in kind (e.g. childcare services) to facilitate desired patterns of work.

Incentives to reduce working hours and take career breaks:
- Financial incentives (benefits, tax credits);
- Increased provision of structured activities outside of paid work which improve well-being and the environment, including volunteering opportunities, community engagement, and creative and other activities;
- Diverse policy instruments to influence cultural and individual values, norms, practices, habits, behaviours and knowledge regarding the role of paid work, consumption and non-paid uses of time in the construction of self-identity and achievement of high levels of well-being.

Targeting and equity:
- Level of time rights and incentives increased for periods outside of paid work which are:
  - » Outside of individual control (e.g. unemployment, illness, disability);

» Used for socially valuable or accepted reasons (e.g. child-care, retirement, lifelong learning, community participation, volunteering, personal and spiritual development);
» Environmentally beneficial (either directly via reduced earnings and consumption, and/or indirectly via use of non-work time in environmental projects).

- Increased support for those who would otherwise not be able to afford to reduce working time.

Wider considerations:
- Rights and support differentially provided by three pillars: state, sector/employer, and individual, i.e. collective and individual provisions, to share responsibilities and to adapt overall outcomes to different contexts;
- Instruments to address employer costs, preferences and behaviours;
- Policy instruments adjusted at these different levels so that the sum of individual working patterns aligns with macro and meso goals.

Opportunities and capabilities
Time rights and financial facilities aim to provide the opportunities and capabilities for all workers to alter their working patterns to match their preferences, by decoupling periods of paid work from the periods in which the resultant income is received and used. A person could save in advance for a period of career break using a special tax-free savings account, as in the Dutch Life Course Savings Scheme, for example. Alternatively, where an individual would like a career break earlier in their career, such as for childcare purposes, before they have had sufficient time to save enough for one, a borrowing facility should be provided (a notable omission in the Dutch scheme).[38] Policy would need to protect employees from any negative impacts on their career from taking a career break, by ensuring that they are allowed to return to their job after the break, for example, similarly to the right provided by maternity leave legislation in the UK. The rights of employers to refuse a career break would need to be limited to special circumstances, as in the Belgian Time Credit Scheme, and consideration of workers with fewer financial resources to be able to afford to reduce working hours would be needed – see 'Targeting and equity' below for more on this.

Incentives

Restructuring of income tax rates and benefits for working time reduction is needed to reduce the financial benefits of working long hours and the income lost from working time reduction. LaJaneusse,[39] for example, suggests levying higher income taxes on long working hours and overtime, while benefits and tax credits could be provided for shorter hours and career breaks. With careful design such changes could be made fiscally neutral for the state, to help maintain state finances.

Working time reduction should also be supported and encouraged by diverse mechanisms, not just financial. Offering financial incentives to the employed population as a whole to reduce working time could be expensive, and may not even be particularly effective. Multiple avenues of influence on behaviour can be used, including use of diverse media channels to highlight the well-being effects of certain activities outside of paid work and the limited effects on well-being of increasing income once a certain level is reached, and providing increased levels of support for doing some of the activities outside of paid work that are beneficial for well-being, including the provision of more courses to challenge prevailing assumptions and ways of thinking, for example, by encouraging 'mindfulness',[40] and more support for voluntary and community activities.

As well as tailoring policy to particular demographic groups, incentives could also be tailored to specific uses of non-paid time. Higher incentives could be provided for socially and environmentally beneficial non-paid activities (such as lifelong learning, child and elderly care, or volunteer work in environmental and social projects), for 'social risk' events (such as redundancy or incapacity), and for activities which promote higher well-being.

The aim here is to provide more opportunities for individuals to pursue non-material routes to well-being outside paid work, and to raise awareness of the evidence regarding routes to happiness – in short to promote and provide the opportunities to adopt lifestyles in which people are 'less attached to carbon intensive consumption and more attached to relationships, pastimes, and places that absorb less money and more time'.[41]

Targeting and equity

Policy should also aim to target and treat particular demographic groups differently. As the results here show, from the environmental perspective it is important to encourage working time reduction among higher income households, as it is reductions in their working time and incomes, and hence consumption levels, that would bring the largest reductions in greenhouse gas emissions. However, policy also needs to consider the risk of a rising inequality in non-paid time, in which only these more affluent households could afford to reduce working hours. To prevent this, it is likely that financial support would need to be provided to particular demographic groups, to enable them to have real capacity to make use of working time reduction rights, notably low income households and those with children, demographic groups in which income is already more likely to be spread thinly and capabilities to reduce it further are more limited. LaJeunesse,[42] for example, suggests ensuring those households on less than median income (equivalised per capita) can reduce their working hours for a period without income loss, through receipt of compensatory benefits.

Generally shorter working hours and more career breaks could also potentially contribute to increasing gender equality, since in couples men are more likely than women to work longer hours and take fewer career breaks for child and other care purposes. By supporting more equal use of working time reduction and career break rights, a more gender-equal distribution of paid work and non-paid care work could potentially be achieved.

Wider considerations
It is likely that regulation would be needed to protect people's wage rates under reduced working hours. An assumption in the modelling here is that people's wage rates are unaffected by working time changes, and hence that gross incomes fall proportionately to the reductions in working hours. Although those taking career breaks often currently face impacts on future job opportunities and wage rates as a result, widespread working time reduction would also reduce labour supply, creating a relatively higher demand than at present, which would tend to encourage wage rate increases. A gradual transition to shorter average working hours modelled in this chapter could also in part ameliorate the resulting reduction in household income. An increase in the wage over time could at least, in part, counter the wage effects of reducing working hours.[43]

As the share of a person's income saved typically increases the more they earn, then pension sustainability becomes an issue under working time reduction. The risk is that as people begin to work and earn less, they would save less into pensions and spend more of their money directly. A range of tax and other incentives might be needed to ensure that people continue to have sufficient income in retirement, either through state, sectoral or individual schemes. Careful tailoring of financial incentives to work less would also be needed to minimise the overall effect on the public sector's financial sustainability, as mentioned above.

It is likely that policy would also be required to address employer concerns regarding working time reduction, and to make it more acceptable, even attractive, to them too. Restructuring taxes and benefits could help with any additional fixed costs of having to employ more people for shorter hours, and to make it financially preferable for the employer to do that rather than encourage long hours and overtime from its current employees. It is worth noting that this would not be purely a cost: employing two skilled part-time workers instead of one full-time worker reduces risks to businesses, as they become less vulnerable to impacts from staff falling ill, retiring, leaving for a new job, or taking a career break.

Sectoral agreements might be necessary to support sectors which are, for example, subject to more intense international competition, which are important export sectors, or which provide key services to society, to ensure that their costs and competitiveness are maintained, and that the country's trade balance and public service levels can be sustained even as private consumption levels fall. A range of wider effects on the economy therefore need to be considered beyond the immediate working time policies needed to support working time reduction.

Future challenges

The scenarios presented here indicate that a substantial level of emissions reductions could be expected as a result of ambitious levels of working time reduction. The scenarios also have outcomes that could result in, or are conducive to, reduced income inequality, greater gender equality in paid work and non-paid care, and increased well-being via non-consumption activities.

The direct reduction in greenhouse gas emissions might seem small for a given level of working time reduction, but the estimates are likely to be low, as there are sources of further reductions in emissions not modelled here. These relate to the need for reduced tax revenue to be matched by reduced expenditure elsewhere in the economy (either by the state or by taxing other groups more, reducing their expenditure), and to reduced household savings rates which imply further curtailment of consumption, and so emissions, in the future. Although not examined in this research, there should also be similarly important reductions in the use of natural resources and the production of other pollutants, benefiting ecosystems, habitats, and the people and species which rely on them.

It is clear that the link between working time reduction and greenhouse gas emissions reductions would continue to hold with greater levels of working time reduction. However, greater policy support is needed to give employees more rights to control their working time. At the same time, novel incentives, not just financial, would be needed to encourage substantial working time reduction. However, there are substantial challenges too. Countries like the Netherlands and Belgium demonstrate that strong working time reduction policy can work, but that careful design is needed to make any scheme accessible to all workers and attractive to them, as well as financially sustainable for government and acceptable to employers. These issues are real and influential, and in a globally free market system there are concerns about how working time reduction would impact on the productive efficiency of a country's economy and on its international competitiveness, trade balance and influence.

In the current economic climate too, how many people would be willing to reduce their working hours even if they had the rights to do so, risking signalling a lack of commitment to their employer? Strong policy support, and support from businesses, would help with this, by reducing the risk to the individual. It makes sense when there is a lower demand for labour, as in the current economic situation, to distribute the work more evenly among the population by reducing average hours rather than having some people overworked and others unemployed. Strong policy would also allow early adopters of shorter hours to act as high profile demonstrators of the benefits (and occasional challenges) of a lifestyle not so focused on long hours and high levels of consumption, showing the way in moving away from the dominant work- and consumption-oriented norms with respect to lifestyles and routes to well-being.

Some of the options in the green life course approach described here are designed to explicitly promote these non-consumption routes to well-being, ways of living focused on family, friends and community, on taking time to live and act creatively for oneself and others, and on appreciating the world mindfully. Encouraging such value change is likely to be as important to working time reduction as any policy, and another genuine challenge. It suggests a step change is needed in approaches to regulating, and thinking about, working time to reconcile and achieve these diverse environmental, well-being and economic goals. While a green life course perspective does not provide all the answers, it provides a framework in which the different goals, needs and preferences of different groups can be considered together, and suggests new ways in which reducing the environmental impacts of our lifestyles through reducing work and consumption can be coupled with human flourishing.

Time, gender and carbon: how British adults use their leisure time

Angela Druckman, Ian Buck, Bronwyn
Hayward and Tim Jackson[1]

In order to meet the challenging reductions in greenhouse gas (GHG) emissions set out in the Climate Change Act 2008,[2] it is increasingly agreed that behaviour change by households will be necessary alongside technological and infrastructure innovations.[3] The challenge of how consumers can reduce their emissions is generally approached from the perspective of changing the basket of goods and services that they purchase. However, an alternative way to consider the problem is to think about how people might change their patterns of time use.[4] Thus, rather than taking the more traditional focus of how people can spend their money differently, we can look through the lens of how they might use time differently.[5]

An important distinction between how people spend their money on goods and services (and the associated carbon emissions) and how they spend their time is that all of us, rich and poor, those who are always time-strapped and those who cannot find enough to do, all have an equal allocation of just 24 hours per day. In contrast, average UK incomes and per capita carbon emissions both vary by more than 1000-fold.[6] We can (and must) cut our carbon emissions per capita, but we cannot cut our 24-hours-per-day time allotment. All we can do is reduce one activity and transfer the time to another activity.

A necessary precursor to exploring the potential GHG reductions that may be possible through changes in time use, is to understand the status quo: although many studies explore the relationship between how households spend their money and the GHG emissions that the expenditure gives rise to, there has to date been much less focus on the GHG implications of how people spend their time. This study aims to contribute to filling this gap. Accordingly, in this study, we investigate the carbon intensity of different uses of time.[7] In other words, are the GHG emissions per unit of time higher for some activities, such as going to the theatre, than for others, such as staying at home and watching television? If so, how much?

We limit the scope of this study to understanding the time use behaviour of people in an average British household outside of their time at work (paid and voluntary) and during routine daily life (holidays are excluded). However, the activities of people outside working time are inextricably linked to their working lives and roles in the wider economy: people play dual roles as both consumers and producers in the wider economy. Therefore our paper also discusses some of the complexities that this interconnection results in and explores the complexity of modelling future scenarios.

This paper is organised as follows: First, we set out an overview of the methodology. Next, we present results, first looking at time use by an average British person, followed by the GHG intensity of time use. We then look at differences between the GHG emissions of men and women with respect to their time use. We conclude with a discussion of the insights that this work might bring in forming policies to move towards lower carbon lifestyles.

Methodology

This study draws on two major datasets: time use data for an average British person, and the GHG emissions of an average UK household. We commence with descriptions of the two datasets followed by an explanation of how they were combined.

Time use data were obtained from the Office of National Statistics (ONS).[8] The aim of the Time-Use Survey was to find out how people spent their time during a typical day. Data collection was done in four waves in February, June, September and November 2005, and thus intended to cover all seasons, with the main holiday periods of Christmas, Easter and August being avoided.

The GHG[9] emissions of an average household can be divided into two distinct categories: direct and indirect (or 'embedded') emissions. Direct emissions are those that arise due to direct fuel use, such as gas for space and hot water heating, electricity for powering lights, appliances and gadgets, and fuel for personal transportation. Indirect or 'embedded' emissions are emissions that arise along supply chains in the production and distribution of products and services purchased by households, such as GHG emissions embedded in food, clothing and vehicles. Embedded emissions that occur in the supply of products that are purchased by UK households are attributed to UK households whether they arise in the UK or overseas.

In this study we obtain direct emissions from the UK Environmental Accounts.[10] Non-travel emissions are then allocated to space heating, water heating, lighting and electricity for powering appliances and gadgets according to the Department of Energy and Climate Change (DECC).[11] Emissions due to travel are allocated according to time spent travelling as recorded in Table 5.17 in the Time-Use Survey,[12] and further disaggregation was carried out using the National Travel Survey[13] Table 4.2, assuming that time travelled is proportional to distance travelled.[14] Embedded emissions were estimated using the Surrey Environmental Lifestyle MApping (SELMA) framework. This framework combines the expenditure of an average UK household with information on the carbon emissions that are generated in the UK and abroad by every pound spent in various categories. Full details of SELMA are given in Druckman and Jackson.[15]

Time use data and GHG emissions data are in different categories and in this study were combined into activity categories selected to be representative of the household activities which incur both GHG emissions and time use. The GHG intensity of each activity category is defined as the GHG emissions that arise (both directly and indirectly) per unit of time while carrying out the activity.

The major limitations within this study arise from the aggregation of the two primary data sets of time use and GHG emissions into activity categories. Jalas,[16] in a similar study, argues that there is 'no single "right" categorisation of activities,' and therefore describes his household activity categories as 'a partly arbitrary attempt to decompose everyday life into sequences, towards which humans orient their attention'.[17] These observations also apply well to this study and it is important to note that the activity categories used are built up of many activities which are often carried out in many different ways by different households. For example, one household member may watch television on a small-screen portable set in the kitchen, while another may use a larger set with amplified sound in the living room. The motivation may be essentially the same in both instances. But the associated GHG emissions could be considerably different.

A further limitation of the study is that several time use and GHG emission categories are excluded, as in other studies of this nature.[18] For instance, paid and voluntary work-time is excluded, since household GHG emissions cannot be allocated to this use of time. Emissions due to furnishings, rent and financial services are excluded due to the difficulty in allocating specific time uses to them. GHG emissions due to holidays are excluded as the focus of this study is time use during routine daily life. A full list of exclusions is shown in Appendix 2. Due to these exclusions it is important to note that the relative intensity of time use activities is of more importance in our analysis than absolute values.[19]

A more detailed account of the methodology, assumptions and limitations of the study is presented in Appendix 1.

Results

In this section we first sketch a picture of how an average British person spends their time. We then present the estimates derived in this study for the GHG intensity of time use.[20]

How an average adult uses their time

The way in which an average British adult[21] uses their time is shown in Figure 1. Unsurprisingly, this shows that the highest single time-use category is Sleep and Rest, at nearly 9 hours per day, with Leisure and Recreation[22] being the next highest category, accounting for on average 5.7 hours per day. In this chart, the category Household, which accounts for an average of 2.7 hours per day, includes cleaning and tidying the house, repairs, gardening, pet care, personal care, clothes care and caring for others. Food and Drink, which accounts for 2.1 hours per day, includes both eating and drinking (including alcohol and eating out) as well as food preparation and dishwashing.

In the results that follow we show the intensity (GHG emissions per unit of time) of different time-use activities. As explained above, several time-use and GHG emission categories are excluded from the study. Time excluded from the study, which includes paid and voluntary work time, is 3.3 hours per day. The GHG emissions excluded from the study account for around $5.2tCO_2e$ per household of the total carbon footprint of $26.1tCO_2e$ per household.

The GHG intensity of time use of an average adult

Figure 2 shows the GHG intensity of some broad categories of time use.[23] From this we can clearly see that Sleep and Rest, as expected, has an extremely low GHG intensity. The graph shows that leisure activities have a relatively low intensity, at around $1kgCO_2e/hr$, compared to the daily average intensity of $1.2kgCO_2e/hr$. The most GHG intensive time use categories are Food and Drink and Commuting, both giving rise to over $3.5kgCO_2e/hr$. One notable feature of this graph is the striking difference in the time use intensities shown: for example time use associated with the category Food and Drink is over 42 times more GHG intensive than Sleep and Rest, and nearly 4 times as intensive as Leisure and Recreation.

One particular aspect that is interesting to explore is the importance of travel in the GHG intensity of time use. Figures 3a and 3b show more disaggregated time use categories. In Figure 3a the contribution of emissions due to transport is shown separately within each category. Here, the GHG intensity of the travel component includes both direct fuels used for transportation, such as petrol and diesel, as well as embedded emissions attributed to travel, such as those from the production and distribution of cars, and those attributed to public transport. This graph demonstrates the importance of travel emissions in activities that take place outside the home such as Entertainment and Culture (which includes, for example, outings to the theatre) and Sport and Outdoor Activities (such as trips to football matches). These activities are dominated by travel emissions. Conversely activities that take place in the home have, in comparison, relatively low emissions per unit of time.

Prominent exceptions to this are the GHG intensities of Eating and Drinking, Food Preparation and Dishwashing, Personal Care, and Repairs and Gardening which have high GHG emissions per unit of time, but relatively low travel emissions.

In order to understand these categories in more detail, Figure 3b shows the same categories of time use with the emissions allocated to: direct household fuel (gas, other fuels and electricity); direct transportation fuel; and embedded emissions. This graph shows that embedded emissions account for around 90 per cent of the emissions due to Eating and Drinking. These are emissions that arise along the food supply chain, including, for example, emissions due to fertilisers, pesticides and transportation. Similarly around 93 per cent of emissions due to Repairs and Gardening are embedded emissions. However, in the time use category Personal Care, embedded emissions only account for around 56 per cent with direct household fuels accounting for around 41 per cent and the balance made up of a small portion of direct transport fuels.

These figures enable us to explore which type of leisure activities are less GHG intensive in more detail than in Figure 2. Spending time with family/friends at home is the least GHG intensive category apart from Sleep and Rest. This category includes both spending time with family and friends when family and friends are physically in the home and also spending time with them remotely, for example talking on the phone or by electronic means such as through email. At around $0.6 kgCO_2e/hr$, this time use category is composed of around 56 per cent emissions due to direct household fuel use (which includes heating, lighting, and electricity for powering equipment) with the remainder being embedded emissions that arise during manufacture and distribution of equipment (such as telephone and computer).

Entertainment and Culture is the most intensive leisure time use category, at around $2.4 kgCO_2e/hr$. From Figure 3a we can see that the total (embedded and direct) emissions due to transport make up around 63 per cent, again demonstrating the importance of travel emissions. The embedded emissions in this category include, for example, GHG emissions due to leisure services such as running theatres and cinemas.

Men, women, time and carbon

Using the time use data identified and the carbon intensities of time use shown above, we now allocate total carbon to different high-level time use categories for British adults. Figure 4 shows the average daily GHG emissions of British men and women allocated to high-level time use categories. A particular concern here is to differentiate household work (and associated activities) from what we might call discretionary time – time spent in leisure and recreational activities. Hence the categories shown in Figure 4 are slightly different from those used in Section 3 above. Specifically, the Household Work and Commuting category has been taken here to include the following subcategories: Food Preparation and Dishwashing; Commuting; Shopping and Study. Other categories have been adjusted accordingly.

Figure 4 shows that the total GHG emissions for an average day are slightly higher for women than for men (around $22kgCO_2e$ for an average woman compared to around $20kgCO_2e$ for an average man). This is perhaps not surprising since women have on average more 'non-work'[24] time than men – 21.3 hours per day compared to 19.8 hours per day.[25] Conversely men spend more time at work and it should be remembered that the carbon emitted from work (production) is attributed in this accounting system to consumption based activities. In fact, the overall carbon intensity of time use for an average woman is almost the same as that for an average man, at around $1.2kgCO_2e/hr$.

There are, however, some differences between men and women in terms of the carbon implications of the way they spend their time. First, it is of course already widely known that women spend more time on household work than men do. So it is perhaps not surprising to find that the carbon associated with household work is higher for women than it is for men, slightly offset by the higher carbon attributable to men commuting to work. Conversely, men spend more carbon in leisure and recreation activities than women do: about 26 per cent of men's carbon footprint is allocated to leisure, compared to 22 per cent for women. This is partly because they spend more time in leisure and recreation than women. But it is also partly because they tend to engage in more carbon intensive leisure activities, spending more time in out-of-home activities than women do. This might be partially a matter of preferences, but it might also be related to the different nature of men's leisure time. This is because men's leisure time is generally more 'usable' than women's, as it is more likely to be in predictable and clearly demarcated blocks, while women's leisure time is less predictable, more fragmented and more likely to be interrupted and/or combined with caring responsibilities.[26]

The differences are admittedly not huge, and it is certainly not possible to draw hard and fast conclusions about sexual politics from these data. It should be remembered in particular, of course, that gender differences in this analysis can only be seen as proxies for role differences. Mary Douglas[27] postulated 'An individual's main objective in consumption is to help create the social world and to find a credible place in it.' From the perspective of this paper, we might paraphrase Douglas to suggest that the main objective of time use is to help create the social world and to find a credible place in it. It is not revolutionary to suggest that men and women approach this task in different ways. The results here indicate that these differences will probably have carbon implications and may well have important ramifications when it comes to carbon emission reduction policies, or indeed to work-time reduction policies.

Comparison with other studies

There are very few comparable studies with which to compare the results of this study, and, in particular there are no studies, to our knowledge, which explore the difference in GHG intensity of time use between men and women. The most comparable studies are those carried out by Jalas.[28] Jalas studied the time use intensity of direct and indirect energy use by Finnish households 1987–90. He used different categories of intensity to those selected in our study, but found similar patterns, with time uses that incur travel having generally higher intensities, and with leisure activities having generally relatively low intensities.

Similarly, in a study of the direct and indirect energy use associated with leisure activities by Norwegians in 2001, Aall et al[29] found that the energy use per hour was lower for leisure activities within the home such as traditional games, and radio and television, and that activities requiring travel were in general more energy intensive per unit of time. A notable exception to this was an exceptionally high energy intensity found for 'Redecoration'. This is similar to the high GHG intensity shown for Repairs and Gardening in our study (see Figure 3). Also in line with our results, Aall also found that reading was more energy intensive than listening to the radio and watching television.

Minx and Baiocchi[30] studied the material intensity of time use in Western Germany in 1990. Again, the categories used were different to those in either Jalas's, Aall's or our study. They found that the highest material intensity categories were Household Production and DIY, with Leisure and Socialising having relatively low material intensities of time use.

Discussion

We started this paper by reminding readers that the challenging reductions in GHG emissions required to meet climate change objectives will not be achieved by technology alone. Behaviour change is essential.

And yet to date we are struggling to engage consumers in the behaviour change actions necessary. This is, in part, because consumers are to a large extent locked-in to the systems of provision within which they carry out their lives. But it is also because carbon emissions are driven by aspiration, by the search for luxury, status and influence, and by the pursuit of the 'good life'.[31] Some of this is closely bound up with individual and collective identity and driven crucially by social norms.[32]

This study recasts these discussions in terms of time use. For instance, it shows that a significant proportion of carbon is 'locked up' in basic systems of household provision: the way we cook, shop, commute, care for ourselves, our clothes, our homes, and for others. Women's carbon footprint tends to be slightly higher because they spend more time in these activities. But this division of carbon simply mirrors a 'division of labour' in the home. And beyond this division of labour there are some potentially more significant 'divisions of leisure'. Men spend more carbon in leisure and recreation than women do, partly because they spend more time in leisure and partly because they spend time differently in leisure, preferring for example to socialise outside the home.

Leisure activities generally have lower than average GHG emissions intensity, at around $1kgCO_2e/hr$ compared to an average of all activities of around $1.2kgCO_2e/hr$. Furthermore, our study has shown, for example, that activities in and around the home, such as reading, playing games, or simply spending time with friends and family, are all relatively low GHG intensity leisure pastimes compared to those that involve travel. So a possible strategy for reducing GHG emissions is to shift leisure activities towards those that take place in and around the home. But such a strategy would clearly have to navigate the subtle and sometimes not so subtle differences that characterise people's use of leisure time. Gender is one those differences. But identity – even within gender – is closely bound up with the way that we socialise and the activities we engage in.

This possibility raises interesting concerns about carbon allocation and social justice – concerns that are likely to be exacerbated by a consideration of wider social and demographic differences between people. For example, Nussbaum discusses the economics of 'tragic choices', where many must choose between leisure time and a decent standard of living, choosing to work longer hours to support their family while knowing that family relations will suffer.[33] She considers the case of a single parent who may effectively have no choice over significant aspects of the use of their time.

Elsewhere Robert Goodin has reflected on our ability to control the use of our time, or the 'capacity to spend time' as one wishes.[34] He frames this discussion as a question of temporal justice. Goodin argues that there are increasing inequalities in particular over '…discretionary control over one's time'. Based on a review of six nations,[35] he argues that the type of person with the greatest capability to exercise control over discretionary time is 'almost invariably' the person in a dual income household with no kids (so-called DINKs). By contrast the person with the least discretionary time is often the 'lone mother'.

When we couple these concerns with the allocation of carbon between non-discretionary and discretionary time, we can see that carbon reduction policies may inadvertently invoke a dual set of injustices: temporal and carbon. As framed by Goodin and Nussbaum, this is generally a gender issue, however, with changing family structures,[36] it might increasingly be seen as an issue of household roles.

The complexity of this terrain should already warn us against simplistic expectations about behaviour change. Both household provisioning activities and the use of discretionary time are likely to be resistant to change without appropriate changes in underlying and supporting physical and social structures. This is clearly true for policies aiming to change leisure practices. It is also true for policies aimed at work-time reduction.

Many observers have advocated a decrease in working hours as a way of enhancing well-being and improving the social, economic and ecological balance of Western economies.[37] But this paper indicates that a simple transfer of time from paid work to the household may be employed in more or less carbon intensive ways. The actual carbon reduction achieved will depend on who works less and where that former work-time is allocated. The methodology employed in this paper could potentially be used to estimate these impacts. But simplistic prescriptions about associated carbon reduction are likely to fail. Much will depend on the whether reduced working time means reduced income, on whether reduced income leads to significant changes in non-working time allocation, and on whether the reduction in working time is shared equally between men and women, for example.

In principle, none of this detracts from the possibility that people could actually work less and still live better lives. But beyond the gender and income implications of this suggestion, it is crucial to identify the appropriate supportive structures that would allow us to lead 'slower' lifestyles, and spend more time, for example, to care for our children and the elderly or simply to have fun in less carbon intensive ways.

For instance, the analysis indicates that travel infrastructure is key to lowering the carbon implications of both household work and leisure activities. Evidence from the past suggests that we have constant time budgets for travel: the amount of time we spend travelling has traditionally not changed whereas the distance we travel has vastly increased.[38] With constrained income this may change, but may also lead to impoverished lives unless there are appropriate changes to planning and infrastructure provision.

One way forward, that might be considered a trail-blazer for future lifestyles in which deep cuts in energy use and GHG emissions might be achieved, is the concept of the '20-minute neighbourhood'. This is a neighbourhood where all basic needs, such as shops, workplaces, health facilities, libraries and recreational facilities can be met within a 20 minute walk or cycle ride.[39] Natural areas such as parks are included within the area and, because people are no longer in their cars and live more locally based lives, community spirit and social capital are increased, resulting in improved levels of well-being.[40]

These more ecologically sustainable types of developments offer two particular benefits that are relevant to our time use study. First, GHG emissions will be lower due to reduced use of motorised transport. Second, importantly, with such a radical change to infrastructure, our constant travel-time budgets (as discussed above) will almost certainly be disrupted, triggering other changes in daily time allocations.[41] Our study importantly gives guidance concerning preferred changes from a carbon perspective. By looking at the chart in Figure 3a, which separates emissions (direct and embedded) associated with transportation from other emissions, we can clearly see that leisure activities are the preferable form of time use, and that even trips to local entertainment centres are likely to have emissions below $1kgCO_2e$ per hour, assuming current technologies. Of course, the actual numbers will change, as (for example) renewables are further introduced into the energy mix and the thermal efficiency of dwellings is improved. But this example demonstrates how the approach used in our study can give insights into the time uses that might be envisioned in a future low carbon society.

Looking at time use by households without taking account of the interconnectedness of the economy is however, generally speaking, a heroic simplification. Households are both producers and consumers: in simplistic economic terms, households receive wages in return for working in industry to produce goods and services for consumption. They also invest their savings in industry, in return for dividends. The mix of goods and services that households choose to consume largely drives industry, and determines which sectors thrive.[42]

From the point of view of time use, the amount of time that households work is, of course, directly related to their amount of non-work time, and this has knock-on effects (although not so straightforward) for wages, prices and spending, and the output of industry.[43] A reduction in working time may generally be expected to reduce incomes and increase non-work time. Traditional economics might say that the mix of goods and services that households choose to spend their resulting income on can be estimated using income elasticities. But this would ignore the issue of time use, as income elasticities for different goods and services are biased when the dimension of time use is omitted.[44]

Nonetheless, the suggestion that reduced work time will lead to lower carbon emissions must at least begin to address the possibility of time rebound. Much depends on how the time freed up is re-spent. Under conditions of constrained income, people (and perhaps more particularly women) may spend more time in household provisioning and shift the balance away from less carbon-intensive leisure time. Not all of these changes lead to positive rebound of course. For example, if we had more time away from work, we may spend more time but less energy in shopping, cooking and eating, and be more careful with the food that we buy.

Estimation of time rebound effects relies crucially on the availability of data, and in particular data that indicates how people would spend time freed up. However, the availability of time use data is generally scarce: in the UK it is limited to data collected by BBC Audience Research in 1961 and 1974/5, ESRC funded studies in 1983–84 (winter) and 1986 (summer), and Office for National Statistics surveys carried out in 2000 and 2005.[45] Hence obtaining a time-series of data from which to estimate 'time-use elasticities' (analogous to income elasticities used in mainstream rebound work)[46] is problematic. An alternative approach would be to conduct surveys to ask how people might use any spare time. However, observed changes in time use allocation have shown that this approach is also problematic. For example, Jalas[47] reports that people have generally replaced saved time by watching TV, even though this is not on their list of desired activities when asked what they would do if they had more free time. Nevertheless, despite these difficulties, it is important that some allowance for time rebound is factored into policy analysis concerning work-time reduction.

Thus we can see that a full analysis of the implications of changes in time use within the home for carbon emissions is intertwined with changes within the entire economy, and any analysis must also recognise that some sections of communities may need additional support if they are to exercise their capability to use time in new, potentially less carbon intensive ways. Modelling this is a challenging task and outside the remit of this paper. Nevertheless, by developing a deeper understanding of how we use GHGs to support UK lifestyles using the time use perspective as in this paper, it is hoped that we can generate more successful strategies to help us move towards a lower carbon future.

Finally of course the astute reader will not have failed to notice that there is considerable potential for carbon reduction to be achieved by both men and women – including the authors of this paper – by getting more sleep.

Acknowledgements

The authors would like to thank members of the New Economics Foundation, and in particular Anna Coote, for the invitation to present this work at the Expert Colloquium 'About Time: Setting the agenda for a shorter working week', held in London in January 2012. We thank the participants of the colloquium and also the following people for the highly informative conversations that have contributed to this paper: Tracey Bedford, Jonathan Chenoweth and Carl Sofield. We would also like to thank two anonymous reviewers for their insightful comments and suggestions.

Appendix 1. Detailed methodology

GHG emissions of an average household

As explained in the main text of this paper, the carbon emissions of an average UK household are estimated separately as two categories: direct and embedded emissions. The year of focus for the estimation is 2004.

Direct household GHG emissions are recorded in the UK Environmental Accounts[48] in which they are recorded as emissions due to direct energy use in the home ('Consumer expenditure – not travel'), and those due to personal transportation ('Consumer expenditure – travel'). As stated in the main text, non-travel emissions are allocated to space heating, water heating, lighting and electricity for powering appliances and gadgets according to DECC.[49] Emissions due to travel are allocated according to time spent travelling as recorded in Table 5.17 in the Time-Use Survey.[50] Further disaggregation is carried out based on National Travel Survey[51] Table 4.2, assuming that time travelled is proportional to distance travelled.[52]

Estimation of embedded emissions is based on expenditure data combined with environmental data. In essence, it is calculated by combining the expenditure by an average UK household with information on the carbon emissions that are generated in the UK and abroad by every pound spent in various categories. In this study we used the Environmentally-Extended Input-Output (EEIO) sub-model within the Surrey Environmental Lifestyle MApping (SELMA), full details of which are given in Druckman and Jackson.[53]

The output of the EEIO sub-model gives carbon emissions according to 122 Standard Industrial Classification (SIC) categories. This classification system tells us about the industry sectors in which emissions arise. As such it contains some very useful information, but to tell us more about how people use GHG emissions to support their lifestyles, and we re-allocated this to 41 Classification of Individual Consumption According to Purpose (COICOP) categories.[54] This re-allocation is based on 'Households final consumption expenditure by COICOP heading' in the Supply and Use Tables ONS.[55] These categories are listed in Appendix 1 of Druckman et al (2012).[56]

Time use by an average household

The Time-Use Survey 2005[57] was an interviewer administered diary with 30 pre-coded activity descriptions. The respondents were members of the household aged 16 and over, and only one member of each household was surveyed. Data collection was done in four waves in February, June,

September and November 2005, and thus intended to cover all seasons. The main holiday periods of Christmas, Easter and August were avoided as the aim was to capture time use during a typical day. Weighting has been applied to the responses to compensate for response rate, and adjusted to ensure that the days of the week were equally represented.[58] The Time-Use Survey categories are shown in Appendix 2 of Druckman et al (2012).

Estimating the GHG intensity of time use
It will be apparent from the discussion above that time use data and GHG emissions data are in different categories. In this study we combine them into activity categories related to time use. Categories were selected to be representative of the household activities which incur both GHG emissions and time use. Details of the allocations used are presented in Appendix 3 of Druckman et al (2012).

The GHG intensity of each activity category is defined as the GHG emissions that arise (both directly and indirectly) per unit of time while carrying out the activity. It is estimated as follows. We estimate the total annual direct and embedded GHG emissions of an average UK household, which we call G, using SELMA. In each day we assume the average adult takes part in n activities. We assume that the average number of adults per household is p. Therefore each activity k gives rise to GHG emissions g_k such that

$$G = 365\, p \sum_{k=1}^{k=n} g_k$$

The GHG intensity $\bar{i}_k$ of activity k is estimated as

$$\bar{i}_k = \frac{g_k}{t_k}$$

where t_k is the time allocated to each activity k. The source of p is Table 5 in ONS (2011).[59] In the following paragraphs we give details of allocations.

As in other studies of this nature (see, for example, Jalas),[60] it was necessary to exclude certain categories of GHGs emissions and time uses from the study due to a lack of available data and difficulties in allocation of time and/or GHG emissions. As this is a household study, time spent in work (paid and voluntary) is excluded as it is not included within the GHG data. Formal education outside the home is also excluded, although study-related travel time and the associated GHG emissions are included. The emissions due to holidays are also excluded as the Time-Use Survey covers typical daily life, as described above. Financial services, housing rental services, furnishings and textiles, postal services and tobacco use have been excluded as it is not possible to match any specific use of time to them. Excluded categories are summarised in Appendix 2.

The category, Spending Time with Family/Friends Outside the Home, includes only the time explicitly recorded for which this was the primary activity, plus the travel emissions allocated to Visiting Friends at private home and elsewhere.[61] Therefore it does not include the emissions that arise in the main destination at which the time was spent. Hence these emissions may appear to be underestimated here, but this allocation was necessary to avoid double counting. For example, in cases where the destination is another person's house then emissions for heating another person's house will be allocated to the other person's household carbon emissions.

The time spent on each indoor activity was used as a guiding factor for the distribution of direct emissions resulting from space heating and lighting. Sleep is one exception, which requires no lighting and little heating. In the absence of better data two hours of heating were deemed to be required for each night's sleep based on the assumption that, on average throughout the year, heating remains on for one hour after the household members go to bed, and comes on again one hour before household members wake. Space heating levels are considered to be constant regardless of the activity being carried out. However, in reality, heating is most effective if adjusted according to the activity being carried out: for example, a sedentary pastime requires a higher temperature for thermal comfort than more active pastimes.[62]

The allocation of lighting according to the time spent on each indoor activity relies on the assumption that the use of lighting remains equal for each activity. However, in reality use may fluctuate depending on the activity. For example, it may require more or less lighting to read than to watch television depending in which room the activity is being carried out or the type of lighting used. However, such discrepancies should have a minimal impact on the results given the relatively low GHG emissions resulting from lighting, which are less than two per cent of households' total carbon footprint.[63]

In modern life, activities are carried out simultaneously, such as listening to music while preparing food, or having a meal while spending time with friends or family.[64] In the time use diaries, respondents were asked to record their primary and secondary activity. The data used in this study is the time spent on the primary activity for all cases except for 'Using the computer', as 87 per cent of time attributed to using a computer in the Time-Use Survey has a secondary activity related to it.[65] Thus computer use is allocated to the relevant secondary activity based on ONS (2006a: Table 15), making the assumption that the remaining 13 per cent can be allocated proportionately in the same way.[66]

Estimating GHGs due to men and women

In order to investigate the emissions due to an average woman or an average man for one day we assume that each activity k has the average GHG intensity i_k as estimated using equation 2. The Time-Use Survey provides estimates of average time use for men and women from which we can calculate the time ${}_m t_k$ that an average man spends on each of the activity categories in our study, and also that for an average woman ${}_w t_k$. We assume that the average intensity of each activity is constant. In other words, we assume, for example, that the emissions per hour due to a man watching television are the same as those for a woman watching television.

The average daily GHG emissions for a man ${}_m g_{day}$ can therefore be estimated:

$$ {}_m g_{day} = \sum_{k=1}^{k=n} {}_m t_k \bar{i}_k $$

where n is the total number of activity categories used in this study. The emissions due to a woman are estimated in a similar manner.

Assumptions and limitations

Inevitably in a study of this nature that draws on different datasets intended for different purposes, many assumptions are required and the limitations of interpretation of the study must be made clear in the light of these assumptions.

The GHG emissions are estimated for the UK. These are divided by an estimate of the number of households in the UK and number of people per household[67] to estimate the per capita GHG emissions. The Time-Use Survey[68] gives estimates of average time use for a sample of the population of Great Britain, and thereby, by using this dataset we assume that emissions and time use are the same in Northern Ireland as in the rest of the UK. In reality, emissions in Northern Ireland will be different as there is a greater proportion of rural households in Northern Ireland and also a greater proportion not connected to mains gas supply. Therefore the emissions associated with space heating and hot water are in particular likely to be higher per capita in Northern Ireland than in the rest of the UK.

A further mismatch is that the GHG emissions data for this study are for 2004 whereas the Time-Use Survey[69] reports survey data taken in 2005. We thus assume that the intensity of time use is the same for both years.

Another mismatch is that the Time-Use Survey included only people 16 years and over, whereas the GHG emissions are on a household basis with children included in the per capita estimates. Furthermore,

GHG emissions vary across different socio-demographic groups and geographical locations,[70] and these variations are not reflected in our study. Another factor to acknowledge is that many of the emissions, such as those due to space heating, are variable throughout the different seasons of the year, and this study presents an average for one year.

It is also important to note that the GHG emissions included in this study are those due to household expenditure. The study thus excludes emissions due to capital investment and government expenditure.[71] This is particularly important for some categories, such as personal care, as the vast majority of health care in the UK is carried out by the National Health Service which is government funded. Therefore the emissions due to Personal Care are underestimated. Similarly, the category Study includes study at home and travel for purpose of studying, but excludes emissions due to formal study outside the home, such as those due to running schools and universities. This is because expenditure for this was, in 2004, generally carried out by government and is therefore outside the scope of this study.[72]

Multi-tasking and multi-purpose goods can also reduce the credibility of set activity categories.[73] Accounting for multi-tasking, except where noted, is outside the realms of this study, however it is clear that this occurs for many household activities. For example, according to the Time-Use Survey[74] Eating and Drinking was often carried out as a secondary activity while Going Out with Family/Friends was recorded as the main activity. Caring for Children, the Elderly or Disabled is frequently a secondary activity during various household activities such as Food Preparation and Dishwashing, particularly in the case of women.[75] Furthermore, the use of multi-purpose goods presents problems for categorisation if use of the goods spans different activities. This is becoming more relevant with the increasing use of 'smart' phones and tablet computers. Such devices can be used for accessing the internet, watching television or reading.[76] Any future time use studies will need to account for the increased proliferation of such devices and their impact on the categorisation of activities.

Jalas[77] argues that it is not possible to allocate the energy use of certain household services and goods to time using activities and this includes furniture and financial services, for example, as in our study (see Appendix 2). However, Jalas[78] excludes heating and lighting whereas in this study, GHG emissions relating to heating and lighting have been allocated according to the time spent on indoor activities. This, arguably, provides a clearer picture of the true GHG intensities of activities taking place within the home. While Jalas[79] makes the point that this type of consumption does 'not require the active and direct participation of consumers in order to be consumed,' this study takes the view that even if heating and lighting are being used while the household members are not present, the related emissions can still be allocated to the activities for which they are required. For example, if the heating is left on while the household members go to work, to provide a comfortable temperature in which to have dinner and watch television on their return, then it stands to reason that the related emissions from the heating can be allocated to having dinner and watching the television. While similar deductions can be made regarding furniture and textiles, the vast differences between these items and their use in different households make any assumptions with regard to activity allocation problematic, therefore emissions associated with furnishings and textiles have been excluded from this study.

In light of the limitations presented here, the results offered in this study should be regarded as a first step towards analysing the GHG emission intensity of activities per unit of time for the UK. There is great potential for future research to provide more accurate and tailored results for households across the UK.

Appendix 2. Categories excluded from this study

Time

- Paid work
- Voluntary work
- Formal education outside the home
- Other

GHG emissions (COICOP Categories)

- Tobacco and narcotics (2.2)
- Rent paid for the housing (4.1)
- Rent paid by owners occupying housing (4.2)
- Furniture and furnishings, carpets and other floor coverings (5.1)
- Household textiles (5.2)
- Postal services (8.1)
- Package holidays (9.6)
- Accommodation services (11.2)
- Retirement homes, wet nurses, counsellors, adoption services etc (12.4)
- Insurance, financial and other services nec (12.5-12.7)
- Holidays: Aviation and shipping emissions.
- Expenditure by UK residents abroad.

Figure 1. Time use of an average British adult. Source ONS (2006b).

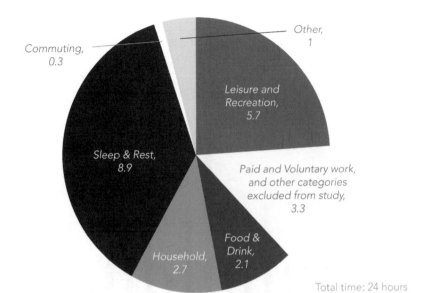

Commuting,
0.3

Other,
1

Leisure and
Recreation,
5.7

Sleep & Rest,
8.9

Paid and Voluntary work,
and other categories
excluded from study,
3.3

Food &
Drink,
2.1

Household,
2.7

Total time: 24 hours

Figure 2. The GHG intensity of time use – broad categories

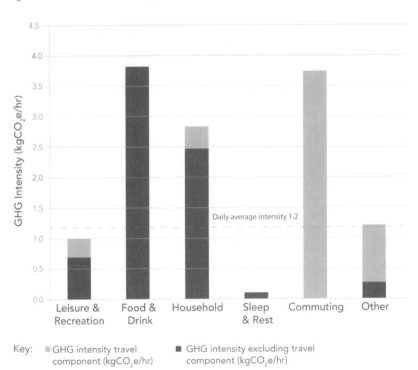

Daily average intensity 1.2

GHG Intensity (kgCO$_2$e/hr)

Leisure &
Recreation | Food &
Drink | Household | Sleep
& Rest | Commuting | Other

Key: ■ GHG intensity travel
component (kgCO$_2$e/hr)
■ GHG intensity excluding travel
component (kgCO$_2$e/hr)

Figure 3a. The GHG intensity of time use – detailed categories with total travel disaggregated.

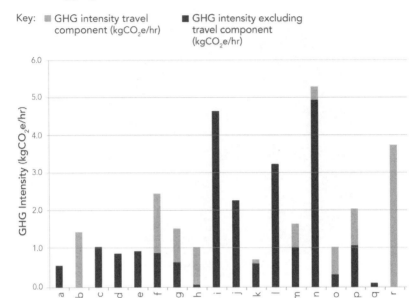

Key: ▨ GHG intensity travel component (kgCO₂e/hr)   ■ GHG intensity excluding travel component (kgCO₂e/hr)

a: Spending time with family/friends at home
b: Spending time with family/friends outside the home
c: Reading
d: TV & Videos/DVDs, Radio & Music
e: Hobbies & Games
f: Entertainment & Culture
g: Sports & Outdoor Activities
h: Shopping
i: Eating & Drinking (incl alcohol & eating out)

j: Food Preparation & Dishwashing
k: Cleaning & Tidying of Household
l: Repairs & Gardening
m: Pet Care
n: Personal Care (incl clothes, clothes washing & health care)
o: Caring for others
p: Study
q: Sleep & Rest
r: Commuting

Figure 3b. The GHG intensity of time use – detailed categories showing direct and embedded emissions.

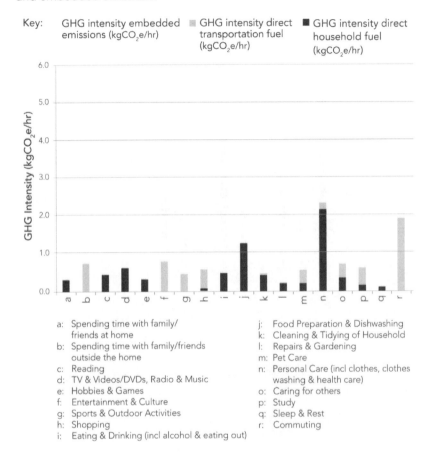

Key: GHG intensity embedded   ▒ GHG intensity direct   ■ GHG intensity direct
        emissions (kgCO₂e/hr)   transportation fuel   household fuel
                                     (kgCO₂e/hr)   (kgCO₂e/hr)

a: Spending time with family/
    friends at home
b: Spending time with family/friends
    outside the home
c: Reading
d: TV & Videos/DVDs, Radio & Music
e: Hobbies & Games
f: Entertainment & Culture
g: Sports & Outdoor Activities
h: Shopping
i: Eating & Drinking (incl alcohol & eating out)

j: Food Preparation & Dishwashing
k: Cleaning & Tidying of Household
l: Repairs & Gardening
m: Pet Care
n: Personal Care (incl clothes, clothes
    washing & health care)
o: Caring for others
p: Study
q: Sleep & Rest
r: Commuting

Figure 4. The average daily GHG emissions of British men and women.

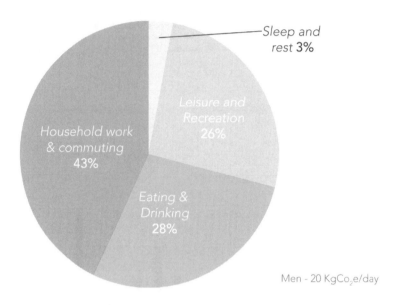

Men - 20 KgCo₂e/day

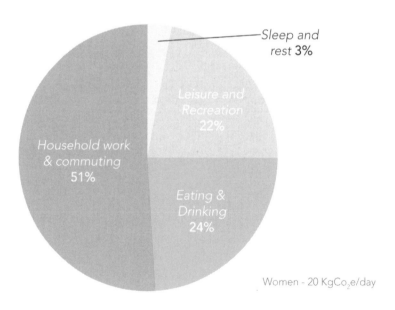

Women - 20 KgCo₂e/day

Learning from other countries

Patterns and purpose of work-time reduction – a cross-national comparison

Anders Hayden

Several years ago, I came across this quotation by former Dutch Prime minister Ruud Lubbers[1] defending his country's economic reforms, which included work-time reduction (WTR) as part of a successful package to escape a deep economic crisis and reduce unemployment:

> 'It is true that the Dutch are not aiming to maximize gross national product per capita. Rather we are seeking to attain a high quality of life, a just, participatory and sustainable society that is cohesive . . . . While the Dutch economy is very efficient per working hour, the number of working hours per citizen are rather limited. . . . We like it that way. Needless to say, there is more room for all those important aspects of our lives that are not part of our jobs, for which we are not paid and for which there is never enough time.'

At the time, I was struck – and I still am – by the way these words encapsulated many of the key reasons to seek WTR. Today, solutions are needed once again to an economic and unemployment crisis, and which also contribute to ecological sustainability, higher quality of life, and a more balanced society, while taking into account workplace efficiency. Another important objective – one not reflected in Lubbers' words – is gender equality, to which WTR can also contribute if structured in certain ways.

This chapter examines the various motivations for work-time reduction, as well as some tensions among them. It provides an overview of the main forms that WTR can take and the leading practices in countries, mainly in Europe, that have been work-time innovators. It considers the main ways to pay for shorter work hours, and concludes with some thoughts on the pros and cons of different work-time options and the opportunities to move forward.

Motivations for work-time reduction

Since the industrial revolution, two main objectives have motivated the struggle for WTR. First, working people and their allies have sought free time away from the job to enable workers to live healthy, dignified, and high-quality lives. In other words, WTR has been seen as a key form of social progress. This logic was reflected in the US labour movement's *Eight Hour Anthem* of the 1880s, which called for, 'Eight hours for work, eight hours for rest, eight hours for what we will'.

Second, work-time reduction has been seen as a way to reduce unemployment by improving the distribution of available work. As the American labour leader Samuel Gompers put it in 1887, 'So long as we have one person seeking work who cannot find it, the hours of work are too long.' Under this work-sharing logic, WTR is not so much a product of social progress, but a solidaristic response to economic hardship.

Today, these historical motivations – jobs and time away from the job – have been joined by new rationales. Advocates of gender equality have argued for work-time norms that enable a more equitable distribution of paid and unpaid labour between women and men. A related goal is reducing work-family conflicts that have grown alongside the increase in women's labour-market participation. These concerns have led to feminist support for a shorter standard workweek – such as calls in Sweden in the 1970s for a 30-hour week or backing in France for the 35-hour week – to enable women to participate as equals in the labour market and to encourage men to play a greater role in family life at home.

An additional reason to revive the historic movement for shorter work hours is the need to reduce environmental impacts. Steady increases in labour productivity – output per hour of labour – present contemporary societies with two basic options. People can work as much as before, resulting in greater production and consumption or, alternatively, increasing labour productivity can be channelled towards the non-material benefits of more 'time affluence'. In the wealthy global North, there are strong ecological reasons to shift emphasis from ever-growing quantities of material output toward potential quality-of-life gains for time-pressed populations. A turn away from endless consumption growth in the affluent North would also help preserve 'ecological space' for growth in the global South, where expanded output is needed to reduce poverty.

In addition to limiting production growth, work-time reduction could reduce ecological footprints in other ways. Time scarcity is often a factor driving individuals to make less environmentally sound lifestyle and consumer choices. By freeing up time, WTR could allow people to participate in more environmentally sound, but time-intensive consumption and lifestyle practices. Examples include cycling or taking public transport rather than driving; avoiding highly packaged, pre-processed convenience foods and other throwaway products; growing more of one's own food; or using a clothesline rather than an electric dryer. WTR is also part of an ecologically sound response to unemployment, as one key alternative to reviving conventional, ecologically damaging growth, alongside efforts to create new green jobs.

While advocates of work-time reduction have long highlighted the ecological benefits,[2] evidence from empirical studies and economic modelling has recently emerged to support these claims.[3] Institutional support for such arguments has also come from the UK Sustainable Development Commission[4] and the United Nations Environment Programme, which acknowledged that 'channelling productivity gains towards more leisure time instead of higher wages that can translate into ever-rising consumption also increasingly makes sense from an ecological perspective'.[5]

A more business-oriented logic has also emerged, one that links WTR for employees to workplace modernisation and, in particular, greater work-time flexibility for employers. Shorter but more flexible work hours for employees can, through new shift arrangements that include more evening or weekend work, enable longer operating hours for firms, allowing capital to work longer while individuals work less. More extensive use of capital equipment can enhance productive capacity and increase the return on capital. Such efficiency gains can, in turn, increase business competitiveness and enable WTR with little or no loss in pay. Furthermore, firms have demanded more variable work hours to respond to fluctuations in business activity, a change that can be linked to shorter average hours per employee. As discussed below, such trade-offs were central to France's 35-hour week and some other recent European work-time reduction initiatives. Even without such flexibility tradeoffs, WTR typically results in increases in hourly productivity in the remaining work hours, which can help offset costs to business. (However, this also means that each hour of WTR will generally produce less than one equivalent hour in new employment.)[6]

Work-time reduction can thus be motivated by various goals, including higher quality of life for employees, creating and saving jobs, gender equality, reducing work-family conflicts, ecological sustainability, and workplace modernisation. Some overlap exists between these logics. For example, the emphasis on quality of life, as an alternative to an ever-growing quantity of consumption, is a key part of the ecological logic – as is the use of work-time reduction as a job-creation tool. Nevertheless, tensions can arise between the different objectives, as discussed below.

Work-time policies and innovations

Work-time reduction can take various forms. The following section provides an overview of the key options and leading-edge practices.

Shorter standard workweek

In most countries, a workweek of 40 hours (or more) is the norm for full-time employment.[7] The United States, one of the rich world's long-hours nations today, was actually an early leader in reaching a 40-hour standard. Henry Ford's auto plants moved to a 40-hour week in 1926, while German autoworkers had to wait until 1967 for a similar standard. In the 1930s, the US and France were among the first countries to legislate for a 40-hour week. Well behind the United States were countries such as the Netherlands, where Saturday was a regular working day until the 1960s, and Sweden, which did not reach a 40-hour standard until 1973.

Since then, numerous European countries have introduced standard workweeks below 40 hours. France cut the standard workweek from 40 to 39 hours in 1982 and later, through two laws in 1998 and 2000, to 35 hours. Employees took their additional time in various ways, including shorter workdays, days or half-days off on a weekly or bi-weekly basis, additional days off on an annual basis, 'annualisation' (allowing companies to vary weekly hours throughout the year), and time-savings accounts to enable longer leaves. The 35-hour week aimed to integrate three work-time reduction logics: work sharing to reduce France's stubbornly high unemployment, maintaining and even improving firms' competitiveness through greater work-time flexibility and productivity-enhancing work reorganisation (as well as reduced payroll taxes and salary moderation by workers), and improved quality of life for employees.[8] Some tensions emerged between these objectives. For example, although numerous jobs – an estimated 350,000 – were created, this was less than originally expected. One reason was that many companies absorbed the change through greater-than-predicted increases in hourly productivity, which, for some workers, also created problems of work intensification.[9] Increased work-time flexibility for firms – which could take the form of more evening and weekend work, and greater variation in weekly hours – eroded some of the quality of life benefits for employees, particularly those with less control over when they could take their additional time off. Reduced income growth was also more keenly felt by lower income workers. Despite these imperfections, most employees who gained shorter hours said their overall quality of life improved.[10]

France's 35-hour week has been more durable than often suggested in the English-language press, which has reported on its 'death' several times.[11] Conservative governments did introduce a series of counter-reforms to encourage French employees to 'work more to earn more'. The original structure of the 35-hour laws was undermined, but neither Presidents Jacques Chirac nor Nicolas Sarkozy dared to eliminate the 35-hour standard, which maintained majority public support.[12] One of the first acts of François Hollande's Socialist government was to re-introduce taxation of overtime in excess of 35 hours per week.

Other countries have taken more gradual steps to shorter workweeks through negotiations between employers and labour unions. These include the Netherlands (36- or 38-hour week), Denmark (37), Norway (37.5), and Belgium (38, which later became a legislated standard). In Germany, labour unions had, by 2004, achieved a 35-hour week in several sectors with about one fifth of the workforce. One controversial element in Germany, as in France, was that employees typically accepted greater work-time flexibility – on employers' terms, including greater variability in weekly hours – in return for shorter hours overall.[13] In the mid 2000s some German employers, notably in metalworking and in public services, pushed to reverse previous hours reductions, claiming that longer hours for the same pay would boost competitiveness and shrink public deficits. The result was an increase in full-time workers' usual weekly hours.[14] However, since the economic downturn, WTR, at least on a temporary basis, has been back on the agenda in Germany as a way to save jobs, as discussed below.

Provisions to limit overtime, such as quantitative limits and taxes on overtime hours, are also important in capping weekly hours. Maximum workweek standards, such as the EU's 48-hour maximum, can also limit the recourse to very long work hours. The UK still maintains its controversial opt-out provision, which allows employees to work more than 48 hours on a 'voluntary' basis. Critics argue that many UK workers feel pressure to accept such long hours as a condition of employment, and so its elimination would be one option worthy of inclusion in a British WTR agenda.

Paid vacations/annual leave
The most striking difference between the EU and North America is the length of paid vacations, a form of work-time reduction that can considerably enhance quality of life. Although 97 per cent of countries have legislated a minimum paid annual leave, the United States is not one of them.[15] The average US private sector worker receives only about nine days of paid vacation annually, while one in four workers has no paid vacation at all.[16] Meanwhile, Canadian laws generally guarantee only two or three weeks' vacation, depending on the province and years of service.

In contrast, the 1993 EU Working Time Directive established a minimum of four weeks paid leave, while many European workers benefit from significantly more time off. Six EU countries – Austria, Denmark, France, Italy, Luxembourg, and Sweden – have a five-week, or 25-day, minimum, while 25 days is the average in collective agreements in several member states, including the UK. Meanwhile, collective agreements give Danish and German workers 30 vacation days on average.[17]

In 1998, Danish workers launched a national strike to demand a sixth week of vacation, which led to a phased in introduction of five additional paid leave days. Some might depict the Danish workers' demands as excessive. However, through a lens that prioritises well-being, equity, and ecological sustainability, the strike could be seen as a way for employees to stake their claim to a fair share of economic progress, and an enlightened choice of time over more consumption as the way to take that share. As a young Danish worker told the press at the time,'Everyone is talking about the good economic results in Denmark. As for me, I want my share in the form of more free time.'[18]

A related policy option is to introduce new public holidays. Again, the United States lags behind. American workers have no legislated right to paid holidays. Private sector US workers receive an average of six paid holidays, but about one quarter receive no paid holidays at all. Other wealthy nations guarantee all employees between 5 and 13 paid holidays annually.[19]

In the UK, the statutory entitlement to paid leave was recently increased to 28 days per year. However, this includes eight bank holidays, and so it could be more accurately considered to be a 20-day vacation standard, which is at the low end compared to other EU member states.[20]

One issue requiring further research is the degree to which the amount of vacation time, and the form it takes, has counter-productive ecological consequences. More vacation time may lead, for example, to more air travel and related carbon emissions; therefore, other complementary policy instruments and campaigns to encourage holidays close to home and lower carbon transportation choices are needed. Whether or not vacation time is taken in one large block or many short breaks will likely have different ecological impacts, and is perhaps even more important than total vacation time. Fewer, lengthier breaks – with enough time to opt for slower, lower-carbon travel such as rail rather than aviation – would appear ecologically preferable to the 'five-a-year' model of short getaways with numerous flights.

Parental leave

Parental leave enables people to scale back their labour time at one of life's most important moments, providing significant quality of life benefits, while creating opportunities – as well as potential pitfalls – for greater gender equity. Again, the US stands out for its meagre standards, with its Family and Medical Leave Act guaranteeing a right to only 12 weeks of unpaid leave, and only in firms with more than 50 employees. However, some US employees have better provision in their workplace.

The most advanced parental leave policies are again found in some EU countries,[21] notably in Scandinavia. For example, in Sweden, each parent can take up to 18 months job-protected leave after a child's birth. Couples can between them take 480 days of paid leave, at up to 80 per cent of their regular pay. The leave can be taken flexibly, at any time until the child reaches eight years of age, enabling parents to choose, for example, a shorter period of continuous leave or a longer period combining part-time leave with part-time work.[22]

Parental leave policies raise important gender equality issues. On the one hand, they are a valuable tool enabling parents to take time off with a guarantee that they can return to their job, which can be particularly important for women seeking to reconcile career goals and family responsibilities. On the other hand, gender inequality concerns arise precisely because mothers tend to take significantly more parental leave days than fathers, and this can put women at a disadvantage in the workplace. Sweden and other Scandinavian countries have been leaders not only in introducing generous parental leave, but also in responding to related gender equity concerns. One innovation is the 'father's quota' – a certain number of leave days that only men can take – to encourage fathers to play a greater role in child care. In Sweden, 60 of the paid leave days are reserved for each parent and cannot be transferred between them, while a 'gender equality bonus' adds a modest financial incentive for men to take a more equal share of leave.[23] Some 90 per cent of Swedish fathers now take parental leave before their child's eighth birthday. In 2010, men accounted for 44 per cent of parental leave benefit recipients and took 23 per cent of the leave days. There is still some way to go to complete gender equality, but a significant evolution is evident in Sweden over time.[24] One country where men take an even greater share (33 per cent) of leave is Iceland, where a 3+3+3 leave system reserves three months of leave for the mother, three for the father, and three for either parent.[25]

In countries, including the UK, where current standards fall short of those in leading nations such as Sweden, longer parental leave and more generous payment can be justified on grounds of quality of life and reduced work-family conflict, while measures to encourage men to take a greater share of leave can promote gender equality. The ecological impacts, however, may be mixed. On the one hand, like other WTR options, longer parental leave represents a form of time affluence that can serve as an alternative to production growth. On the other hand, if more generous leave results in higher fertility – and some countries, such as Russia, have lengthy paid leave in part because they hope to boost population growth – then the net ecological impact becomes more complicated to assess. Indeed, some studies suggest that lengthier parental leave does increase fertility,[26] although others find no evidence of an impact on fertility.[27]

A right to choose shorter hours – with equal conditions

Some countries have shifted emphasis from collective forms of work-time reduction, such as a shorter standard workweek or expanded vacation rights for all employees, to individualised options – or what some call 'time sovereignty' – over the life cycle. One example is establishing an individual right to choose shorter hours, with equal conditions to full-time work. The Netherlands has been a leader in this area. Under the Working Hours Adjustment Act of 2000, Dutch workers have the right to reduce their work hours, while part-timers who want more work can adjust their hours upwards.[28] Germany has introduced similar legislation. If a Dutch or German employee wants, for example, a four-day week for four days' pay, the employer can only refuse if he or she can show that significant business or organisational interests stand in the way. Such legal provisions give people more power to balance work with the rest of their lives and are particularly important for parents with young children. A central goal in the Netherlands has been to allow parents to work roughly 75 per cent of regular hours when they have young children. In practice, however, gender differences persist as women are more likely to reduce their hours than men and to do so by a greater amount.

An important element of the Dutch model, which makes the choice of shorter hours more attractive, is a legal requirement that part-time workers be treated equally to full-timers with respect to issues such as hourly pay, pro-rated benefits, and promotion opportunities. This principle of equal treatment for shorter-hours workers was also incorporated in the EU's 1997 directive on part-time work. The contrast is again substantial with North America, where employees seeking shorter hours often have no option to do so in their current job, and must instead consider finding a different part-time job with lower hourly pay, few or no benefits, and reduced promotion prospects. The combination of a right to adjust one's hours and equal treatment for shorter-hours workers helps explain why the Netherlands not only has the highest rate of part-time work among rich nations and shortest average hours per employee, but also the lowest share of involuntary part-time as a percentage of part-time employment.[29] Although the rate of part time work is high among men as well as women in the Netherlands, a considerable gender gap does exist; an estimated 76.7 per cent of women work less than full-time hours compared to 25.4 per cent of men, according to Eurostat.

Some nations give employees with special needs the right to reduced hours. Parents with young children have such a right in countries including Austria, Finland, Norway, Portugal, Spain, and Sweden.[30] The UK has gone some way in this direction by giving parents with children under 17, and some carers, the right to request flexible work arrangements, including job-sharing, part time work, and other options. However, unlike the above mentioned countries, UK parents have only the right to ask for flexible work and employers can refuse after seriously considering the request where there are legitimate business grounds. Meanwhile, older employees have special rights to reduce their hours in countries including Austria and Belgium. In the latter, workers over 55 have the right to work half-time or an 80 per cent schedule, while receiving an income top-up through the 'time credit' system discussed below.[31]

Until now, reducing work–family conflict has been the primary motivator of policies to enhance employee rights to reduce their hours. However, such rights could also serve an ecological logic, particularly if they are guaranteed to all employees and not just working parents or others with special needs. A general right to reduce one's hours can be an important tool for downshifters and others who reject the consumerist vision of the good life, enabling them to work only as much as necessary to meet their needs, while experiencing a higher quality of life, blazing a trail toward lifestyles with a greater emphasis on time affluence than ever more material affluence. Proposals in the UK to extend the right to flexible working to all employees can thus be seen to have potential ecological merit as well.

Sabbaticals and career breaks

Another form of individualised WTR involves enabling employees to take career breaks and leave for various reasons, not only for parenting. One pioneer was Denmark, which in the 1990s introduced a system of sabbatical, educational, and child-care leaves, with the aim of opening up opportunities for the unemployed, while allowing employees to upgrade skills and improve their quality of life. Other countries, such as Austria, Belgium, Finland, and Sweden, also introduced similar policies. The core idea is that an employee can take up to one year off to pursue their own personal projects, subject to their employer's agreement, and receive unemployment benefits or a paid allowance. The cost is partly offset by the money that the government saves when an unemployed person is hired as a replacement. This allows 'job rotation' between the employed and unemployed, in effect, converting one person's unemployment into another's leisure. Denmark and Sweden later scaled back their sabbatical policies as they grew more concerned with a perceived need to increase labour supply. However, Austria, Belgium, and Finland continue to provide such options.

Belgium's career breaks have evolved into a 'time credit' system, through which all employees can take a one year sabbatical, or a half time sabbatical over two years, while receiving a modest income from the social security system. Alternatively, Belgians can choose a four-day week for up to five years, while receiving an income top up on the fifth day. Employees with particular justifications, such as caring for young children or sick family members, can take lengthier leaves, while older workers, as noted, have the right to a shorter-hours job at the end of their careers.[32] After 2002, hiring an unemployed person as a replacement was no longer required – the primary goal became improving work–life balance.[33] Nevertheless, time credits have been one of the WTR options used in response to the economic crisis, helping Belgium to avoid a significant increase in unemployment despite a large drop in output.[34] In 2011, 2.8 per cent of Belgium's workforce took part in this system.[35] Conceptually, the Belgian programme is not unlike an extension of the public pension system, allowing people to enjoy paid time off even before retirement. Although some cost-saving restrictions were introduced in 2012, such as increasing the age when older workers gain special rights to reduce their work time from 50 to 55, the basic elements remain in place.[36]

Work sharing and short time work to avoid layoffs
The recent economic crisis, unlike the downturn in the 1990s, has not given rise in Europe or North America to widespread demands for further reductions in standard work hours. However, some countries have made considerable use of temporary work sharing to avoid layoffs. Most notable is Germany, a leader in using *kurzarbeit* (short time working) to absorb economic downturns. For example, instead of laying off 20 per cent of the workforce, a company could move to a four-day workweek for all employees, who receive payments from the unemployment insurance system on the fifth day. Such measures to cut hours rather than jobs not only spare workers from unemployment's heavy costs. Firms benefit by keeping their skilled employees and avoiding rehiring and training costs when demand picks up. In mid-2009, some 1.4 million German workers used the *kurzarbeit* system, which saved an estimated 200,000 jobs in 2008–09.[37] Short time working and other forms of WTR less overtime, reduction of regular hours, paying workers out of the 'time savings' or working time accounts built up in the pre-crisis years – played a central role in helping Germany avoid a large jump in unemployment despite the economic crisis.[38] Similar work sharing policies exist in other EU nations, including Austria, Belgium, France, Italy, Luxembourg, Netherlands, Poland, and Slovenia. One analysis concluded that, as a result of these measures, 'nearly two million European workers in 2009 did not lose their jobs, and retained much of their take-home pay'.[39]

The UK does not have a formal work sharing programme;[40] nevertheless, reduced hours at many British companies appear to have been important in preventing unemployment from rising as much as one might have expected given the depth of the crisis.[41]

In North America, Canada has a work sharing programme that, like Germany, uses the unemployment insurance system to finance shorter hours rather than layoffs. So do 23 American states; however, knowledge of such programmes is not widespread and their take-up rate is low. Even so, such policies saved an estimated 166,000 jobs in the US in 2009.[42] An important step toward the wider use of work sharing came in February 2012 with new federal legislation that provides financial support for US states that launch or expand work sharing programmes.[43] Among other countries to make considerable use of work sharing is the Republic of Korea, which gained experience with the idea in response to the 1997–98 Asian financial crisis.[44]

How to pay for shorter hours?

Just as shorter hours can take various forms, numerous ways exist to answer the question of how to pay for work time reduction.

The main option historically has been to take advantage of hourly productivity gains, which enable employees to receive a higher hourly income and shorter hours without loss in pay. Indeed, as has been emphasised throughout this chapter, from an ecological perspective it is increasingly important for WTR to serve as an outlet for continued increases in hourly productivity. In addition to productivity gains result- ing from external factors (improved technology, better management practices, higher education levels, etc.), WTR itself typically stimulates increased hourly productivity for reasons including less mental and physical fatigue, identifying and eliminating non-productive uses of time, and improved employee motivation. As a result, WTR will partly pay for itself, although the degree to which it enables higher hourly productivity can vary considerably.[45] There are both pros and cons in situations where WTR can be absorbed primarily through productivity gains. On the one hand, the problem of how to pay for shorter hours largely solves itself. On the other hand, there may also be less employment creation and concerns over excessive intensification of work, which can undermine quality of life gains for employees.

Efforts to link WTR to workplace modernisation – through greater work-time flexibility, longer operating hours, and other forms of work reorganisation – can also generate labour and capital productivity gains that can help pay for shorter hours without loss in pay. Some scope exists for 'win-win' negotiation on such issues between labour and business; however, negative consequences can arise for workers when, in return for shorter hours, they experience large and unpredictable variations in schedules to serve business needs. It is important to ensure that such forms of workplace modernisation and flexibility trade-offs are not taken to extremes that undermine quality of life benefits.

Another way to pay for WTR is simply for employees to accept lower incomes. This has certainly not been the norm historically, as work hours have been roughly cut in half in many advanced capitalist countries since the 1870s even as per capita incomes have risen tenfold.[46] However, contexts exist where it can be the appropriate option. It is the norm in cases where individuals chose to reduce their hours below the collectively agreed standard, such as the choice of a four-day week at four days' pay. Also, with work sharing to avoid layoffs, employees typically see some income reduction, although top-ups from unemployment insurance funds can allow for, say, a 20 per cent cut in hours with less than a 10 per cent cut in pre-tax income (and an even lower percentage cut in after tax income).

Historically, labour unions have typically sought WTR without loss in pay. It is indeed important for reasons of equity to avoid imposing pay cuts on low income earners. However, the option of a 'solidaristic wage policy' with income reductions among wealthier employees – who tend to have the strongest preference for time relative to money – should not be ruled out. Such a policy is worth considering particularly if it can be linked to commitments to increase employment and ensure that fewer wage moderation and work time flexibility sacrifices are required of low income earners. Some observers argue that a policy of this kind would have improved the outcomes and overall equity of France's 35-hour week.[47]

Work time reduction can also receive state financial support. Such support can allow hours to be reduced more rapidly than the rate of productivity growth, enabling bigger gains in free time and employment, while helping to avoid labour cost increases for business and large income reductions or other sacrifices by employees. When jobs are created or saved through WTR, state financial support can largely pay for itself through savings on unemployment insurance and other social costs of joblessness. This was the original justification in France for the provision payroll tax reductions to firms that introduced a 35-hour week.[48] Other options – such as leave policies that enable 'job rotation' between the employed and unemployed and work sharing policies to avoid layoffs – have similarly benefitted from state financial support in many countries. The cost of payments to those on leave or short-time working can be offset, in whole or in part, by the savings generated when unemployed workers are hired or layoffs avoided.

Societies may also decide that it is worth providing public funds to top-up the incomes of individuals who choose a shorter workweek or take leave of various kinds, even without any compensating savings on the costs of unemployment. This kind of support for WTR – seen, for example, in Belgium's time credit system – can be justified as an expansion of social rights by enabling all employees to enjoy periods of paid time off.

Of course, financially strapped governments have limited resources, raising the question of where to find additional funds to support WTR. One proposal has been to use revenues from new ecological taxes to support reductions in hours. This is a potentially interesting combination that would provide incentives to shift production in a greener direction, while at the same time shifting emphasis away from production to leisure.

Another possibility is redistributing income from capital and wealthy elites to enable the majority of the population to enjoy shorter hours. While cutting into the profit shares of productive enterprises could have negative consequences in discouraging investment and hiring, a redistribution of financial sector profits – which are of more questionable social legitimacy – could support further WTR. Such demands have appeared, for example, in France among advocates of a 32-hour week who hope to build on the 35-hour week's achievements, while avoiding imposition of income and flexibility sacrifices on less privileged workers.[49] Such redistributive proposals are obviously politically contentious. However, they deserve serious consideration as a way to reverse rising social inequality and promote WTR's various benefits.

In summary, there is no single right answer to the question of how to pay for WTR. However, the above options provide numerous possible combinations that can allow a path to be found that is appropriate to the context.

Weighing the options

Many options are available for reducing work time, all of which have positive features, but they differ in the degree to which they fulfil the various motivations for WTR: employment, quality of life, gender equality, work-family integration, ecological sustainability, and workplace modernisation. Another factor to consider is the degree to which political opportunities exist for the various options. With those issues in mind, the following section offers some thoughts on the path ahead.

A societal project to reduce the standard workweek – with a flexible range of options for how free time is actually taken – has much in its favour. By taking advantage of hourly productivity gains, a shorter workweek can be phased in gradually without loss in pay. Alternatively, the workweek could be reduced more rapidly than the rate of productivity growth, enabling bigger gains in free time and employment, but it is also likely to require employees to accept lower take-home pay. In either case, it represents a centrally important option for breaking from the current growth centred economic model. Shorter standard hours also enable parents to benefit from reduced work–family conflict, in a way that promotes gender equality in the workplace and at home, unlike separate shorter-hours options for working parents that, in practice, tend to reinforce gender inequalities. Likewise, a shorter standard workweek avoids creating different standards for older and younger workers, unlike proposals – which have both benefits and drawbacks – to phase in a four day workweek at 80 per cent pay by making it the norm for new hiring.[50] From an ecological perspective, a shorter standard workweek – and other collective forms of WTR – have another advantage. If the choice of shorter hours is left solely to individual downshifters and seekers of voluntary simplicity, their numbers are likely to be limited due to the challenges of swimming against the current and the consumption norms made possible by long hours. Shorter standard hours go further in establishing a new collective norm that challenges the dominance of 'work-and-spend' lifestyles more broadly across society.

A large-scale, collective reduction of work time will, however, be likely to generate strong business resistance – and will also face some resistance from those employees who prefer income growth over more time. Individualised shorter hours choices are likely to face less employer resistance. That is not to say that individualised options will face no resistance. For example, any measure that guarantees workers the right to choose shorter hours will be likely to face objections from some employers who see it as a regulation that impedes their autonomy and pursuit of profit. Nevertheless, some possibility exists to link individual employees' choices of shorter hours with employer desires for more work time flexibility to enhance efficiency. For example, having more shorter hours workers gives employers a greater range of scheduling possibilities, allowing more employees to be available at times of the greatest production need, with time off concentrated during times of less demand. Furthermore, individual choices of shorter hours typically involve employees giving up some income – a more appealing option for employers than shorter hours for all with no loss in pay.

On the employee side, individualised WTR options, such as a Dutch-style right to choose shorter hours with equal conditions to full-time workers, have the benefit of giving people greater power to shape their working lives. They respond to the diversity of employee preferences regarding time and money and ensure that hours reductions are concentrated among those who want them most. Campaigns to expand such options can appeal to the value of 'free choice', which is supposed to be a core value in a market economy, but plays a surprisingly limited role in the labour market in many countries when it comes to options regarding time versus money. Individualised WTR options have, as noted, particular value for working parents seeking a greater work-family balance. It is important, however, to be aware of the possible risk that such options could reinforce gender inequalities in the workplace if women end up being the ones who reduce their hours the most – as has been the case in the Netherlands. (That said, in places such as the UK where the right to request shorter hours is already available to parents – and, in practice, taken up mostly by working mothers – then extending such a right to all employees who want shorter hours for whatever reason would be a move in a gender-neutral direction.) Meanwhile, a right to choose shorter hours could enable individual pioneers to show possibilities of less-consumptive lifestyles, perhaps paving the way for wider collective change later – although it does not go as far in breaking from the logic of the growth model as would a broader societal commitment to use future productivity gains to reduce hours collectively rather than increase output. In summary, expanding individualised options for shorter hours could be a politically pragmatic way to enhance quality of life, reduce work-family conflict, share employment more widely, and promote less consumerist lifestyles, but it does have some potential pitfalls and limitations.

Sabbatical and other leave options are one way to combine some of the benefits of collective and individual WTR. Expanding such options represents a collective choice of shorter work time, but the individual employee has considerable autonomy over when to take advantage of opportunities for more free time over the life cycle. Variations such as the Belgian time credit system illustrate the possibilities of giving people a right to withdraw fully or partially from the workforce at different points in their lives for a limited time, while still receiving an income. Such policies can improve quality of life and reduce work-family conflict, while also potentially reducing unemployment through 'job rotation'. In addition, to the extent that time off is used for further education or training, there are possible benefits to businesses in increasing workplace productivity by enhancing worker skill levels. Such leave policies have not been motivated to date by ecological concerns, but they stand out as one appealing way to channel rising hourly productivity towards more free time rather than production and consumption growth. While paid leave options or a time-credit system have great appeal, introducing or expanding them will face significant political obstacles in countries currently focused on scaling back public expenditure.[51]

Much greater political opportunity has been evident recently in many countries for work sharing or short time working as an alternative to layoffs. These work sharing policies have proven benefits in preserving jobs and limiting the social costs of economic downturns – offering a potential 'win-win-win' option for workers, firms, and governments.[52] They can also serve a workplace modernisation/productivity enhancement logic, as they give employers greater internal flexibility and provide a lower cost response to business cycle demand fluctuations. The net effect is a form of 'flexicurity' – flexibility for firms with job and income security for workers.[53] While some limited income reduction typically comes with cuts in hours to preserve jobs, and some employees may experience this negatively, the added security can contribute significantly to quality of life.

Work sharing policies deserve to be part of the toolkit for an ecologically sound response to unemployment. The question arises whether they can also help to undermine the work and spend culture and give people a taste of the benefits of less stressed, less consumerist lifestyles with more 'time affluence'. Schor[54] has argued, for example, that work sharing in response to the crisis represents a 'golden opportunity' for Americans who otherwise have few opportunities to experience shorter hours if they wish to retain a good job with benefits coverage. Indeed, cases exist of workers who at first resisted downturn induced hours reductions and the associated income reduction, but later discovered that they preferred the new arrangement and tried to hold onto it once economic conditions picked up again.[55] More research would be beneficial on how different categories of employees experience temporary work sharing and whether it can contribute to longer lasting changes in priorities, but the potential appears considerable.

Work sharing could become much more than a temporary measure if the current period of little or no economic growth becomes a prolonged one, whether due to a lasting hangover from the bursting of the financial bubble, the political choice to respond to the crisis through austerity policies, or other forces. Rubin[56] for example, argues that as cheap conventional oil becomes more scarce, rising energy prices will erode future growth prospects, creating strong pressures to share the employment that is available. In such a context, the task will be to respond to possible hardship in an equitable way, and to turn the threat of chronic unemployment into opportunities for less stressed, less consumerist, higher quality lives.

Conclusion

One should be under no illusion that further work time reduction will be easy to achieve. History since the industrial revolution has shown that it has typically required significant political mobilisation to overcome resistance from most employers, who have over the years argued that competitive pressures and other obstacles made ideas such as a reducing the work day to 10 or 8 hours impractical.[57] The weakening of the labour movement in many countries also creates new obstacles to further reducing work hours in ways that simultaneously improve quality of life and preserve adequate employee incomes. In some countries, demographic concerns related to the aging of the population have led to arguments that employees need to work more to increase labour supply to pay for pensions and other welfare state programmes. Indeed, budgetary pressures have led to some scaling back of work-time policies that involve state financial support, such as the recent tightening of eligibility criteria for older workers to make use of Belgium's time-credit system. Such concerns cannot be simply dismissed, however, given the urgency of addressing ecological challenges and, in particular, reducing emissions leading to climate change, the case can be made for alternatives to a vision of progress premised on endless output growth. And, as noted, an extended period of slow growth driven by other factors could very well push the need for WTR onto the agenda.

Although there are considerable obstacles to overcome and some tensions between different objectives to navigate, it is worth remembering the significant achievements in reducing work time since the industrial revolution and also the contemporary examples of places that have given their citizens a taste of greater time affluence. For example, a British expat recently described her experience of moving from London to Copenhagen.[58] 'The greatest change has been the shift in work–life balance,' she writes. 'Whereas previously we might snatch dinner once [my husband] escaped from work at around nine, he now leaves his desk at five. Work later than 5.30 and the office is a morgue. Work at the weekend and the Danes think you are mad.' By these standards – and others – the world many of us inhabit is mad. Building on some of the most advanced work-time initiatives could make things somewhat less mad, and take us at least part of the way toward an ecologically sustainable society with high levels of employment, greater gender equality, less work-family conflict, and a high quality of life.

The French experience

Dominique Méda

The introduction of the two 'Aubry laws' to reduce working hours in France (RTT[1]), in 1998 and 2001, was preceded by a considerable amount of academic and intellectual debate. On the one hand, it was argued (by myself and others) that it was necessary to commit to large-scale reduction in working hours to make more room for citizenship activities (political involvement), and for family and personal development. The idea was to recover some lost individual freedom and to stimulate collective action. The 'depoliticisation of the masses' identified by Habermas could be combated through a reduction in hours, while changes in society had to begin with changes in the sphere of work.[2] Furthermore, a reduction in working hours would allow for a rebalancing of time investment by men and women. It could lead to an increase in responsibility for household and family tasks by men and, as a result, to an improvement in employment opportunities and financial independence for women, although of course this would not happen automatically.[3]

On the other hand, it was argued, mainly by economists, that the main purpose of the RTT was to support the fight against unemployment. Jacques Rigaudiat, for example, (author of *Réduire le Temps de Travail*[4] in 1996 and later advisor to Prime Minister Lionel Jospin) believed above all in the capacity of the RTT to create jobs when French unemployment was at a peak. In 1998, a study carried out by the Banque de France[5] and the Observatoire Français des Conjonctures Economiques (OFCE),[6, 7] had calculated that the number of jobs likely to be created by the reduction in working hours would be 750,000. Another author, Pierre Larrouturou, was arguing at the time for a four-day week, on the grounds that it would create more jobs as well as easing the pressure on travel between work and home.

When the left came to power in France in 1997, plans to reduce working hours were still under-developed. Nevertheless, this became one of the new government's priorities for action. In October 1997, it was announced that a bill to reduce working time to 35 hours a week would be presented to Parliament by the end of the year, with small businesses being allowed an extra two years preparation. The reduction in hours would operate without a reduction in salaries, and the bill set out financial incentives for companies negotiating an hours reduction before the deadline.

The first RTT law, in June 1998, set the new legal working hours at 35, to be reached by the year 2000 by companies with more than 20 employees. It made provision for financial support for companies that negotiated RTT agreements and maintained or increased employment levels. To benefit from the financial incentive, companies had to commit to calculate working hours before and after RTT in the same way and in a consistent fashion. This meant that established breaks, such as national holidays, had to be left untouched. The reduction had to be considerable and to be implemented at one stroke. This was to avoid incremental change leading to productivity gains that could pre-empt the need to create new jobs. The Minister for Employment, Martine Aubry, was to say repeatedly throughout the years when the RTT was being implemented that this measure was also designed to increase employees' leisure and 'fun' time. But the primary objective was the creation of jobs. Secondary objectives were the improvement of work time flexibility and revival of workplace negotiation.

The employers' organisation, Mouvement des Entreprises de France (MEDEF),[8] immediately opposed the 35-hour week becoming a legal obligation. Between 1998 and 2000, employers signed numerous voluntary agreements to reduce working time in exchange for greater flexibility and a low level of job creation, without recourse to state finance. Just before the second law was enacted in 2000, 122 professional branches covering over ten million employees had signed an agreement on reduction of working time.[9] The second law ratified these negotiations and introduced a new form of hours flexibility that was less restrictive, notably in terms of the obligation to create jobs and to calculate hours consistently. In 2005, 60 per cent of employees were working in companies which had made the transition to 35 hours. The reduction in working time was lower than 10 per cent because many companies did not adhere to the agreed calculation of working time and achieved increases in productivity or had recourse to flexible working. Studies have demonstrated that between 1995 and 2001, working hours had been reduced, on average, by only one hour and 20 minutes per week.[10]

So, in summary, whereas the first law aimed for a substantial reduction in working hours and the creation of a large number of jobs, the opposition of employers and the introduction of a second law which was far less restrictive transformed the trial. It is for this reason that many researchers in France are keen to distinguish between the two laws: the first being considered as the draft of a rigorous project to reduce working hours aiming to fight against unemployment and to share out jobs; the second as bearing witness to a kind of employer victory which succeeded in weakening the first objective considerably. The second law did less to reduce the working hours of individuals, than to make their hours more flexible, largely to the advantage of employers. A distinction can thus be made between employees whose working time was reduced under the influence of the first law (1998 to 2000) and those whose working hours were reduced after this time.

The impact of working hours reduction

The RTT was the object of intense debate and passionate opposition in France. The head of the employers' organisation resigned at the end of the conference during which the RTT was announced, and the MEDEF ceaselessly opposed the application of this law. In 2002 and above all in 2007, the RTT and its effects were at the centre of debate during the presidential campaign. The political right insisted that the RTT had fostered the perception of work as drudgery. This led to a focus, before and during the presidential campaign of 2007, on the theme of the 'work ethic'. The right maintained that

- the RTT had diminished enthusiasm for work and effort among the French,
- it had been enormously costly,
- companies had been, and would continue to be, impeded by the RTT, and
- France would be among the countries working the least, which would explain a considerable gap in standard of living between France and other countries, for example the United States.

Meanwhile, critical elements on the political left insisted that the RTT was the root cause of

- a significant escalation of work, and of a deterioration in working conditions,
- a significant increase in flexible working and irregular hours,
- a significant reduction in salaries, and
- a worsening of the inequalities between employees.

To examine the effects of the RTT, several surveys were conducted, not only by the Minister for Employment, but also by independent research-ers. A special issue of *Economie et Statistique*[11] was devoted to this topic in 2005. The principal findings were as follows.

There is no tangible indication of 'reduction of work ethic' in France, on the contrary: in Europe the French attribute the most importance to work and have the strongest desire to fulfill their potential at work.[12]

The RTT was directly accompanied by the creation of 350,000 jobs between 1998 and 2002, though it is not known whether this is attributable to the *RTT* itself or to the reduction of *cotisations sociales* (social contributions).[13]

The implementation of the RTT was accompanied by the re-organisation of working practices which were beneficial to companies and by an increase in flexible working for employers: Askenazy[14] demonstrated that the Aubry laws can therefore be interpreted as a tool to facilitate organisational change by (large) French companies to achieve productive flexibilities that were necessary in the context of technological change and increased competition.

It is incorrect that France is the country where people work the least. Essentially, it depends which formulae are used to measure working hours. The reduction in average working hours per week was significantly lower than four hours. This was partly due to many companies changing the way they calculated working hours (some, for example, removed break times from their calculation). In addition, there was no maximum limit on the working week.

France, along with the United Kingdom, is in an intermediate position, between those countries with a relatively low number of working hours (Germany, but above all the Netherlands), and those where the number of working hours is high (Italy, Spain and in particular the United States). The report puts the issue regarding legal or contractual hours relating to full-time employees into perspective. Since the implementation of the legislation relating to the 35-hour working week, France is distinct in having the lowest legal and contractual number of working hours of the group of industrialised countries studied. In fact, in most of the other countries, the legal or contractual weekly hours of full-time employees is slightly higher than 38 hours. When one compares not the weekly legal or contractual hours of full-time employees, but the usual weekly number of hours stated by the whole group of employees, part-time and full-time, the dispersal is distinctly higher mainly due to the part-time impact. Germany and the Netherlands, where part-time jobs of very short duration are the most developed, are distinguished by a very low weekly number of working hours, as stated by employees, less than 30 hours.

Contrary to commentary during the RTT process, the legislation did not bring about a massive reduction of hours, or a massive increase in irregular hours: about 5 per cent of company employees who moved to 35 hours and who had previously worked the same number of days per week with the same hours, moved to regular patterns organised over longer periods than the week, or saw their days and hours of work vary in an erratic fashion. The irregularity of days worked occurred more in industry than in the service sector, while irregularity of times worked only affected management.[15]

Again, contrary to commentary during the RTT process, the working conditions of employees who had moved to 35 hours do not appear to have been worsened by the 35-hours rule, quite the reverse. Coutrot[16] shows that the employees who benefitted from a reduction in working hours in 2002–03 had a working time which was markedly more flexible that the other employees, though their hours were more predictable. Their work was organised in a more restrictive manner but they were subjected to less pressure in terms of time. Moreover, these employees benefitted from more support from their colleagues. These relatively favourable working conditions did not, of course, necessarily result in shorter hours, and could have existed before the implementation of the RTT. Nevertheless, half of the employees thought that the reduction in their working hours had improved their situation, one third that it had changed nothing, and one in seven that it had worsened it. Another study by Estrade, Méda and Orain[17] found that half of the full-time employees whose hours were reduced under the first law considered that their working conditions had not changed. A quarter said they had worsened and a quarter that they had improved.

The RTT was at the root of an unprecedented contractual operation: it was informative and encouraged professional relations within companies.[18] It has been found that 9 out of 10 establishments with at least 20 employees claim to have moved to a reduction in working time between 1996 and 2003. For those who did so in 1999 or before, professional relations differed greatly from the others. The larger companies who were the best equipped with trade union representatives and with institutions representing staff, maintained their professional relations. In companies (mainly smaller in size) who reduced the length of working time belatedly or not at all, professional relations were weaker. Those establishments that applied the RTT in 2000 and afterwards gained the most in terms of introducing or strengthening trade union representation. Organisations that reduced working hours belatedly also progressed more in terms of worker representation by an elected body. Where organisations implemented RTT, negotiations were intense – not only around working time, but also extending into other aspects of work and working conditions.

The impact on employees

There are few studies on the effects of the RTT on employees. The only large-scale survey, *Reduction in Working Time and Lifestyles*[19] (initiated by this author at the Ministry of Work and Employment), was carried out in 2001 using a sample of more than 1,000 people who worked full time before the RTT and experienced a reduction in their working hours mainly as a result of the first Aubry law. The results were as follows.

When interviewed about the overall outcome with regard to the reduction in working hours on their daily life, 'at work as well as outside of work', 59 per cent of employees interviewed said that these effects were 'heading in the direction of an improvement', 13 per cent were 'heading in the direction of a deterioration' and 28 per cent said that 'nothing had changed'. Female managers were by far the most satisfied: almost three female managers out of four referred to an improvement in their daily life (at work and outside of work), whereas this was only the case for 40 per cent of women with an unskilled job (clerks or manual workers). For the men, the corresponding proportions were 65 per cent and 57 per cent. Overall the number of women who considered that the effects of the RTT on their daily life had been more in the direction of improvement was moderately higher than men.

Sixty-five per cent of employees working in companies which had reduced their working hours within the framework of the incentive scheme of the Aubry law noted an improvement in their daily life. Among employees working in companies which had reduced the working hours without an incentive payment, 43 per cent considered that the RTT had had no effect on their daily life. Overall, employee satisfaction was higher in companies where working time was reduced in real terms and jobs created.

For 46 per cent of employees interviewed, the reduction in working time did not affect working conditions on the whole. A quarter of the employees claimed to have experienced some degree of improvement in this area and a quarter some degree of deterioration. The perception of the RTT outcomes in the area of working conditions is therefore ambivalent. According to the surveys:

- There was an intensification of work: the RTT did not translate into a 'proportional' reduction in workload. Four employees out of ten claimed that they had less time to carry out the same tasks. In the same way, 22 per cent of employees who had to adhere to rigid deadlines or production processes saw these deadlines shortened, whereas the reverse was extremely rare.
- There was an increased demand for versatility, which affected almost one in two employees and is frequently associated with an intensification of work. Conversely, the relinquishment or outsourcing of some tasks affected about one employee in five. The intensification of work was closely correlated to reorganisation linked to the RTT. This was more moderate where the workforce was increasing in the department where the employee was working, and more marked when the workforce remained stable or decreased.

- While improving employment in a given department meant that the consequences of the RTT for working conditions were better accepted, an increase in the workforce also seemed to facilitate better management of new distributions of workload.

This intensification of work was anticipated, because the gains in terms of hour-for-hour productivity were generally necessary in order to guarantee the durability of the RTT from the company point of view. Perception of this depended strongly on employees' level of qualifications. The effects of intensification were more frequently felt by the intermediary professions and above all by management. Almost a third of employees claimed to be more stressed in their work. The increase in stress affected more women, in particular unskilled workers. It was in this last category that the outcome of the RTT on working conditions was the least favorable.

The conditions of negotiation and the implementation of the agreement were determining factors with regards satisfaction. A quarter of employees claimed not to have been consulted. This mainly related to employees in the manual worker category, notably unskilled.

In the same way, adhering to the agreement from the point of view of the actual working hours contributed to the satisfaction of those interviewed. A quarter of employees referred to actual working hours above the number set out in the agreement – one employee in ten benefitting (at least partially) from time off in lieu, whereas payment for overtime in terms of extra hours was marginal. Exceeding the anticipated number of hours was mainly an issue for management-level employees, where extra hours were most often worked without pay. For all socio-professional categories, the overall feeling that there had been an improvement was less widespread when the actual working hours exceeded those set out in the agreement.

The opinion of employees with regard to changes to their daily life and working conditions tended to be better when the level of staffing increased.

The feeling of improvement or deterioration of daily life (at work and outside of work) was also closely correlated to the financial outcomes of the agreement. On average, 12 per cent of employees experienced a reduction in salary. The reduction in salaries contributed towards making the overall outcome more negative for employees, even though it frequently took place in compensation for avoided redundancies.

The terms of the RTT also had a crucial influence. The RTT mostly translated into practice through the attribution of a day (or a half-day) on a regular basis and/or extra days of annual leave, more than by a daily reduction. The employees who referred to an overall feeling of improvement in the conditions of their daily life (at work and outside of work) were those who were able to benefit from a half-day or a day which could be taken regularly, or extra days of annual leave. The employees whose working time was adjusted less predictably made less reference to an improvement in their life and working conditions.

The biggest winners were the parents of young children: if a large number of female managers claimed to be satisfied with the RTT, this was because they more often had children, while the majority of women from the unskilled sample did not have children. Men and women with children under the age of 12 came out overwhelmingly in favour of the RTT. Almost half of the parents of children under 12 years claimed to spend more time overall with their children since the RTT (almost as many men as women). These employees spent more days of holiday with their children or more time on Wednesdays[20] or another day of the week. Parents noted that they had more time to spend on family outings, walks, accompanying children to activities, talking with them and playing at home. Around three parents in ten with school-age children devoted more time to the education of their children. In total a third of those interviewed claimed that the reconciliation of work and family life became somewhat easier after the RTT (32 per cent for men, 38 per cent for women).

The RTT relaxed the time restrictions which weighed on women with young children and was without doubt a 'facilitating' factor in maintaining full-time employment or entry into full-time employment by women with children. Méda and Orain[21] showed that men and women working full-time with young children were the most satisfied with the measures introduced in the first of the Aubry laws. Claiming to lack time for their families before the RTT, they afterwards increased the amount of time spent with their children. In the same way, Ulrich[22] showed that the RTT had made it possible for women who had been working part-time on a long-term basis to move to full time.

For 42 per cent of the people interviewed, their spouse also experienced a reduction in working hours. More than one in two employees living as a couple discussed the repercussions of the new organisational structure on their daily life with their partner but only a quarter found that they discussed more, or indeed, more often the allocation of activities with their children between the partners. Four out of ten employees claimed to spend more time with their spouse since the arrival of the RTT (48 per cent for the men, 35 per cent for the women).

The survey showed that RTT had an effect on the sharing of household tasks between men and women, and in terms of how much and the time of day when these tasks are carried out. Forty-two per cent of those interviewed indicated that they had devoted more time to domestic activities since the RTT, including DIY, gardening, tidying, housework, shopping, washing, cooking, and that they had modified the time when they carried these out. Since the RTT, some of these activities were carried out at a different time of day or of the week (notably DIY and gardening for the men, tidying of the house, housework and shopping for the women) and, in the vast majority of cases, this took place in time released by the RTT. Ninety per cent of people who had adjusted the timing of household activities in this way claimed to have done so in order to release time to do other things at the weekend or to carry out these tasks in a more leisurely fashion.

As well as these domestic activities, employees mainly made the most of the time released by the RTT to relax: this was the case for four out of ten women and one man in three. Nonetheless, the RTT did not lead to a major upheaval of leisure time, apart from the fact that women gave more priority to activities such as reading, listening to music, sewing or 'looking after themselves', while men gave preference to sporting activities and leisure time spent on the computer. With regard to breaks spent away from home, 28 per cent of employees (50 per cent of managers but only 13 per cent of unskilled workers) claimed that the RTT had allowed them to go away more often for short breaks or long weekends.

Other surveys, carried out on more limited samples, and completed amongst employees who had experienced the RTT later on, and notably under the influence of the second 'Aubry law', made reference to less satisfying results for employees – notably due to the increase in flexible working and to adjustments in working hours over which they had little or no control.

Conclusion

In conclusion, it can be said that the laws relating to the reduction in working hours in France were affected by several limitations. They came up against fierce management opposition, to such an extent that the second law did not remain an effective tool for creating jobs, but instead became a vehicle for increasing the intensity and flexibility of work, which contributed to a deterioration in working conditions. In addition, the Aubry laws did not have the time to demonstrate their full potential since, from 2003 onwards, they were 'unpicked' after the election of the incoming government. Finally, they were not used as a tool to facilitate a rebalancing of work and family responsibilities between women and men, or of gendered time use.

Research focusing on employees who had moved to 35 hours under the influence of the first Aubry law demonstrated that it became possible to have a strong policy of working hours reduction, paying particular attention to improvement of working conditions, access to employment and balancing activities. However, certain issues still need to be addressed. I have argued elsewhere that a new standard in working time of 32 hours is necessary to adapt to current and future impacts of low economic growth. In addition, a new standard in working time is necessary to allow for gains in quality of life as well as for a reduction in damage to the environment.

Then there is the issue of the management of public services, which has constituted a major problem in France, notably in hospitals where the RTT has not been accompanied by the creation of jobs. Finally, new standards of working time might open up more time and democratic space for collective action, as defended by Bruno Théret in *Les Chemins de la Transition.*[23]

A provocation

National Gardening Leave[1]

Andrew Simms and Molly Conisbee

Finding the time

'The mass of the people can hardly conceive of a time when the Saturday half-holiday did not exist... Latterly, controversy over hours of work has resolved itself into the question: to work or not to work on Saturday morning.'

E. S. Turner,
Roads to Ruin: A Shocking History of Social Progress, 1950

If you could get by working a shorter week, with more time available for family, friends, gardening, going places, making music, making anything for that matter, picking up new skills, walking, joining clubs, or reading a book, would you? In this chapter we set out the case for a new, voluntary scheme to introduce a shorter working week, and for the rapid expansion of productive and pleasurable gardening in Britain's towns and cities.

To achieve a better rather than simply bigger economy, time as much as money is the resource required. At the turn of the 1900s there was a progressive social campaign in the US to establish a shorter, eight-hour working day. It was vehemently opposed by the American National Association of Manufacturers (NAM), who claimed it could ruin the economy.

Much the same argument was used to oppose the abolition of slavery, the introduction of life-preserving safety measures in shipping, and almost every other progressive labour reform throughout history. In the 1920s NAM lobbied against a shorter, five-day working week. In the 1930s, however, the very same lobby group paid for an billboard campaign boasting that the US now had the 'world's shortest working hours' adding, with the zeal of the converted: 'There's no way like the American way'.

The industrial revolution robbed men, women and children of the privileges that they had once enjoyed even under feudal lords. Calculations of the number of weeks worked in some medieval periods suggest that annual hours of labour were shorter than in the industrial era. In fifteenth-century France one in every four days was an official holiday.[2] But with the advent of industrialisation it took until 1825 to limit child labour to 12 hours a day in the week, and 9 hours on Saturday. Each reduction in hours was fought tooth and nail by economic interests. A reduction to ten hours, it was argued in familiar fashion, would be utterly ruinous to the economy. Not so long ago, it was said that the idea of giving workers a half-day holiday on a Saturday would lead to 'immorality.'

The art of living

The French have a saying, 'The English kill themselves to live.' But this is not innate. 'We English certainly do not like working for work's sake,' wrote J. B. Priestly in the *New Statesman* in 1949. 'There is nothing inside us that cries to be set going at an early hour and kept at it until a late hour. We have no private passion for being industrious.' As other authors have noted in this book, JM Keynes imagined that progressive economic, social and technological developments would lead to a 15-hour week by the twenty-first century. The rest of our time, thought Keynes, would be devoted to the art of living.

Yet, according to the Office for National Statistics (ONS), the UK has the third longest working hours in Europe. The UK Trade Union Congress (TUC) calculates that a rising number of people are doing unpaid overtime in their jobs. Over five million of us are estimated to be providing the equivalent of a whole day's free work to our employers every week, worth £29.2 billion to the economy in 2011.[3]

Contrarily, we have created an economic system that generates both high levels of overwork for those in employment (including unpaid overtime), and high levels of unemployment (a condition now demonised). Considering that few people have the privilege to enjoy work as vocationally-driven and fulfilling, it begs the question, Have we forgotten that our economy should serve us, rather than the other way round?

In 1909 Sir Sydney Chapman argued in his presidential address to the Section on Economic Science and Statistics of the British Association for the Advancement of Science, that 'competitive pressures would tend to set the working day at a longer than optimal length'. His empirical evidence showed a rise in productivity after shorter working hours were introduced. This suggests that, where working hours exceed an optimum, reducing them can lead to relative improvements in wages, productivity and employment, as well as to other social, well being and environmental advantages. Multiple benefits can flow from sharing available work more equitably.[4]

If we make the necessary shift from today's culture of passive consumption and disposability, to one of more active engagement and production, we'll find there are more genuinely useful things to do with paid as well as unpaid time. Low carbon economies need people for all the repairing, re-using and recycling demanded in a closed-loop system. And if work is better shared-out between those who are over-worked and those who are unemployed, or underemployed, we can also solve a raft of other problems, as **nef** (the new economics foundation) argued in its report *21 hours: Why a shorter working week can help us all to flourish in the twenty-first century.* This calls for a radical redistribution of paid and unpaid time. It would not be compulsory or introduced as a kind of shock therapy. Several other simultaneous reforms would be needed, especially to tackle low pay. The main benefits would be threefold.

Firstly, economic. It would help to resolve the paradox of overwork and unemployment, and ameliorate the impact of the deep, intractable recession and rising unemployment that has followed from the credit-induced collapse of the global financial systems. It would also help to shift the balance of the global economy to serve the needs of society and the environment, rather than depending on passive over-consumption.

Secondly, social. The redistribution of paid and unpaid work would address widening inequalities, and the fact that working and earning more beyond a certain point doesn't make us happier. It would give more people more time to be better parents, carers, friends, neighbours and gardeners, and everyone a better chance to earn a living. We'd save money by being able to do more things for ourselves. With more people around to help each other the pressure on public services would be eased, and it would reduce the accumulating stresses of retirement.

Thirdly, and crucially, environmental. It would help us escape the consumer hungry and environmentally depleting treadmill in which we are persuaded, as Professor Tim Jackson puts it, 'to spend money we don't have on things we don't need to create impressions that won't last on people we don't care about'. These are things which, we add here, we probably won't use, don't make us happy and which the planet cannot afford. Neither, it seems, do we have the space in our homes to keep them. Yellow Box, the company which provides units to store surplus household goods, is expanding by 40 per cent a year in the UK.

Creating a new social norm of a shorter working week could turn negative prevailing economic circumstances from a problem into an opportunity. It would also be the next step on a long historical path that, designed well, could ensure that everyone benefits, especially those who are currently unemployed and poor. So-called 'time affluence', or reduced working hours, relates positively to improved well-being. We can already glimpse the possibilities.

Utah and other experiments

In Utah the recession following the 2008 financial crisis hit hard, worsened by rapidly rising energy prices. Queues lengthened at food banks, unemployment and mortgage foreclosures both rose dramatically. Money needed to be saved. The task fell to Jon Huntsman, the State's Republican Governor. He surprised people with a new approach.

He took his inspiration from an American management consultant called Riva Poor who wrote a book in 1970 advocating a revolution in work and leisure called *4 Days, 40 Hours*. It caused a stir at the time arguing that great benefits would flow from a longer weekend, and working fewer but longer days. Then the issue went away. Quietly, though, in the ensuing years, a four-day week became a less uncommon option for public employees at city and county level. As a public administrator Huntsman knew this, and saw the opportunity to go further.

He realised that if swathes of public sector workers all worked a shorter week in unison, he'd be able to close public buildings on the extra day, saving money. But something like this hadn't been tried state-wide before. All kinds of problems might emerge, from childcare to public anger over lack of access to services. The state, though, was in dire straits. 'We can study this for another six months or we can do it, and figure it out as we go,' said Huntsman.

At only a month's notice 18,000 of the State's 25,000 workforce were put on a four-day week. Around 900 public buildings closed on Fridays, with more partially closing. The non-essential vehicle fleet was left garaged on the extra day, saving three million miles' worth of petrol. Only essential safety services and a few staff facing particular problems were exempt. Such a quick and significant change you might expect to cause turmoil.

'It started with a one year test period. There were hiccups at the beginning,' says Prof. Rex Facer, from Brigham Young University, who advised on the initiative and analysed its impact. 'Some businesses complained about access to public officials on the day departments closed. But the agencies figured out the problems, the State communicated what it was doing better and in six months complaints pretty much dropped to zero.'

Facer looked into how the public and state employees responded. Eight out of ten employees liked it and wanted it to continue. Nearly two thirds said it made them more productive and many said it reduced conflict both at home and at work. Only three per cent said it made childcare harder. Workplaces across the state reported higher staff morale and lower absenteeism. There were other surprises. One in three among the public thought the new arrangements actually improved access to services. 'The programme achieved exactly what was intended. The public and businesses adapted to it,' says Facer. 'The extended opening times on the four days when employees worked were actually preferred by many. It was more convenient for them being able to contact public bodies before and after conventional working hours.'

Falling energy prices reduced the expected savings, but it still saved the State millions of dollars. Staff well-being improved with the longer weekend, and having less and easier commuting outside the normal rush hour, which benefited other commuters too by reducing congestion. It wasn't the explicit objective, but at a stroke the four-day week also reduced carbon emissions by a substantial 14 per cent.

Then President Obama made the Governor of Utah ambassador to China. In autumn 2011 the State-wide four-day week ended. Not because it had failed, but because it fell victim to a power struggle between the State legislature and the new, less committed governor's office. The legislature was annoyed at how the programme was introduced initially over their heads. Yet, in spite of the repeal, the shorter week's popularity meant it was kept by the State's larger cities including West Valley City and Provo, and was copied elsewhere, for example by the Forestry Department in Virginia. Far from being an evolutionary dead end for the workplace the idea – of changing the conventional five day, 9 am to 5 pm working week to reap a range or social, economic and environmental benefits – is catching on more widely.

In early 2013 Gambia, a relatively poor West African country, announced a four-day week for public sector workers. It wasn't because of economic necessity, but to allow more time to pray, socialise and tend the fields. In Ghana there were subsequent calls for the country to follow Gambia's example to allow time for the popular cultural activity of attending funerals on a Friday.

Many French businesses kept their 35-hour week after President Sarkozy tried to end it in 2008. And in the Netherlands a four-day week is quite normal. As in Utah, the Dutch public sector led the way in response to recession, this time in the early 1990s, by hiring new staff on 80 per cent contracts. Now job sharing is common in health and education. There are part time bankers, surgeons and engineers. One in three men works either part time or compresses their hours as in Utah, with the term 'daddy days' now part of the language. Polling suggests that almost all Dutch part time workers do not want to increase their hours. The approach, backed by decent State childcare provision, has raised levels of female employment (although there remains a severe gender imbalance, with many more women than men working part time).

How the garden grows: from suburban escape to urban salvation

'If you have a garden and a library, you have everything you need.'
Cicero

'The sustainability movement motivated it, the internet facilitated it, and the economic downturn mainstreamed it, as cash got scarce and time got more abundant,' says Juliet Schor of the rising interest in a shorter working week. All sorts of opportunities open up when we have more time on our hands. One is the chance to make our towns and cities more convivial and resilient places to live, and in the process reap a further range of social, health, environmental and well-being benefits.

Resilience – emotional and environmental – is a well-planted garden, both literally and metaphorically. The language of planting, growing and harvesting permeates our culture like a deep root system, recalling a time when our ancestors were literally dependent on their (personal) ability to produce food to survive. There was, and still is, no culture without agriculture. Settled farming allowed for food surplus, and created time for other expressions of being beyond simple survival. This must have included planting for beauty and aesthetics as well as edibility. New discoveries repeatedly force us to recognise how humankind previously used its spare time in the creation of art, ornament and culture, rather than excess productivity for its own sake.

In an era of mass food production, which has divorced most of us at least in the global North, from the daily slog of growing our own, the renewed interest in allotments and other growing schemes is on one level a curiosity. Even with the sharp rise in global food prices since 2008, we still spend considerably less of our budgets on food than our grand-parents did (around 10 per cent compared to around 25 per cent a couple of generations ago). Food is cheap – in part 'thanks' to the supermarket squeeze on producers, industrialisation of a once labour-intensive sector, and increased yields leveraged from soil and aquifer depletion, oil-based fertilisers, pesticides and other practices of farming intensification.

Much contemporary interest in food growing has been attributed to the ongoing recession. Undoubtedly, growing your own – if you have a few quid for seeds and access to some reasonable soil – is the cheapest way to access fruit and vegetables. But there is also a longer view that makes a more overtly political point about access to land, growing space, and the well-being engendered by green environments. Not as a prelapsarian 'back to nature' mythology – gardening and growing involves working with, while also controlling, pruning and taming – but as a model of rugged self-reliance, drawing on political traditions of both the left and right.

Plots past and present

'Certain gardens are described as retreats when they are really attacks.'
Ian Hamilton Finlay

Access to land for growing is intimately bound up with the transition in the UK from feudal to an early modern economic system. Common land was one of the bedrocks of the feudal system, whereby Lords of the Manor allowed access to grazing and growing land to their bonded labour. The Acts of Enclosure between the twelfth and nineteenth centuries gradually eroded this space. And the consequent move to private housing and gardens, the transition to an industrial economy, further encroached on plots for planting.

This is in part why planting has often become a site of resistance and political activism, rather than what George McKay describes as 'suburban, as leisure activity, as television makeover opportunity'.[5] The Levellers, and more radically the Diggers, argued for access to (common) land. William Cobbett's vision of the sturdy, self-sufficient rural family was predicated on their ability to produce their own food. The pioneers of the Garden City movement, although often ridiculed in their time as utopian dreamers, proved remarkably prescient in their visualisation of the potential of the self-sufficient urban realm. And contemporary urban farmers and guerrilla gardeners are increasingly busy planting the cityscape with food to eat and plants to enjoy.

One of the features of the mass move from rural to urban was the creation of allotments. Intended to help supplement the diet of working people, the Allotments Act of 1887 compelled the provision of growing spaces where there was demand. Provided from a range of sources – from private landlords to major industrial employers, such as the railway companies – by 1895 there were well over 450,000 allotments in use in the UK.

Allotments were to prove a major part of national food provision during the two world wars; over 1.5 million thrived during World War I ('everyman his own gardener'). Post-war allotments were provided to returning soldiers. A similar movement existed in the United States – and indeed provided crucial food supplies in the inter-war depression years: the so-called 'self-help' or 'thrift' gardens.

The Dig for Victory and Victory Gardens campaigns during both world wars are well documented; but what Jane Brown has described as 'digging fatigue' gripped the nation after the war years and allotments fell into rapid decline, not really to experience a revival until during the oil crisis of the 1970s when the number of people on waiting lists for allotments increased by 1,600 per cent, at the same time that some were being concreted over for industrial or housing estates.

Today there are around 330,000 allotments, over 90 per cent of which are owned by local authorities who are often under pressure to give them up for development (a notorious recent example being Newham Council's decision on behalf of the Olympic Park). There has been a strong revival of 'allotmenteering', partly a response to rises in food prices, but also to a growing desire to reconnect in some way to the land, food production and forms of community engagement. And this is not a phenomenon of latter-day middle-class 'good lifers'. Some of the UK's most deprived communities have created a local form of resilience and regeneration from growing their own, with thriving schemes everywhere from Sandwell in the West Midlands to Hackney in London. There are around 100 community gardens and 16 city farms in London alone.

The town of Sandwell in the West Midlands has been a pioneer of urban food growing, thanks in part to the Director of Public Health, Dr John Middleton, who made it a priority to tackle the links between obesity and the difficulty of accessing fresh, healthy food for some communities in this deprived area. His solution has been to get local people involved in growing their own. There are now 1,600 allotment plots and a working dairy farm. The flagship project, Salop Drive, is a three-acre market garden and community growing project, which provides fresh vegetables to local families, and has a greenhouse, polytunnels, and outdoor beds, as well as allotments for the local community.[6]

'Incredible Edible Todmorden' is a practical, hands-on campaign based in a Yorkshire market town, for growing local food, with widespread fruit and vegetable planting across the town and a growing patch in every local school. The growing is done by volunteers, and members of the public are free to pick anything they see growing around the town.[7]

Many US cities, abandoned by the industrial and manufacturing heritage that built them, have also turned to urban growing. When Detroit's car industry crumbled, the city rescued and reinvented poor and abandoned neighbourhoods through urban farming, dubbed 'Mo-town to Gro-town.' Grown in Detroit, for example, is a co-operative of 37 market gardens in the city. It developed out of the city's Garden Resource Program, a joint project of several not-for-profit organisations, which provides compost and seeds to Detroit's 1,200 vegetable gardens. Years of decline and growing deprivation are slowly being reversed as more than one third of the city has been 'greened' through fruit and vegetable growing in abandoned factories, empty lofts and once desolate spaces. Something similar is happening in New York, where one study found 5,000 acres of land suitable for urban farming, with a further 1,000 acres in housing projects and under-used land.[8]

For all of us, exercise in green spaces brings enormous physical and mental health benefits.[9] The therapeutic power of landscapes and gardens appears to be greater the more natural features they contain. The range of specific health benefits attributable to gardening is extraordinarily diverse, including lower incidence of dementia and premature mortality, less brittle bones from osteoporosis, fewer problems with blood pressure, heart disease, and a range of conditions relating to depression and anxiety. The presence of trees in urban areas, many of which depend on gardens, is shown to correlate with lower levels of hostility, ranging from psychological aggression to severe violence.[10]

There is strong evidence that if children have contact with nature this will have a positive effect on their physical and mental health, as well as contributing to their educational development.[11] Studies reveal that active involvement in a school garden helps young people to develop more sustainable lifestyles.[12] Practical community-based environmental learning programmes have been found to improve 'young people's attachment to place, civic engagement, and environmental stewardship.'[13] Meanwhile, re-offending by ex-prisoners in England and Wales is estimated to cost £11 billion a year.[14] Nature-oriented programmes for offenders can reduce re-offending on release and have shown a 39 per cent success rate in helping them through the processes of gaining employment.'[15]

In a warming world, the heat island effect of built-up urban areas can lethally exacerbate weather extremes such as heat waves, and lack of natural drainage worsens flooding after heavy rainfall. Increasing the amount of green space can help to reduce temperatures and ameliorate floods. Trees aid cooling, directly by providing shade, and through moisture exchange.[16] Gardens too, can be arks of biodiversity. One detailed study over a 30-year period of an 'ordinary garden' in the English town of Leicester revealed it to be visited by one in four of all the known insect species in the country, while a concentrated 3-year study discovered 15 species of wasp previously unknown in the UK and 4 more that were unrecorded anywhere.[17] The energy, carbon and water footprints of gardens and green spaces vary enormously depending on how they are managed. Broadly speaking, however, following permaculture principles produces the most environmentally friendly results, that is: minimum soil cultivation, low chemical use, plant diversity, using recycled water and organic matter.

It takes time and care to do this. The busier you are, the less time you have at your disposal, the more likely it is that you will want machines to help you garden 'efficiently', to prefer decking or paving, to grass and plants, or to use chemical fertilisers and pesticides. So there are strong links too between more ecological types of gardening and a shorter working week. Altogether we believe the case is strong that Britain would be better off if we combined fewer hours in paid employment with rapid expansion of productive and pleasurable gardening in Britain's towns and cities.

Could it catch on?

'The most difficult thing to find is the way to the signposts.'
Wieslaw Brudzinski

Could national gardening leave catch on in Britain, where, as the French saying goes, allegedly we, 'kill ourselves to live?' The last place you might expect a new, more progressive work culture to take root, is in the stress and bonus fuelled City of London. But Nick Robins, who analyses climate risks and challenges for the bank HSBC, suggests the City could be hiding a secret. 'There's not much discussion,' says Robins, 'But if you want to work less, it seems to be quite open.' He turned his back on the City's conventional long hours for a four-day week. 'You get a sense of incredible liberation,' he says. 'You may get 20 per cent less pay but you get 50 per cent more free time.' Others are doing so too, says Robins, but without drawing attention to the fact. He finds the lack of discussion peculiar. 'It is an extremely strange thing that in the UK we haven't thought in a cultural sense about time. The debate is oddly absent, and then it comes up only to do with family, in other words swapping one type of work for another.' One of the things he does in the time left fallow is tend an allotment.

Some businesses though, are less shy about the benefits of a shorter week. Michael Pawlyn is one of the architects who worked on the Eden Centre in Cornwall and went on to become a world expert on 'biomimicry,' taking lessons from nature on how to make things better. He'll explain how a beetle can teach you to harvest water in the desert or make fire detectors more sensitive. A big lesson from nature is the importance of fallow time. No ecosystem can be 100 per cent productive all the while. Pawlyn gives staff at his own company 'exploration days' when people can just go away and think. 'It helps you to distinguish the things that are important from the things that are merely urgent,' he says.

Caroline Thould, a 39-year-old radiographer, and her husband Peter decided that they would both go part time and share childcare after the birth of a second child. They approached their boss at London's University College Hospital. 'She agreed to "suck it and see". It was a completely new thing to try. We'd both been full time, but she knew that if the kids got sick, she wouldn't lose staff,' explains Caroline. 'It was hard to lose the equivalent of a full time salary, and it still is, but we save on childcare. We still manage a holiday each year, and I think the children will benefit in the long run.'In the time they claimed back they helped build gardens at their children's nursery in Flitnick, Bedfordshire.

It's not only senior, relatively well-paid professionals who are choosing to work less. Kathleen Cassidy is a 26-year-old community organiser on a low income, who chose to work a 25-hour week. 'I didn't have huge outgoings. I have rent, not much on travel, some on food. I've never been much of a spendthrift, never really spent on holidays, cars or things like that.' says Cassidy,'It simplifies life having less money.'She has spent her time helping male former prisoners rehabilitate, building a community garden for a housing association, and was one of the anti tax-evasion activists of the campaign group UK Uncut.'It's about balance and having a passion for not being on a treadmill, when you just work, eat and sleep,'she says.'I felt like I wanted to produce things rather than consume all the time.'

These people made choices to work less and adapt their lives. Choice matters. Research by **nef** (the new economics foundation) shows that voluntarily working less is positive for our well being, but compulsion, especially in the context of an economy not designed to support part time work, ruins the benefit.

There are several reasons now though, why more of us may want and need to adapt. Recent research from the Centre for Economic and Policy Research suggested that a worldwide shift to shorter, European style working, could reduce carbon emissions enough to halve the global warming not already locked-in by current emissions, but which would otherwise be expected up to the year 2100.[18]

We have high unemployment making for a divided country burdened with related social costs. Nick Robins anticipates a long-term future of low to no growth, meaning we might all have to reconsider how we work.'Personally I think we'll have to recognise that the norm of a five-day week for everyone is not possible or desirable,'he says. Even when economists mistily recall periods of so-called full-employment in Britain, they refer to periods when women were homebound, providing the free maintenance of a mostly male, paid work force. To make shorter working weeks viable for low income families means tackling big distributional issues. As Nick Robins observes:'In my personal opinion, we will need to look deep into welfare law, tax levels, credits, starting incomes and work availability.'

In conclusion: two recommendations
There are broad benefits to Britain of a shorter working week and an expansion of opportunities to garden (in the broadest sense) in towns and cities. Gardening's therapeutic power is felt across the social and demographic spectrum, from a child's simple pleasure at seeing a seed

grow, to the wired executive shedding stress with pruning shears, to the depressed, and those in prison, finding comfort and rehabilitation as they dig the soil. Global food and energy markets are shifting and increasingly volatile. Even a modest shift in the balance of our dependence on imported food would leave us stronger, more resilient, and better insulated from upheaval in world markets and climate system.

To reap all these benefits requires two main ingredients: time and physical space. With that in mind, we make just two recommendations.

Firstly, that all employers, public and private, offer all new recruits (and where possible all existing staff) the voluntary option of working a four-day week. How this is done can remain flexible. Some might prefer working a full week in four days, so-called 'compressed hours'. Some may discover opportunities for cost savings when they have more time to do things for themselves. Others may find it sufficiently attractive simply to work a shorter week. In the time people are able to claim back, they wouldn't, of course, have to garden. They could do any number of other things. But the rising popularity of gardening, with growing awareness of its many benefits could make it an attractive option. Any firm or body that adopts this scheme could call itself a 'National Gardening Leave Employer'. Joining would make employers attractive in the job market, and single them out as innovative, modern and trusting. Experience suggests that they would be rewarded with added commitment, higher morale and stronger motivation from staff.

Secondly, and in tandem, we recommend that all work places establish 'growing areas.' The spaces adapted could range from roofs (Thornton's Budgens, the community supermarket in Crouch End, North London, have shown how this is possible with their 'food from the sky' initiative), to window sills and sections of car park. In Los Angeles, citizens have taken to commandeering one or two spaces in car parks and digging them up to create 'parklets'. As shared endeavours, gardening in the work place could bring countless benefits – not least by reducing stress and by engendering a sense of joint enterprise and co-operation.

There is a more detailed agenda for market reform that is beyond the scope of this chapter. Two significant changes are worth mentioning, however. Firstly, to encourage a positive, self-reinforcing dynamic, public and private bodies should be encouraged to favour locally based and owned horticultural and food provision. The loop of localism provides for a reciprocal economy and will strengthen the local economy through the multiplier effect. Less spending tends to leak out of the local economy.

The second change will be intuitive to any gardener who has to battle super-weeds like knotweed, bindweed or ground elder: if you want a productive garden with a satisfying and nutritious variety of plants, you have to keep weeds in their place as part of a garden ecology. As in nature, so in the economy. A diverse and enterprising local economy requires markets that are kept open and not dominated by just one or two powerful corporations. The UK Competition Commission concluded that the ability to manipulate the supply chain through market share and company power can begin by having captured as little as eight per cent of the market. Competition policy is, then, an important concern for those interested in a thriving, food and plant growing economy.

National Gardening Leave – imagined as a positive, progressive social policy, committed to help create the circumstances for human flourishing – would, in our view, be a creative response to a number of the challenges now facing us: under- and over-employment; environmental degradation; de-skilling; a lack of time to develop community and social networks. A forward-thinking economy should help give its citizens time to grow – both literally and metaphorically – and to lead more engaged, embedded lives in their communities. Philosopher Martin Heidegger said, 'To dwell is to garden.' We say: To start living, we need to plant seeds of change, for now and for a sustainable future.

Acknowledgements

First thanks go to Tania Burchardt and to the Centre for Analysis of Social Exclusion at the London School of Economics, who hosted the conference and seminar held in January 2012, 'About Time: examining the case for a shorter working week'. They made it possible for **nef** (the new economics foundation) to bring together more than 600 people for the conference and to commission a series of expert papers for the seminar, which now form the basis of this book. We are immensely grateful to Juliet Schor for her keynote introduction to the conference, and to this volume, and to all our authors for their contributions to this work. We also thank David Fell, Robert La Jeunesse, Paul Cann and Chris Ball for their contributions to the seminar, and Ian Gough for his invaluable advice and support.

Other colleagues at **nef** have encouraged and supported this work, especially Mike Harris, who helped design and co-ordinate the conference and the early stages of the book. Our thanks also go to Carys Afoko, Ross Haig, Jessie Barnard and Angela Greenham for publication and publicity, and to the Hadley Trust for their initial support of **nef**'s work on income, time and carbon.

Notes

Introduction – Anna Coote (p. ix)

1 Office of National Statistics, Labour force Survey Eurostat April to June 2011, via *Guardian* Datablog.

2 Employees in the US work on average 1,787 hours a year, compared with 1,625 for UK employees, equivalent to more than four 8-hour, 5-day weeks: http://www.ons.gov.uk/ons/dcp171778_299752.pdf. As they have much shorter holidays, US averages for weekly hours (38.5 for all workers and 42.5 for 'full-timers') are not comparable: http://www.bls.gov/cps/cpsaat19.pdf.

The triple dividend – Juliet Schor (p. 3)

1 The author would like to thank Tom Laidley for research assistance, and Kyle Knight and Gene Rosa, her collaborators on the models of working hours and eco-impact.

2 Chinese exports have a comparatively high carbon intensity and account for a significant portion of importing nations' total emissions. The US is estimated to have outsourced 20 per cent of its emissions to China (Ghertner and Fripp 2007). Similarly, embodied CO_2 from Eastern Europe is estimated to account for 23 per cent of Germany's emissions. (Ahmad and Wyckoff 2003: 35).

3 York, R. Rosa, E. A. & Dietz, T. (2009). A tale of contrasting trends: three measures of the ecological footprint in China, India, Japan, and the United States, 1961–2003. *Journal of World-Systems Research*, 15(2): 134–146.

4 Calwell, C. (2010). *Is Efficient Sufficient? The case for shifting our emphasis in energy specifications to progressive efficiency and sufficiency*. Stockholm: European Council for and Energy Efficient Economy; Hertwich, E. G. (2005). Consumption and the rebound effect. *Journal of Industrial Ecology* 9, (1–2): 85–98; Sorrell, S. (2007). *The Rebound Effect: An assessment of the evidence for economy-wide energy savings from improved energy efficiency*. London: UK Energy Research Centre.

5 Baer, P. & Athanasiou, T. (2008) The right to development in a climate constrained world. Executive summary, Revised Second Edition. Retrieved from http://www.in.boell.org/web/113-397.html

6 Simms, A. Johnson, V. & Chowla, P. (2010). *Growth Isn't Possible*, new economics foundation.
The Conference Board. (January 2011).The Conference Board Total Economy Database. Retrieved from http://www.conference-board.org/data/economydatabase/; Jackson, T. (2009). *Prosperity Without Growth: Economics for a finite planet*. London: Earthscan; Schor, J. B. (2010). *Plenitude: The new economics of true wealth* (New York: Penguin).

7 Hayden, A. (2010). From growth to sufficiency? A political economic analysis of climate change responses in the UK and Canada. Ph.D., Boston College, Department of Sociology.

8 Jackson (2009) *op. cit.*

9 Meadows, D. H. Meadows, D. L. Randers, J. & Behrens W. W. (1972). *The Limits to Growth*. New York: Universe Books.

10 Daly, H. E. (1977). *Steady-State Economics: The economics of biophysical equilibrium and moral growth*. San Francisco: W. H. Freeman; Daly, H. E. (1996). *Beyond Growth: The economics of sustainable development*. Boston: Beacon Press; Sachs, W. Loske, R. & Linz, M. (1998). *Greening the North: A post-industrial blueprint for ecology and equity*. London: Zed Books; Schor, J. B. (1991). Global inequality and environmental crisis: an argument for reducing working hours in the north. *World Development* 19, (1): 73–84; Schor, J. B. (1995). Can the north stop consumption growth? Escaping the cycle of work and spend. In *The North, the South and the Environment*. Bhaskar, V. & Glyn, A. (eds) London: Earthscan; Schor, J. B. (2010). *Plenitude: the new economics of true wealth*. New York: Penguin; Victor, P. A. (2008). *Managing without Growth: Slower by design, not disaster*. Cheltenham, UK: Edward Elgar; Speth, J. G. (2008). *The Bridge at the Edge of the World: Capitalism, the environment, and crossing from crisis to sustainability*. New Haven, CT: Yale University Press; Jackson (2009) *op. cit.*

11 Freeman, R. (Summer-Fall 2008). The new global labour market. *Focus*. Volume 26, number 1. Retrieved from http://www.irp.wisc.edu/publications/focus/pdfs/foc261a.pdf

12 Schor, J. B. (2010) *op. cit.*

13 Sachs, W. & Santarius, T. (eds). (2007). *Fair Future: Resource Conflicts, Security and Global Justice*. London: Zed Books; Ackerman, F. DeCanio, S. J. Howarth, R. B. & Sheeran, K. (2009). Limitations of integrated assessment models of climate change. *Climatic Change* 95, (April 2): 297–315. Retrieved from http://www.springerlink.com.proxy.bc.edu/content/c85v5581x7n74571/fulltext.pdf;Baer and Athanasiou (2008) *op. cit.*

14 Victor (2008) *op. cit.*

15 For a discussion of this issue, see Schor, J. B. (1992). *The Overworked American: The unexpected decline of leisure*. New York: Basic Books; Golden, L. (2009). A brief history of long work time and the contemporary sources of overwork. *Journal of Business Ethics*, 84: 217–227.

16 Alesina, A. Glaeser, E. & Sacerdote, B. (2005). Work and leisure in the US and Europe: Why so different? *NBER Macroeconomic Annual 2005*.

17 Becker, G. (1965). A theory of the allocation of time. *Economic Journal* 75: 493–517; Lancaster, K. (1966). A new approach to consumer theory. *Journal of Political Economy*, 74, (2): 132–157.

18 Jalas, M. (2002). A time use perspective on the materials intensity of consumption. *Ecological Economics* 41: 109–23.

19 *Ibid.*

20 Nassen, J. Larsson, J. & Holmberg, J. (2009). The effect of working hours on energy use: a micro analysis of time and income effects. ECEEE Summer Study.

21 Devetter, F. X. & Rousseau, S. (2011). Working hours and sustainable development. *Review of Social Economy*, LXIX(3): 333–355.

22 Rosnick, D. & Weisbrot, M. (2006). *Are Shorter Work Hours Good for the Environment? A comparison of US and European energy consumption*. Washington, DC: Center for Economic and Policy Research.

23 Hayden, A. & Shandra, J. M. (2009). Hours of work and the ecological footprint of nations: an exploratory analysis. *Local Environment: The International Journal of Justice and Sustainability*, 14: 575–600.

24 Knight, Rosa and Schor (2012). We utilise the STIRPAT model (York et al 2003) which is a stochastic version of the well known IPAT identity of Ehrlich and Holdren (1971). IPAT includes four variables – impact, population, affluence, (measured as GDP), and technology, although the inability to measure technology means it is typically not included as a variable, and is assumed to enter the error term. The STIRPAT formulation allows the coefficients of the independent variables to differ from each other – the original IPAT constrained all the coefficients to be equal to one – and converts all variables into logarithms and estimates a linear multiple regression model. We estimated all our models using fixed effects panel regression to control for unmeasured time-invariant variables on which countries differ. More details on our estimates, as well as our full results, can be found in Knight, K. W. Rosa, E. A. & Schor, J. B. (2012). Reducing growth to achieve environmental sustainability: the role of work hours. Pollin, R. & Wicks-Lim, J. (eds). *Capitalism on Trial: Explorations in the tradition of Thomas Weisskopf.* Cheltenham: Edward Elgar.

25 Global Footprint Network. (2010). *Ecological Footprint Atlas 2010.* Oakland, CA: Global Footprint Network; Rees, W. E. (2006). *Ecological Footprints and Bio-Capacity: Essential Elements in Sustainability Assessment.* pp. 143–158 in Dewulf J. & Van Langenhove, H. (eds). *Renewables Based Technology: Sustainability assessment.* Chichester, UK: John Wiley and Sons.

26 Mishel, L. Bernstein, J. & Shierholz, H. (2009). *The State of Working America 2008/2009.* An Economic Policy Institute book. Ithaca, NY: Cornell University Press for trends in hours from the Current Population Survey.

27 Reynolds, J. (2004). When too much is not enough: actual and preferred working hours. *Sociological Forum,* 19(1): 89–120.

28 Galinsky, E. Bond, J. T. Kim, S. S. Backon, L. Brownfield, E. & Sakai, K. (2004). *Overwork in America: When the way we work becomes too much.* New York: Families and Work Institute, Executive Summary.

29 Stier, H. & Lewin-Epstien, N. (2003), Time to work: a comparative analysis of preferences for working hours. *Work and Occupations,* 30(3): 302–326.

30 Jacobs, J. A. & Gerson, K. (2005). *The Time Divide: Work, family and gender inequality.* Cambridge, MA: Harvard University Press on the relation between education and preferences to work less.

31 Otterbach, S. (2010). Mismatches between actual and preferred work time: empirical evidence of hours constraints in 21 countries. *Journal of Consumer Policy,* 33: 143–161.

32 For more on these explanations, see the discussion in Schor (1992) *op. cit.* and Best, F. (1980). Exchanging Earnings for Leisure: Findings of an exploratory national survey on work time preference. US Department of Labour, Employment and Training Administration.

33 On behavioral economics, Kahneman, D. & Tversky, A. (2000). *Choices, values and frames.* New York: Cambridge University Press.

34 Solnick, S. J. & Hemenway, D. (1998). Is more always better? A survey on positional concerns. *Journal of Economic Behavior and Organization,* 37: 373–83; Frank, R. (1985). *Choosing the right pond.* New York: Oxford on the positionality of free time. Pouwels, B. Siegers, J. & Vlasblom, J. D. (2008). Income, working hours, and happiness. *Economics*

Letters, doi:10.1016/j.econlet.2007.05.032; Kasser, T. & Sheldon, K. M. (2009). Time affluence as a path toward personal happiness and ethical business practice: empirical evidence from four studies. *Journal of Business Ethics*, 84: 243–255, on the relation between hours and well-being.

35 Bowles, S. & Park, Y. (2005). Emulation, inequality and work hours: was Thorsten Veblen right? *The Economic Journal*, 115: 397–413.

Clock time: tyrannies and alternatives – Barbara Adam (p. 31)

1 In this paper I draw on my research on time and work that extends over some 30 years; for example, Adam 1990, 1993, 1995, 1998, 2003 and 2004. In this discussion paper I will not reference each work separately as I go along but will provide the relevant details in the reference section only.

2 For example: anthropology (Evans Pritchard 1940/1969, Bourdieu 1979, Hall 1983), business studies and organisation theory (Blyton 1989, Clark 1982, de Grazia 1974, Hassard 1989, Hay and Usunier 1993, Starkey 1988), economics (Hill 1989, Shackle 1967, Sharp 1981), geography (Hägerstrand 1975, Harvey 1989, Carlstein et al. eds 1978), history (Landes 1983, LeGoff 1980, Kern 1983, O'Malley 1992, Thompson 1967), social policy (Lee and Piachaud 1992, Rinderspacher 1989), social psychology (McGrath and Rotchford 1983, Jacques 1982, Jahoda et al. 1972/1933, Yaker et al. eds 1972), sociology (Cottrell 1939, Grossin 1969, 1974, 1992, Moore 1963, Nguyen 1992, Rinderspacher 1985) and women's studies (Davies 1990, Balbo and Nowotny eds. 1986, Hantrais 1993, Leccardi and Rampazi 1993, Lefeuvre 1994, Nowotny 1989/1986). This list is a brief selection from an output of several hundred publications. The journal *Time & Society* provides a rich current resource base for publications on working time covering the last 20 years.

3 A bamboo, for example, flowers only every 100 years or so, a rat can reproduce as many as 5 times in a single year whilst a bacterium such as E Coli 0157 can multiply to a staggering 30 million times in just 5 days.

4 I have worked with the idea of the complexity of times throughout my work but developed and theorised the concept of 'timescape' in Adam (1998 and 2004) as well as numerous journal articles.

5 On the issue of commodified time, see Marx (1976/1867) and, for contemporary examples, see Giddens (1981: 118–120; 130–135), Harvey (1989), and Ingold (1995).

6 Marx, K. (1976/1867). *Capital, Volume I.* Harmondsworth: Penguin.

7 Gregory, L. (2009). Change Takes Time: Exploring the structural and development issues of time banking. *International Journal of Community Currencies*, 13: 19–36.

Hurried and alone: time and technology in the consumer society – Mark Davis (p. 41)

1 Shiels, M. (10 May 2010). Tech President Obama disses iPads and Xboxes. BBC online. Retrieved from http://www.bbc.co.uk/blogs/thereporters/maggieshiels/2010/05/tech_president_obama_disses_ip.html

2 Bauman, Z. (2010). *Living on Borrowed Time: Conversations with Citali Rovirosa-Madrazo.* Cambridge: Polity Press, p. 57.

3 Maffesoli, M. (2003). *L'instant Eternel: Le retour du tragique dans les sociétés postmodernes.* Paris: La Table Ronde.

4 Bauman (2010) *op. cit.* p. 149.

5 Bauman, Z. (1992). *Intimations of Postmodernity.* London: Routledge; Bauman, Z. (1995). *Life in Fragments: Essays in post-modern morality.* Oxford: Basil Blackwell; Bauman, Z. (1993) *Postmodern Ethics.* Oxford: Basil Blackwell.

6 BBC. (19 August 2010). Ofcom report highlights 'multi-tasking media users. BBC online. Retrieved from http://www.bbc.co.uk/news/technology-11012356

7 Griffin, J. (May 2010). *The Lonely Society?* Mental Health Foundation. Retrieved from http://www.mentalhealth.org.uk/publications/the-lonely-society/

8 Gershuny, J. (2005).Busyness as the badge of honour for the new super-ordinate working class, *Social Research*, 72, 2: 287–314.

9 Murphy, C. (25 May 2010). Young more lonely than the old, UK survey suggests. BBC online. Retrieved from http://news.bbc.co.uk/1/hi/8701763.stm

10 Morrison, C. M. and Gore, H. (2010). The Relationship between excessive internet use and depression: A questionnaire-based study of 1,319 young people and adults. *Psychopathology*, 43: 121–126.

11 Goffman, E. (1972). *Relations in Public.* Harmondsworth: Penguin.

12 Goffman, E. (1984). *The Presentation of Self in Everyday Life.* Harmondsworth: Penguin [originally published in 1959].

13 Žižek, S. (2010). *In Defence of Lost Causes.* London: Verso.

14 Sullivan, O. & Gershuny, J. (2004). Inconspicuous Consumption: Work-Rich, Time-Poor in the Liberal Market Economy. *Journal of Consumer Culture*, 4: 79–100.

15 To give a sense of the growing problem, the UK self-storage industry made £310 million in 2005 and has grown by 40 per cent each year until 2008. In the US, the self-storage company 'Yellow Box' occupied three-times the area of Manhattan Island with over 40,000 depots across the nation. It currently makes more money than the nation's movie theatres or its music business! And this is not a preoccupation of the wealthy – more than a third of all 'Yellow Box' storage units are rented by people earning less than £15,000 per year.

16 Dobson, R. and Thompson, J. (6 June 2006). Cash-rich, time-poor Britons waste £1,725 a year on must-have gear they'll never use. *The Independent*. Retrieved from http://www.independent.co.uk/news/uk/this-britain/cashrich-timepoor-britons-waste-acircpound1725-a-year-on-musthave-gear-theyll-never-use-6168330.html

17 Clement, B. (23 February 2006). Britons work longer hours than anyone else in Europe. *The Independent*. Retrieved from http://www.independent.co.uk/news/uk/this-britain/britons-work-longer-hours-than-anyone-else-in-europe-467467.html

18 Yang, H. (2006). Work hours and self-reported hypertension amongst working people in California. *Hypertension*, 48, 4: 744–750.

19 Kanavos, P., Ostergren J. & Weber M. A. (2007). *High blood pressure and health policy: where we are and where we need to go next.* London: Ruder Finn Inc.

20 Zimbardo, P. The secret powers of time. Royal Society of Arts (RSA) website. Retrieved from http://www.thersa.org/events/video/archive/philip-zimbardo-the-secret-powers-of-time. Zimbardo, P. (24 May 2010). 'The secret powers of time'. RSA Animate on the RSA website. Retrieved from
http://comment.rsablogs.org.uk/2010/05/24/rsa-animate-secret-powers-time/

21 Žižek, S. (2006). *How to Read Lacan*. London: Granta Books.

22 Carr, N. (2010). *The Shallows: What the internet is doing to our brains*. London: W. W. Norton & Company.

23 Fisher, M. (2009). *Capitalist realism: Is there no alternative?* Ropely, Hants: Zero Books, p. 23

24 Transition Network. *Homepage*. Retrieved from http://www.transitionnetwork.org/

25 Thompson, C. J. & Coskuner–Balli, G. (7 November 2007). Enchanting Ethical Consumerism: The case of community supported agriculture. *Journal of Consumer Culture*. 3: 275–303.

26 There are currently 147 Cittaslow towns in 24 countries across the world. 'Cittaslow is an accreditation that acknowledges the dedication and commitment of community members who work hard to make their part of the world a healthier, greener, happier, slower place to inhabit.' Cittaslow UK. Homepage. Retrieved from http://www.cittaslow.org.uk/

27 The Long Now Foundation was established in 1996 to develop the Clock and Library projects, as well as to become the seed of a very long-term cultural institution. 'The Long Now Foundation hopes to provide a counterpoint to today's accelerating culture and help make long-term thinking more common. We hope to creatively foster responsibility in the framework of the next 10,000 years'. Long Now Foundation. Homepage. Retrieved from http://longnow.org/

28 *Ibid.*

Time, care and gender inequalities – Valerie Bryson (p. 55)

1 Some of the arguments in this paper are developed further in Bryson, V. (2007). *Gender and the Politics of Time: Feminist theory and contemporary debates*. Bristol: The Policy Press.

2 Gershuny, J. (2011). *Time-Use Surveys and the Measurement of National Well-Being*. Oxford: ONS and University of Oxford Centre for Time Use Research. Retrieved from ONS http://www.ons.gov.uk/ons/rel/environmental/time-use-surveys-and-the-measurement-of-national-well-being/article-by-jonathan-gershuny/index.html . The reasons for this rise in the second half of the twentieth century are complex, but include a shift to greater 'at home' provision of services such as laundry and also an increase in life expectancy which has meant both that a larger percentage of the population are retired and that more people (including many who are themselves retired) provide unpaid care for elderly relatives, friends and neighbours.

3 Miliband, E. Speech to the Labour Party Conference. Retrieved from http://www.politics.co.uk/comment-analysis/2011/09/27/ed-miliband-s-conference-speech-in-full

4 For an elaboration of this point, see Bryson, V. (2008). Time-Use studies: A potentially feminist tool? *International Journal of Feminist Politics*, 10 (2).

5 Gershuny (2011) *op. cit.*

6 Woodroffe, J. (2009). *Not Having It All: How motherhood reduces women's pay and employment prospects.* London, Fawcett and Oxfam, p. 3.
  Overall, 43 per cent of women but only 13 per cent of men work part time. TUC. (2012). *Women's Pay and Employment Update: A public/private sector comparison.* Retrieved from http://www.tuc.org.uk/tucfiles/251/Womenspay.pdf

7 A recent survey for the Equality and Human Rights Commission found that six in ten fathers worked over 40 hours a week. See Equality and Human Rights Commission. (2009). *Working Better: Fathers, families and work – contemporary perspectives.* Research summary 41. Retrieved from http://www.equalityhumanrights.com/uploaded_files/research/41_wb_fathers_family_and_work.pdf

8 Around 17.2 per cent of men in work are low paid, compared with 28 per cent of women workers, with those women who work part time the most likely to be in low paid employment. See TUC. (2012) *op. cit.* p. 3. See also Woodroffe (2009) *op. cit.*

9 Working Families (2011) *Working and Fathers: Combining family life and work,* Lancaster University Management School., p. 5. Retrieved from Working Families website, http://www.workingfamilies.org.uk/admin/uploads/WF_WorkingAndFathers-Report-FINAL.pdf

10 TUC (2012) *op. cit.*

11 At £210 a week, electrotechnical apprentices (99 per cent male) earn most of all, partly reflecting the higher qualifications required. See TUC and YWCA. (2010). *Apprenticeships and gender.* Available at http://www.tuc.org.uk

12 See for example Ofsted. (2011). *Girls' Career Aspirations.* Retrieved from http://www.ofsted.gov.uk/resources/girls-career-aspirations

13 For an expansion of this point, see Bryson (2008) *op. cit.*

14 Lynch, K. and Walsh, J. (2009). Love Labouring: Nurturing rationalities and relational identities. Lynch, K. Baker, J. and Lyons, M. (eds). *Affective Equality: Love, care and injustice.* Basingstoke: Palgrave Macmillan, p. 49.

15 Future Foundation, (2006). *The Changing Face of Parenting: Professional parenting, information and healthcare.* London: An Experian Company.

16 Boyd, E. (2002). 'Being there': Mothers who stay at home, gender and time. *Women's Studies International Forum,* 25 (4): 463–70, p. 466, quoting Anne Manne.

17 Everingham, C. (2002). Engendering Time: Gender equity and discourses of workplace flexibility. *Time and Society,* 11 (2/3): 335–351, p. 338.

18 Quoted in Connolly, M. (22 November 2010). Western trust cuts nursing home places. BBC News Northern Ireland. Retrieved from http://www.bbc.co.uk/news/uk-northern-ireland-11808727 . For a recent critical report on the home care industry, Equality and Human Rights Commission. (2011). *Close to Home: An inquiry into older people and human rights in home care.* Retrieved from http://www.equalityhumanrights.com/uploaded_files/homecareFI/home_care_report.pdf

19 Bryson, V. and Deery, R. (2010) Public policy, 'men's time' and power: the work of community midwives in the British National Health Service. *Women's Studies International Forum,* 33: 91–98, p. 96.

20   For a discussion of this, see Bryson (2007) *op. cit.*

21   Boyd (2002) *op. cit.* p. 466.

22   Brines, J. (1994) Economic dependency, gender, and the division of labor at home. *American Journal of Sociology,* 100 (3): 652–88, p. 652.

23   Working Families (2011) *op. cit.*

24   Equality and Human Rights Commission (2009) *op. cit.*

25   Equality and Human Rights Commission (2009) *op. cit.*

26   Working Families (2011) *op. cit.*

27   See Skills for Care. (2010). *Men into care: A research-based contribution to a recruitment and retention issue.* Retrieved from http://www.skillsforcare.org.uk/research/latest_research_reports/men_into_care.aspx

28   On the poor quality of much home care and the link with the low pay and status of care workers, see Equality and Human Rights Commission (2011) *op. cit.*

29   Blau, R. Kenyon, A. and Lekhi, R. (2007). Stress at Work: A recent report for the Work Foundation's principal partners. London: The Work Foundation, p. 26.

30   As with the 2 weeks paternity leave at birth, the first 13 weeks of this transferred leave are currently (August 2012) paid at £135.45, the remainder are unpaid. The 2012 Queen's Speech indicated that the right to transfer leave would be extended. Details have not yet been announced, but are highly unlikely to include increased financial support.

31   Working Families (2011) *op. cit.* p. 22.

32   Childs, S. (2004). *New Labour's Women MPs*: London: Routledge.

33   For a discussion of the policy-making implications of time-use studies, Esquivel, V. (2011). Sixteen Years after Beijing: What are the new policy agendas for time-use data collection? *Feminist Economics,* 17 (4).

Time, income and freedom – Tania Burchardt (p. 69)

1   For a full version of this paper please see: Burchardt, T. (2010). Time, income and substantive freedom: A capability approach. *Time and Society,* 19(3): 318–344.

2   Rawls, J. (1971). *A Theory of Justice.* Oxford: Oxford University Press.

3   Bojer, H. (2003). *Distributional Justice, Theory and Measurement.* London: Routledge.

4   Sen, A. (1985). *Commodities and Capabilities.* London: New Holland; and Sen, A. (1999). *Development as Freedom.* Oxford: Oxford University Press.

5   The series of papers culminating in Goodin, R. Rice, J. Parpo, A. and Eriksson, L. (2008). *Discretionary Time: A new measure of freedom.* Cambridge: Cambridge University Press.

6   Gershuny, J. (2003). *Time, Through the Life-course, in the Family.* ISER Working Paper Number 2003–03. Essex: Institute for Social and Economic Research.

7   As in Goodin et al, (2008).

8   Burchardt, T. (2008). *Time and Income Poverty.* York: Joseph Rowntree Foundation.

9 The implicit assumption is that an increase in free time is worth the same as a proportional increase in income. This is because we are modelling the time-income capability set as an *area*. In practice, additional time, or additional income, is likely to produce decreasing marginal returns. Moreover, the relative value of additional time and additional income is likely to vary between people, depending on their interests and preferences.

10 For example Brown, S. and Pudney, S. (2005). Hours constraints and in-work poverty. *Bulletin of Economic Research*, 57 (3): 305–315; Kodz, J. et al (2003). Working Long Hours: A review of the evidence. *Volume 1 – main report.* Employment Relations Research Series no. 16. London: DTI; Organisation for Co-operation and Development (OECD). (2006). *Babies and Bosses: Reconciling work and family life.* Paris: OECD.

The 'green life course' approach to designing working time policy – Martin Pullinger (p. 83)

1 *This essay draws on research that formed part of my PhD on working time reduction: Greening Our Working Lives: The environmental impacts of changing patterns of paid work in the UK and the Netherlands, and implications for working time policy (2011), undertaken at the University of Edinburgh and funded by the Economic and Social Research Council (ESRC). Award reference number PTA-031–2005–00233.

2 Coote, A. Franklin, J. & Simms, A. (2010). *21 Hours: Why a shorter working week can help us all to flourish in the 21st century.* London: **nef**; Hayden, A. (1999). *Sharing the Work, Sparing the Planet.* Sydney: Zed Books; LaJeunesse, R. (2009). *Work Time Regulation as Sustainable Full Employment Strategy.* Routledge; Robinson, TJC. (2006). *Work, Leisure and the Environment: The vicious circle of overwork and over consumption.* Cheltenham: Edward Elgar; Schor, J. B. (2005). Sustainable consumption and worktime reduction. *Journal of Industrial Ecology* 9(1–2): 37–50.

3 Spangenberg, Omann & Hinterberger (2002) and Victor (2008, 2011) look at how various macroeconomic variables change under different scenarios of transition to environmental sustainability. They include average working time per capita as one of these variables, and find that it must reduce, but do not look at patterns of work in the population in detail.

4 I use the terms carbon footprint and greenhouse gas emissions interchangeably in this essay. They are used to refer to emissions of the six greenhouse gases that are the principle contributors to human-induced climate change: carbon dioxide, methane, nitrous oxide, hydrofluorocarbons, perfluorocarbons and sulphur hexafluoride (UNFCCC 2008: 106). They are measured on a common scale of tonnes of carbon dioxide equivalent, CO_2e, which provides a standard unit of measurement for different greenhouse gases expressed in terms of their potential for contributing to global warming compared to that of carbon dioxide. A household's carbon footprint or greenhouse gas emissions refers here to the tonnes of greenhouse gas emissions (CO_2e) that are produced as a result of manufacturing and distributing all the goods and services which that household purchases, i.e. it is a measures of the environmental impact of the household's level of consumption.

5 Coote et al (2010) *op. cit.*

6 Speth, J. G. Costanza, R. Hassol, S. J. & Kasser, T. (2007). Some convenient truths: Scaling back our energy-hungry lifestyles means more of what matters, not less. Grist.

7   Layard, R. (2006). *Happiness: Lessons from a new science*. London: Penguin Books, pp. 62–70.

8   Jackson, T. (2009). *Prosperity without Growth? Economics for a finite planet*. London: Sustainable Development Commission, pp. 55–61

9   Delhey, J. (2009). From materialist to post-materialist happiness? National affluence and determinants of life satisfaction in cross-national perspective. *World Values Research* 2(2): 30–54; Layard (2006: 62–70) *op. cit.*; Kasser, T. (2006). Csikszentmihalyi, M. & Selega Csikszentmihalyi, I. (eds). *Materialism and its alternatives. A Life Worth Living: Contributions to positive psychology*. Oxford: Oxford University Press. pp. 200–214.

10   Coote et al (2010) *op. cit.*

11   Committee on Climate Change. (2008). *Building a Low-Carbon Economy: The UK's contribution to tackling climate change. The first report of the Committee on Climate Change*, December 2008. London: The Stationery Office, p. 117.

12   I used the 2004–05 UK Expenditure and Food Survey and the 2000 Dutch Budgetonderzoek (Budget Survey).

13   These data were calculated by two research groups and kindly provided to me for use. Grateful thanks are extended to both for this generosity: in the UK, everyone at the Stockholm Environment Institute, University of York, and in the Netherlands, Kees Vringer and colleagues. Paul et al. (2010) and Vringer et al. (2010) for details of the data and the work related to them.

14   Hertwich, E. G. & Peters, G. P. (2009). Carbon footprint of nations: a global, trade-linked analysis. *Environmental Science and Technology* 43(16): 6414–6420.

15   Pullinger, M. (2011). *Greening Our Working Lives: The environmental impacts of changing patterns of paid work in the UK and the Netherlands, and implications for working time policy*. Edinburgh: University of Edinburgh, pp. 262–263.

16   Pullinger (2011) *ibid*.

17   Carbon Footprints of Nations. Homepage. Retrieved from www.carbonfootprintofnations.com.

18   The OECD equivalence scale is used. Under this scale, household income is divided by an 'equivalence factor', which is the sum of the values from the following: the first adult in the household has a value of 1; subsequent adults (aged 14 or over) have a value of 0.5; children (13 and under) have a value of 0.3. The equivalised income is essentially an attempt, albeit approximate, to compare households with equivalent living standards, measured as an equivalised per capita income, based on the assumption that a certain proportion of household expenditure is on goods and services which can be shared by the household members (such as heating, living space, economies of scale in food purchasing, etc), and also that children need fewer resources than adults.

19   Pullinger (2011) *op. cit.*: pp. 259–261.

20   *Ibid.*

21   Knijn, T. Martin, C. and Millar, J. (2007). Activation as a common framework for social policies towards lone parents. *Social Policy and Administration*. 41(6): 638–652; p. 638.

22   Plantenga, J. 2005. Dutch debates: Modernising social security by introducing the life course as a frame of reference. De Gijsel, P. & Schenk, H. (Eds). *Multidisciplinary*

Economics: The birth of a new economics faculty in the Netherlands. Dordrecht Pp. 53–64: Springer, p. 55.

23 Van der Meer, M. & Leijnse, F. (2005). *Life-course savings schemes and social policy reform in the Netherlands: On the relationship between the welfare state, social pacts and the management of new social risks.* Amsterdam: SISWO/Social Policy Research, p. 5.

24 Leijnse, F. Goudswaard, K. Plantenga, J. & Van den Toren, J. P. (2002). *A Different Attitude to Security: Life course, risk and responsibility.* The Hague: Ministry of Social Affairs and Employment, pp. 16–17; Plantenga, J. (2005). The life course and the system of social security: Rethinking incentives, solidarity and risks. *European Journal of Social Security* 7(4); pp. 302–303.

25 International Labour Organisation. (24 April 2011). Social pacts in Netherlands. Retrieved from http://www.ilo.org/public/english/dialogue/ifpdial/info/pacts/netherlands.htm

26 Fouarge, D. J. A. G., and Baaijens, C. (2004). *Changes in Working Hours and Job Mobility: the effect of Dutch legislation.* Tilburg.

27 Van der Meer & Leijnse, F. (2005). *op. cit.,* pp. 17–18.

28 Groenendijk, H. & Keuzenkamp, S. (2010). 2.19 The Netherlands. International Review of Leave Policies and Related Research 2010. Moss, P. (ed). *Employer Relations Research Series.* London: Department for Business, Innovation and Skills, pp. 161–168.

29 Debacker, M. de Lathouwer, L. & Bogaerts, K. (2004). Time credit and leave schemes in the Belgian welfare state. *Work Package 6: Quality in Labour Market Transitions: A European challenge.* Amsterdam: Royal Academy of Sciences.

30 Debacker et al. (2004) *op. cit.,* pp. 6, 8–9.

31 Merla, M. & Deven, F. (2010). 2.4 Belgium. International Review of Leave Policies and Related Research 2010. Moss, P. (ed). *Employer Relations Research Series.* London: Department for Business, Innovation and Skills, pp. 59–64.

32 Merla, M. & Deven, F. (2010). *op. cit.* p. 64; Devisscher, S. & Sanders, D. (2007). Ageing and life-course issues: the case of the career break scheme (Belgium) and the life-course regulation (Netherlands). Modernising Social Policy for the New Life Course. D'Addio, A. C. & Whiteford, P. Paris: OECD, pp. 117–132.

33 Devisscher & Sanders (2007) *ibid.,* p. 123.

34 *Ibid.*

35 Debacker et al (2004) *op. cit.*

36 Delsen, L. & Smits, J. (2010). Does the life course savings scheme have the potential to improve work–life balance? *British Journal of Industrial Relations* 48(3): 583–604.

37 Committee on Labour Market Participation. (2008). *Towards a Future that Works: Main recommendations.* Netherlands: Committee on Labour Market Participation.

38 Plantenga 2005a:59–61.

39 LaJeunesse (2009). Op cit., pp. 235–242.

40 Kabat-Zinn, J. (2004). *Wherever You Go, There You Are: Mindfulness meditation for everyday life.* London: Piatkus Books.

41 Coote et al (2010). *op. cit.*, p. 3.

42 LaJeunesse (2009). *op. cit.*, pp. 235–242.

43 Coote et al (2010). *op. cit.*, p. 28.

Time, gender and carbon: how British adults use their leisure time – Angela Druckman, Ian Buck, Bronwyn Hayward and Tim Jackson (p. 101)

1 Originally published as: Druckman, A. Buck, I. Hayward, B. & Jackson, T. (2012). Time, Gender and Carbon: A study of the carbon implications of British adults' use of time. *Ecological Economics.* Volume 84; pp. 153–163.

2 HM Government (2008). *Climate Change Act 2008.* London: The Stationery Office Limited.

3 Jackson, T. (2009). *Prosperity Without Growth: Economics for a finite planet.* London: Earthscan; Moriarty, P. & Honnery, D. (2010). A human needs approach to reducing atmospheric carbon. *Energy Policy* 38(2): 695–700; OECD (2011). *Greening Household Behaviour: The role of public policy,* OECD Publishing. Retrieved from OECD iLibrary at http://dx.doi.org/10.1787/9789264096875-en

4 Jalas, M. (2006). *Busy Wise and Idle Time.* Ph.D. Thesis. Helsinki: Helsinki School of Economics; Reisch, L. (2001). Time and Wealth: The role of time and temporalities for sustainable patterns of consumption. *Time & Society* 10(2/3): 367–385.

5 Ropke, I. & Godskesen, M. (2007). Leisure activities, time and environment. *International Journal of Innovation and Sustainable Development* 2: 155–174.

6 Gough, I. Adbdallah, S. Johnson, V. Ryan-Collins, J. & Smith, C. (2011). *The Distribution of Total Greenhouse Gas Emissions by Households in the UK, and Some Implications for Social Policy'.* LSE STICERD Research Paper No. CASE152. London: Centre for Analysis of Social Exclusion, London School of Economics, and **nef**; Jin, W. Joyce, R. Phillips, D. & Sibieta, L. (2011). *Poverty and Inequality in the UK. 2011.* London: Institute for Fiscal Studies.

7 In both cases GHG emissions arise due to expenditure on goods and services. However, in this study we go one step further than general consumption studies and allocate consumption to categories of time use.

8 ONS (2006a). *The Time-Use Survey 2005.* London: Office for National Statistics.

9 In this study 'GHGs' refer to a basket of six GHGs: carbon dioxide, methane, nitrous oxide, hydro-fluorocarbons, perfluorocarbons and sulphur hexafluoride (ONS 2008). The unit of measurement is carbon dioxide equivalent (CO_2e) (OECD 2005).

10 ONS. (2008).'Environmental Accounts'. Accessed 07.11.08, available from http://www. statistics.gov.uk/statbase/explorer.asp?CTG=3&SL=&D=4261&DCT=32&DT=32#4261.

11 DECC. (2009). Energy Consumption in the UK: Domestic data tables 2009 update. Retrieved from http://www.decc.gov.uk/en/content/cms/statistics/publications/ecuk/ ecuk.aspx.

12 ONS (2006a) *op. cit.*

13 Department for Transport. (2009b).'National Travel Survey: 2008'. Accessed 02.06.10, available from http://www.dft.gov.uk/pgr/statistics/datatablespublications/personal/ mainresults/nts2008/

14 This is based on the premise that the distribution of travel modes is the same for all journey purposes.

15 Druckman, A. & Jackson, T. (2008a). *The Surrey Environmental Lifestyle MApping (SELMA) Framework: Development and key results to date.* RESOLVE Working Paper 08–08, University of Surrey, Guildford. Retrieved from http://resolve.sustainablelifestyles. ac.uk/sites/default/files/RESOLVE_WP_08-08_0.pdf; Druckman, A. & Jackson, T. (2009a). The carbon footprint of UK households 1990–2004: a socio-economically disaggregated, quasi-multiregional input-output model. *Ecological Economics* 68 (7): 2066–2077.

Druckman, A. & Jackson, T. (2009b). *Mapping Our Carbon Responsibilities: More key results from the Surrey Environmental Lifestyle MApping (SELMA) framework.* RESOLVE Working Paper 02–09, University of Surrey, Guildford. Retrieved from http://resolve. sustainablelifestyles.ac.uk/sites/default/files/RESOLVE_WP_02-09_0.pdf.

16 Jalas, M. (2005). The Everyday Life Context of Increasing Energy Demands: Time-Use Survey Data in a decomposition analysis. *Journal of Industrial Ecology* 9(1–2): 129–145, p. 136.

17 *Ibid.*

18 Jalas, M. (2002). A time use perspective on the materials intensity of consumption. *Ecological Economics* 41(1): 109–123; Jalas 2005 *ibid.*; Minx, J. & Baiocchi, G. (2009). Time-use and sustainability. Suh, S. (ed). *Handbook of Input-Output Economics in Industrial Ecology.* Dordrecht, the Netherlands: Springer.

19 It is however interesting to note that the average daily intensity of a British adult of 1.2kgCO$_2$e/hr estimated according to this study is in fact only very slightly lower than the average intensity of 1.3kgCO$_2$e/hr if no exclusions in either time or GHG are made.

20 Readers who are interested in looking at detailed estimates of the GHG emissions of an average UK household allocated to high-level functional uses are referred to Druckman and Jackson (2010).

21 The Time-Use Survey excludes children under 16 years old.

22 Leisure and Recreation includes the following categories:
Spending Time with Family/Friends at Home
Spending Time with Family/Friends Outside the Home
Reading
TV and Videos/DVDs, Radio and Music
Hobbies and Games
Entertainment and Culture
Sport and Outdoor Activities.

23 In Figure 2 'Other' is Shopping and Study.

24 By 'non-work' time we refer to time outside (formal) paid and voluntary work.

25 ONS (2006a) *op. cit.*

26 Bryson, V. (2007). *Gender and the Politics of Time: Feminist theory and contemporary debates.* Bristol: The Policy Press.

27 Douglas, M. (1976). Relative poverty, relative communication. Halsey, A. (eds). *Traditions of Social Policy.* Oxford: Basil Blackwell.

28 Jalas (2002; 2005; 2006) *op. cit.*

29 Aall, C. Klepp, I. G. Engeset, A. B. Skuland, S. E. & Stoa, E. (2011). Leisure and sustainable development in Norway: part of the solution and the problem. *Leisure Studies* 30(4): 453–476.

30 Minx & Baiocchi (2009) *op. cit.*

31 Carrillo-Hermosilla, J. (2006). A policy approach to the environmental impacts of technological lock-in. *Ecological Economics* 58(4): 717; Jackson, T. & Papathanasopoulou, E. (2008). Luxury or 'Lock-in'? An explanation of unsustainable consumption in the UK: 1968 to 2000. *Ecological Economics* 68(1–2): 80–95; Sanne, C. (2002). Willing consumers – or locked-in? Policies for a sustainable consumption. *Ecological Economics* 42(1–2): 273–287; Unruh, G. C. (2002). Escaping carbon lock-in. *Energy Policy* 30(4): 317–325.

32 Gregson, N. Metcalfe. A. & Crewe, L. (2007). Identity, mobility and the throwaway society. *Environment and Planning D: Society and space.* 25: 682–700; Hamilton, C. (2010). Consumerism, self-creation and prospects for a new ecological consciousness. *Journal of Cleaner Production* 18(6): 571–575; Jackson (2009) *op. cit.*

33 Nussbaum, M. (2011). *Creating Capabilities: The human development approach.* Cambridge, Massachusetts. Harvard University Press.

34 Goodin, R. E. (2010). Temporal justice. *Journal of Social Policy* 39(01): 1–16.

35 US, Australia, Germany, France, Sweden and Finland.

36 Allan, G. Hawker, S. & Crow, G. (2001). Family Diversity and Change in Britain and Western Europe. *Journal of Family Issues* 22(7): 819–837; Patterson, C. J. (2000). Family relationships of lesbians and gay men. *Journal of Marriage and Family* 62(4): 1052–1069.

37 Coote, A. Franklin J. & Simms, A. (2010). *21 hours: why a shorter working week can help us all to flourish in the 21st century.* London: new economics foundation; Gorz, A. (1994). *Capitalism, socialism, ecology.* New York and London: Verso Books; Hayden, A. (1999). *Sharing the Work, Sparing the Planet.* London and New York: Zed Books Ltd; Jackson (2009) *op. cit.*; Reisch (2001) *op. cit.*; Schor, J. B. (2005). Sustainable Consumption and Worktime Reduction. *Journal of Industrial Ecology,* 9(1): 37–50; Victor, P. (2008). *Managing Without Growth: Slower by Design, Not Disaster.* Cheltenham, UK, and Massachusetts, USA, Edward Elgar.

38 Binswanger, M. (2001). Technological progress and sustainable development: what about the rebound effect? *Ecological Economics* 36(1): 119–132; Hofstetter, P. Madjar, M. & Ozawa, T. (2006). Happiness and Sustainable Consumption: Psychological and physical rebound effects at work in a tool for sustainable design. *International Journal of Life Cycle Assessment* (Special Issue 1): 105–115.

39 Larabee, M. (2008). Portland's walking neighborhoods seen as guide to future. Retrieved from http://www.oregonlive.com/news/oregonian/index.ssf?/base/news/121280911730720.xml&coll=7

McNeil, N. (2010). A twenty minute neighborhood for bicycles? Retrieved from http://nathanmcneil.files.wordpress.com/2010/05/mcneil20minuteposter2.pdf

40 Benfield, K. (27 October 2009). Living smart and well in a '20 minute neighbourhood'. Retrieved from http://switchboard.nrdc.org/blogs/kbenfield/to_live_smart_and_well_choose.html

Costanza, R. Alperovitz, G. Daly, H. Farley, J. Franco, C. Jackson, T. Kubiszewski, I.

Schor, J. B. & Victor, P. (2012). *Building a Sustainable and Desirable. Economy-in-Society-in-Nature.* New York: United Nations.

41 In 2005 British adults spent on average 82 minutes per day travelling ONS (2006a) which translates to an average of around two 20-minute return trips per day. The actual time spent travelling in a '20-minute neighbourhood' would depend on how many trips are made per day, whether they are multi-purpose or not, and the location of each destination within the 20-minute range.

42 As different sectors have very different carbon intensities, this has important implications for supply chain carbon emissions [Carbon Trust (2006). *The Carbon Emissions Generated in all that we Consume.* London, UK, Carbon Trust.]

43 Becker, G. (1965). Theory of the Allocation of Time. *Economic Journal*: 75, pp. 493–517.

44 *Ibid.*

45 Gershuny, J. (2011). *Time-Use Surveys and the Measurement of National Well-Being, Centre for Time-use Research,* Department of Sociology, University of Oxford; ONS (2006a) *op. cit.*

46 Druckman, A. Chitnis, M. Sorrell, S. & Jackson, T. (2011). Missing carbon reductions? Exploring rebound and backfire effects in UK households. *Energy Policy* 39: 3572–3581.

47 Jalas, M. (2009). Time-Use Rebound Effects: An activity-based view of consumption. Herring, H. & Sorrell, S. (eds). *Energy Efficiency and Sustainable Consumption.* Basingstoke, Hampshire: Palgrave Macmillan.

48 ONS (2008) *op. cit.*

49 DECC (2009) *op. cit.*

50 ONS (2006a) *op. cit.*

51 DfT (2009b) *op. cit.*

52 The National Travel Survey allocates a small portion of travel distance to 'personal business' which includes visits to hairdressers, dry-cleaners, libraries, churches, medical appointments and so on (DfT 2009a). In the absence of further data these are allocated as follows: Personal Care 85 per cent; Cleaning and Tidying of Household 11.5 per cent; Repairs and Gardening 2 per cent; Entertainment and Culture 1 per cent; Reading 1 per cent: Watching TV and Videos/DVDs, Listening to Radio and Music 1 per cent.

53 Druckman and Jackson (2008a; 2009a; 2009b) *op. cit.*

54 UN (2005). Classification of Individual Consumption According to Purpose, (COICOP). United Nations Statistics Division.

55 ONS. (2006b). 'Input-Output (I-O) Supply and Use Tables (SUTs)'. Table 4. Accessed 30.04.08, available from http://www.statistics.gov.uk/about/methodology_by_theme/inputoutput/latestdata.asp.
  One exception to this is the SIC sector 'Retail Distribution', as examination of this showed inconsistencies. For example, in the 2006 version of the Supply and Use Tables, 51 per cent of Retail Distribution is allocated to Other Personal Effects. In the 2009 version this is reduced to 25 per cent, and furthermore, the percentage given for the year 2007 in the 2009 version of the tables is 17 per cent. Carbon emissions due to Retail Distribution are therefore allocated according to distribution margins from 'Supply of Products' in the Supply and Use Tables (ONS 2006b: Table 4) following Jackson et al (2006) and Carbon Trust (2006).

56 Druckman, A. Buck, I. Hayward, B. & Jackson, T. (2012). *Carbon and time: A study of the carbon implications of British adults' use of time*. RESOLVE Working Paper Number 01–12. Guildford, UK, University of Surrey. Retrieved from http://resolve.sustainablelifestyles.ac.uk/sites/default/files/resolve_wp_01-12.pdf

57 ONS (2006a) *op. cit.*

58 More details can be found in ONS (2006a) *op. cit.*

59 ONS. (2011). 'Families and households data tables. United Kingdom, 2001–2010'. Accessed 04.08.11, available from http://www.statistics.gov.uk/StatBase/Product.asp?vlnk=1614

60 Jalas (2002; 2005) *op. cit.*

61 DfT (2009b: Table 4.2) *op. cit.*

62 Hong, S. Oreszczyn, T. & Ridley, I. (2006). The impact of energy efficient refurbishment on the space heating fuel consumption in English dwellings. *Energy and Buildings* 38: 1171–1181; Summerfield, A. J. Lowe, R. J. Bruhns, H. R. Caeiro, J. A. Steadman, J. P. & Oreszczyn, T. (2007). Milton Keynes Energy Park revisited: Changes in internal temperatures and energy usage. *Energy and Buildings* 39(7): 783–791.

63 Druckman, A. & T. Jackson (2010). *An Exploration into the Carbon Footprint of UK Households*. RESOLVE Working Paper Series 02–10, University of Surrey, Guildford, November 2010. Retrieved from http://resolve.sustainablelifestyles.ac.uk/sites/default/files/RESOLVE_WP_02-10.pdf.

64 Godbey, G. (1996). *No Time to Waste: Time Use and the Generation of Residential Solid Waste*. PSWP Working Paper #4. New Haven, Connecticut, Yale School of Forestry and Environmental Studies; Godbey, G., Lifset, R. & Robinson, J. (1998). No Time to Waste: an Exploration of Time Use, Attitudes Toward Time, and the Generation of Municipal Solid Waste. *Social Research* 65(1): 101–140.

65 ONS (2006a) *op. cit.*

66 *Ibid.*

67 Both taken from Table 5 in ONS (2011) *op. cit.*

68 ONS (2006a) *op. cit.*

69 *Ibid.*

70 Brand, C. & Boardman, B. (2008). Taming of the Few – The Unequal Distribution of Greenhouse Gas Emissions from Personal Travel in the UK. *Energy Policy* 36: 224–238; Brand, C. & Preston, J. M. (2010). 60–20 Emission – The Unequal Distribution of Greenhouse Gas Emissions from Personal, Non-business Travel in the UK. *Transport Policy* 17: 9–19; Druckman, A. & Jackson, T. (2008b). Household energy consumption in the UK: a highly geographically and socio-economically disaggregated model. *Energy Policy* 36(8): 3167- 3182; Druckman & Jackson (2009a) *op. cit.*, Gough et al (2011) *op. cit.*

71 Druckman & Jackson (2009a; 2009b) *op. cit.*

72 *Ibid.*

73 Alcala, R. & Antille, G. (1999). Technical Change in the Private Consumption Converter. *Economic Systems Research* 11(4): 389; Jalas (2009) *op. cit.*

74 ONS (2006a) *op. cit.*

75 Bryson (2007) *op. cit.*

76 Grossman, L. (1 April 2010). 'Do we need the iPAD? A TIME Review.' *Time Magazine.* Retrieved from http://www.time.com/time/magazine/article/0,9171,1977106,00.html.

77 Jalas (2005) *op. cit.*

78 *Ibid.*

79 Jalas (2009) *op. cit.*

Patterns and purpose of work-time reduction – a cross national comparison – Anders Hayden (p. 125)

1 Lubbers, R. (Autumn 1997). The Dutch Way. *New Perspectives Quarterly.* p. 15.

2 Coote, A. Franklin, J. & Simms, A. (2010). *21 Hours: Why a shorter working week can help us all to flourish in the 21st century,* London: **nef**; de Graaf, J. (2010). Reducing Work Time as a Path to Sustainability. *State of the World 2010: Transforming cultures from consumerism to sustainability.* New York: W. W. Norton & Company. pp. 173–177; Gorz, A. (1994). *Capitalism, Socialism, Ecology.* London: Verso; Hayden, A. (1999). *Sharing the Work, Sparing the Planet: Work Time, Consumption and Ecology.* London: Zed Books; Schor, J. B. (2010). Plenitude: The New Economics of True Wealth. New York: The Penguin Press.

3 Hayden, A. and Shandra, J. M. (2009). Hours of work and the ecological footprint of nations: an exploratory analysis. *Local Environment,* 14(6), pp. 575–600; Jackson, T. and Victor, P. (2011). Productivity and work in the 'green economy': Some theoretical reflections and empirical tests. *Environmental Innovation and Societal Transitions,* 1, pp. 101–108; Knight, K. W. Rosa, E. A. and Schor, J. B. (19 August 2012). *Could working less reduce pressures on the environment? A cross-national panel analysis of OECD Countries, 1970–2007.* Annual Meeting of the American Sociological Association. Denver, CO; Rosnick, D. and Weisbrot, M. (2006). *Are shorter hours good for the environment? A comparison of US and European energy consumption.* Washington, DC. Center for Economic and Policy Research; Victor, P. (2008). *Managing Without Growth: Slower by design, not disaster.* Cheltenham, UK. Edward Elgar.

4 Jackson, T. (2009). *Prosperity Without Growth? The transition to a sustainable economy.* London: Sustainable Development Commission.

5 UNEP. (2008). Green Jobs: Towards decent work in a sustainable, low-carbon world, Nairobi. United Nations Environment Programme.

6 One rule of thumb has been that increased labour productivity will absorb roughly 50 per cent of the hours-reduction, with the other half enabling higher employment, although this percentage will vary greatly depending on the workplace and conditions in which the change takes place. Bosch, G. & Lehndorff, S. (2001). Working-time reduction and employment: experiences in Europe and economic policy recommendations. *Cambridge Journal of Economics,* 25(2), p. 227; Golden, L. (2012). *The Effects of Working Time on Productivity and Firm Performance: A Research Synthesis Paper.* Conditions of Work and Employment Series No. 33. Geneva: International Labour Organisation.

7 ILO. (2011). *Working Time in the Twenty-First century.* Geneva. International Labour Organisation, pp. 12–13.

8 Hayden, A. (2006). France's 35-hour week: attack on business? Win-win reform? Or betrayal of disadvantaged workers? *Politics Society*, 34(4), pp. 503–542; Méda, D. (2001). Les 35 heures dans l'histoire séculaire de la réduction du temps de travail. Brunhes, B. Clerc, D. Méda, D. & Perret, B. (eds). *35 heures: Le Temps du Bilan,* Paris: Desclée de Brouwer, pp. 13–20.

9 Other factors behind the lower-than-expected employment gains included the fact that fewer employees than expected gained a 35-hour week before a new centre-right government halted the shorter week's further spread. Work time also fell less than originally expected, as many firms avoided a full ten per cent cut in hours by changing their way of calculating work time, e.g. by no longer counting breaks.

10 Méda, D. (2001). Travailler moins pour vivre mieux? Brunhes, B. Clerc, D. Méda, D. & Perret, B. (eds). *35 heures: Le temps du bilan,* Paris: Desclée de Brouwer. For a more detailed review of the 35-hour week, see Hayden (2006) *op. cit.*

11 For example, Evans-Pritchard, A. (24 March 2005). France to abandon the 35-hour week. *Telegraph*, p. 38.

12 For example, a poll by BVA (2011, pp. 5, 12–15) in December 2011 found that 56 per cent were against abolishing the 35-hour week versus 43 per cent in favour. The only age group favouring abolition were those over 65 years of age, who do not benefit from it.

13 Bispinck, R. (2006). Germany: Working time and its negotiation, in Keune, M. & Galgóczi, B. (eds). *Collective bargaining on working time: recent European experiences.* Brussels: ETUI, pp. 111–129.

14 Lehndorff, S. (2011). Before the Crisis, in the Crisis, and Beyond: The upheaval of collective bargaining in Germany. *Transfer*, 17(3), pp. 346–7.

15 ILO (2011b) *op. cit.*, p. 15.

16 BLS. (2012). *Employee Benefits in the United States – March 2012.* Washington DC. Bureau of Labor Statistics, p. 16; Ray, R. and Schmitt, J. (2007). *No-Vacation Nation.* Washington DC. Center for Economic and Policy Research.

17 Cabrita, J. (16 August 2012). *Working time developments – 2011.* European Industrial Relations Observatory Online. Retrieved from http://www.eurofound.europa.eu/eiro/studies/tn1204022s/tn1204022s.htm

18 Truc, O. (1998). Ces Danoises qui préfèrent le temps à l'argent. *Libération*, 8 May.

19 Ray and Schmitt (2007) *op. cit.*; BLS (2012) *op. cit.:* p. 16

20 Cabrita (2012) *op. cit.*

21 In 2010, the EU extended the minimum leave to four months per parent, in addition to a minimum 14 weeks maternity leave, although it is up to member states to determine the level of pay.

22 Moss, P. (2012). *International Review of Leave Policies and Related Research 2012.* International Network on Leave Policies and Research, pp. 260–261

23 *Ibid.,* p. 260

24 Swedish men took only about seven per cent of parental leave days in 1987 (Moss 2012) *ibid.,* p. 263.

25 Moss (2012) *op. cit.*, pp. 42–43, 151–154.

26 Björklund, A. (2006). Does family policy affect fertility? *Journal of Population Economics*, 19(1), pp. 3–24; Lalive, R. & Zweimüller, J. (2009). How does Parental Leave Affect Fertility and Return to Work? Evidence from Two Natural Experiments. *Quarterly Journal of Economics*, 124(3), pp. 1363–1402.

27 Gauthier, A. (2007). The impact of family policies on fertility in industrialised countries: a review of the literature. *Population Research and Policy Review*, 26(3), pp. 323–346.

28 Grünell, M. (28 February 2000). Part-time Employment Act seeks to promote combining work and care. *European Industrial Relations Observatory Online*. Retrieved from http://www.eurofound.europa.eu/eiro/2000/02/feature/nl0002182f.htm; ILO. (2011). Database of Conditions of Work and Employment Laws. Geneva: International Labour Organisation. Retrieved from http://www.ilo.org/dyn/travail/travmain.home

29 ILO (2011) *op. cit.*, p. 27; OECD. (2012). Incidence of involuntary part time workers. Retrieved from http://stats.oecd.org/Index.aspx?DatasetCode=INVPT_I; OECD. (2012). Part-time employment % of total employment. Retrieved from http://www.oecd-ilibrary. org.ezproxy.library.dal.ca/employment/part-time-employment_20752342-table7

30 Moss (2012) *op. cit.*

31 ILO (2011a) *op. cit.*; Moss (2012) *ibid.*, p. 65.

32 Corbanie, S. and Cousin, S. (July 2012). New austerity measures: restrictions on 'time credit' (career breaks). International HR briefing. Belgium. Retrieved from http://www. lexology.com/library/detail.aspx?g=793288a7-fb15-4029-948a-dd76ebd7d261; Gyes, G. V. (July 2009). Reducing working time as anti-crisis measure. *European Industrial Relations Observatory Online*, July. Retrieved from http://www.eurofound.europa.eu/eiro/2009/06/ articles/be0906029i.htm. Moss (2012) *ibid.*, pp. 64–65.

33 Devisscher, S. (2004). *The career break (time credit) scheme in Belgium and the incentive premiums by the Flemish government*. Discussion paper. Retrieved from http://www.mutual-learning-employment.net/uploads/ModuleXtender/PeerReviews/7/Discussion%20 paperBEL04.pdf

34 Defeyt, P. (2010). *Pourquoi le chômage n'augmente-t-il pas plus?* Ottignies, Belgique: Institut pour un Développement Durable; Gyes (2009) *op. cit.*; RTL. (23 March 2012). Chômage: au niveau le plus bas depuis 20 ans. *RTL info*. Retrieved from http://www.rtl. be/info/belgique/societe/865551/chomage-au-niveau-le-plus-bas-depuis-20-ans

35 Moss (2012) *op. cit.*, p. 67.

36 Corbanie & Cousin (2012) *op. cit.*; Moss (2012) *op. cit.*, p. 66.

37 OECD. (2010). *Employment Outlook 2010: How does Germany compare?* Paris: Organisation for Economic Co-operation and Development.

38 Lehndorff. (2011). *op. cit.*; Schmitt, J. (2011). *Labor Market Policy in the Great Recession: Some lessons from Denmark and Germany*, Washington DC. Center for Economic and Policy Research.

39 Mandl, I. (2010). *Extending Flexicurity – The potential of short-time working schemes: ERM Report 2010*, Dublin: European Foundation for the Improvement of Living and Working Conditions.

40 Wales, however, does have its own regional short-time working programme known as ProAct.

41 Wolf, M. (2011). Britain's curiously continental job market. *Financial Times*, 16 June, p. 9.

42 Schor, J. B. (9 August 2010). The work sharing boom: exit ramp to a new economy? *Yes! Magazine*.

43 Woo, N. and Baker, D. (May 2012). *States Could Save $1.7 Billion per Year with Federal Financing of Work Sharing*. Issue Brief. Washington, DC. Center for Economic Policy and Research.

44 Messenger (2009) *op. cit.*, p. 3.

45 See endnote 1, above.

46 Bosch, G. and Lehndorff, S. (2001). Working-time reduction and employment: experiences in Europe and economic policy recommendations. *Cambridge Journal of Economics*, 25(2), p. 215.

47 Hayden (2006) *op. cit.*, p. 529.

48 In the first Aubry law of 1998, payroll tax reductions were given to firms that reduced hours by ten per cent and increased employment by at least six per cent. The second Aubry law of 2000 gave payroll tax reductions to any firm that moved to a 35-hour week, without a specific hiring requirement. Due to the lack of hiring requirements, the payroll tax reductions were no longer fully self-financing via the savings on the costs of unemployment.

49 Azam, G. et al, (13 January 2011). Pour la semaine de 32 heures. *Le Monde*. Retrieved from http://www.lemonde.fr/idees/article/2011/01/12/pour-la-semaine-de-32-heures_1464577_3232.html

50 Hiring new workers on a four-day schedule was common in the Netherlands in the 1980s to maximise employment. Such ideas certainly merit consideration today. They have a pragmatic appeal as new workers are not yet accustomed to the income from a full five-day week and, in a context of high unemployment, will be likely to welcome the improved job opportunities that result. However, where other significant generational inequalities are at play, as young employees are increasingly saddled with student debt and face difficulties in getting on the housing ladder, separate work time (and income) standards for younger and older workers may face greater resistance.

51 Improving one particular leave option, parental leave, may face better short-term political prospects in some countries due to its relatively broad appeal, ranging from those seeking to expand employee rights on the left to more conservative voices in favour of 'family values'.

52 ILO (2011b) *op. cit.*, pp. 60–63; Messenger, J. C. (2009). *Work sharing: A strategy to preserve jobs during the global jobs crisis*. Geneva: International Labour Organization.

53 Mandl (2010) *op. cit.*

54 Schor (2010b) *op. cit.*

55 This was the case, for example, with a move by Bell Canada in 1994 to a 36-hour, four-day week as an alternative to 5,000 planned lay-offs. Hayden. (1999). pp. 122–123; White and Goulet (1998).

56 Rubin, J. (2012). *The End of Growth*, Toronto. Random House Canada. pp. 179–183.

57 However, some innovative employers have played pioneering roles along the way, such as W. K. Kellogg, who introduced a six-hour day at his US cereal plants in the 1930s.

58 Strongman, C. (2012). Copenhagen really is wonderful, for so many reasons. *The Observer*, 8 April, p. 29.

The French experience – Dominique Méda (p. 143)

1 RTT = Réduction du Temps de Travail (Reduction in working hours). Loi du 13 juin 1998 d'orientation et d'incitation relative à la réduction du temps de travail et loi du 19 janvier 2000 relative à la réduction négociée du temps de travail.

2 Méda, D. (1995). Le travail: une valeur en voie de disparition. Paris. Aubier, Coll. Alto, 1995, rééd. Paris, Champs-Flammarion, 1998, p. 358

3 Boulin J.-Y. Lallement M. Lefèvre G. & Silvéra R. (1998). Temps de travail et mode de vie: quelques résultats d'une enquête empirique. *Futuribles*, n° 237, décembre.

4 Rigaudiat J. (1996). *Réduire le Temps de Travail*, Syros. Translation: *Reducing working time.*

5 Translation: Bank of France

6 Translation: French Observatory for Economic Situations

7 Dares (1998), L'impact macroéconomique d'une politique de réduction de la durée du travail, *Premières Synthèses*, n° 05–2, DARES.

8 Translation: Business Action France

9 Askénazy P. Bloch-London C. & Roger M. (2005). La réduction du temps de travail 1997–2003: dynamique de construction des lois 'Aubry' et premières évaluations, *Économie et Statistique*, n° 376–377.

10 Afsa C. & Biscourps P. (2005). L'évolution des rythmes de travail entre 1995 et 2001: quel impact des 35 heures? *Economie et Statistique*, n° 376–377.

11 *Economie et Statistique*, n° 376–377, 2005.

12 Philippon, T. (2007). *Le Capitalisme d'Héritiers : La crise française du travail.* Paris: Seuil; Davoine, L. & Méda, D. (February 2008). *Place et sens du travail en Europe: une singularité française? Document de travail*, Centre d'Etudes de l'Emploi, n° 96–1, p. 116. Retrieved from http://www.cee-recherche.fr/fr/doctrav/travail_europe_96_vf.pdf ; Davoine, L. & Méda, D. (February 2008) *Importance and Meaning of Work in Europe: a French Singularity*? *Document de travail*, Centre d'Etudes de l'Emploi, n° 96–2, p. 105

13 *Cotisations Sociales* – Translation: social contributions. Definition: In France, *cotisations sociales* are deducted directly from salaries in France (so a form of 'payroll tax').

14 Askenazy, P. (2003). La dynamique de l'organisation du travail lors de la réduction du temps de travail. *Économie et Prévision*, n° 158, pp. 27–46.

15 Afsa and Biscourp (2005) *op. cit.*

16 Coutrot T. (February 2006). Les conditions de travail des salariés après la réduction du temps de travail. *Premières Synthèses*, n ° 06.3, Dares, Ministère du Travail et de l'Emploi.

17 Estrade, M.-A., Méda, D. et Orain, R. (2001). Les effets de la réduction du temps de travail sur les modes de vie: qu'en pensent les salaries un an après? *Premières Synthèses*, n° 21.1, MES, Dares.

18 Ulrich, V. & Zilbermann, C. (January 2007). La réduction du temps de travail: révélateur et source de développement des relations professionnelles en entreprise. *Premières Synthèses*, n ° 03.2, DARES, Ministère du Travail et de l'Emploi.

19 The Reduction of Working Time and Lifestyles Survey, MES-DARES, Ministère du Travail et de l'Emploi. 2001.

20 French school pupils, especially younger ones, often have the day or half-day off on Wednesdays. They often go to school on Saturday mornings.

21 Méda D. et Orain R. (April 2002), Transformations du travail et du hors-travail: le jugement des salariés sur la RTT. *Travail et Emploi*, n° 90.

22 Estrade M.-A., et Ulrich, V. (2002). La réorganisation des temps travailles avec les 35 heures: un facteur de segmentation de la main-d'oeuvre? *Travail et Emploi*, n° 92, pp. 71–94.

23 Théret, B. (2010). Réduction du temps de travail et développement démocratique. Coutrot T. Flacher D. & Méda, D. (2010). *Pour en finir avec ce vieux monde. Les chemins de la transition.* Editions Utopia.

National Gardening Leave – Andrew Simms and Molly Conisbee (p. 155)

1 A different version of this chapter was originally prepared for the Garden Futures Conference, London, in October 2012 and published as the pamphlet, *National Gardening Leave*.

2 Ehrenreich, B. (2007). *Dancing in the Streets: A history of collective joy*. Granta, London.

3 TUC. (22 February 2012). Surge in older workers doing unpaid overtime. Retrieved from http://www.tuc.org.uk/workplace/tuc-20663-f0.cfm

4 Walker, T. (2002). 'The 'lump-of-labor' case against work sharing: populist fallacy or marginalist throwback?' *Working Time: International trends, theory and policy perspectives*, Lonnie Golden, L & Figart, D. M. (eds).

5 McKay, G. (2011). *Radical Gardening: Politics, Idealism and Rebellion in the Garden*. London: Frances Lincoln, 2011.

6 http://sandwellfoodnetwork.blogspot.co.uk/

7 Incredible Edible Todmorden. (2013). *Homepage*. Retrieved from www.incredible-edible-todmorden.co.uk [accessed 20 June 2013]

8 Ackerman, K. (2011). *The Potential for Urban Agriculture in New York City*. The Earth Institute. Columbia University.

9 Mind. (May 2007). *Ecotherapy: The green agenda for mental health*. Mind: London. Retrieved from http://www.mind.org.uk/assets/0000/2139/ecotherapy_executivesummary.pdf

10 Kuo, F. E. & Sullivan, W. C. (May 2001). Environment and crime in the inner city: does vegetation reduce crime? *Environment and Behavior*, Vol. 33 No. 3.

11 Sustainable Development Commission (SDC). (2009). *Every Child's Future Matters*. 3rd Edition. London: SDC; Frumkin, H. (2001) Beyond toxicity: human health and the natural environment. *American Journal of Preventive Medicine*, 20(3); Faber T. A. & Kuo

F. E. (2006) Is contact with nature important for healthy child development? State of the evidence. In Spencer, C. & Blades, M. (eds). *Children and Their Environments: Learning, using and designing spaces*. Cambridge: Cambridge University Press; Louv, R. (2005). *Last Child in the Woods: Saving our children from nature-deficit disorder*. Chapel Hill: Algonquin Books; Chawla, L. & Flanders Cushing, D. (2007). *Benefits of Nature for Children's Health, Fact Sheet Number 1*. Denver: Children, Youth and Environments Center for Research and Design, University of Colorado at Denver and Health Sciences Center.

12 Esteban, A. (2012). *Natural solutions: Nature's role in delivering well-being and key policy goals – opportunities for the third sector*. **nef**, London.

13 *Ibid.*

14 BTCV (March 2010). Reducing re-offending by ex-prisoners: report by the Social Exclusion Unit. *BTCV position paper, Employment and Skills*

15 BTCV (March 2010). *BTCV Position Paper, Employment and Skills*.

16 Cameron, R. W. F. Blanuša, T. Taylor, J. E. Salisbury, A. Halstead, A. J. Henricot, B. & Thompson, K. (2012). The domestic garden: its contribution to urban green infrastructure. *Urban Forestry & Urban Greening Volume 11*, Issue 2.

17 *Ibid.*

18 Rosnick, D. (2013). *Reduced Work Hours as a Means of Slowing Climate Change*, Centre for Economic and Policy Research.

Bibliography

Aall, C. Klepp, I. G. Engeset, A. B. Skuland, S. E. & Stoa, E. (2011). Leisure and sustainable development in Norway: part of the solution and the problem. *Leisure Studies* 30(4): 453-476.

Ackerman, F. DeCanio, S. J. Howarth, R. B. & Sheeran, K. (2009). Limitations of integrated assessment models of climate change. *Climatic Change* 95, (April 2): 297–315. Retrieved from http://www.springerlink.com.proxy.bc.edu/content/c85v5581x7n74571/fulltext.pdf

Ackerman, K. (2011). *The Potential for Urban Agriculture in New York City*. The Earth Institute. Columbia University.

Adam, B. (1990). *Time and Social Theory.* Cambridge: Polity Press.

Adam, B. (1993). Within and beyond the time economy of employment relations. *Social Science Information,* 32: 163–84.

Adam, B. (1995). *Timewatch: The Social Analysis of Time.* Cambridge: Polity Press.

Adam, B. (1998). *Timescapes of Modernity: The Environment and Invisible Hazards.* London: Routledge.

Adam, B. (2003). When time is money: contested rationalities of time in the theory and practice of work'. *Theoria* 102: 94–125.

Adam, B. (2004). *Time.* Cambridge/Boston, MA: Polity Press.

Afsa C. & Biscourps P. (2005). L'évolution des rythmes de travail entre 1995 et 2001: quel impact des 35 heures? *Economie et Statistique,* n° 376–377.

Ahmad, N. & Wyckoff, A. (2003). Carbon dioxide emissions embodied in international trade of goods. *OECD Science, Technology and Industry Working Papers,* 2003/15, OECD Publishing.

Alcala, R. & Antille, G. (1999). Technical Change in the Private Consumption Converter. *Economic Systems Research,* 11(4): 389.

Alesina, A. Glaeser, E. & Sacerdote, B. (2005). Work and leisure in the US and Europe: why so different? *NBER Macroeconomic Annual 2005.*

Allan, G. Hawker, S. & Crow, G. (2001). Family diversity and change in Britain and Western Europe. *Journal of Family Issues* 22(7): 819–837.

Askenazy, P. (2003). 'La dynamique de l'organisation du travail lors de la réduction du temps de Travail'. *Économie et Prévision,* n° 158, pp. 27–46.

Avdagic, S. Rhodes, M. & Visser, J. (2011). *Social Pacts in Europe: Emergence, evolution and institutionalisation.* Oxford: Oxford University Press, xi, p. 322. Retrieved from http://labordoc.ilo.org/record/457201?ln=en

Azam, G. et al, (13 January 2011). Pour la semaine de 32 heures. *Le Monde*. Retrieved from http://www.lemonde.fr/idees/article/2011/01/12/pour-la-semaine-de-32-heures_1464577_3232.html

Baer, P. & Athanasiou, T. (September 2008). 'The Right to Development in a Climate Constrained World,' Executive Summary, Revised Second Edition. Retrieved from http://www.in.boell.org/web/113-397.html

Balbo, L. and Nowotny, H. (eds) (1986). *Time to Care in Tomorrow's Welfare System*. Vienna: Eurosocial.

Bauman, Z. (2010). *Living on Borrowed Time: Conversations with Citali Rovirosa-Madrazo*. Cambridge: Polity Press.

Bauman, Z. (1995). *Life in Fragments: Essays in Postmodern Morality*. Oxford: Basil Blackwell.

Bauman, Z. (1993). *Postmodern Ethics*. Oxford: Basil Blackwell.

Bauman, Z. (1992). *Intimations of Postmodernity*. London: Routledge.

Becker, G. (1965). Theory of the Allocation of Time. *Economic Journal*: 75, pp. 493–517.

Benfield, K. (27 October 2009). Living smart and well in a '20 minute neighbourhood'. Retrieved from http://switchboard.nrdc.org/blogs/kbenfield/to_live_smart_and_well_choose.html

Best, F. (1980). *Exchanging Earnings for Leisure. Findings of an Exploratory National Survey on Work Time Preference*. U.S. Department of Labour, Employment and Training Administration.

Binswanger, M. (2001). Technological progress and sustainable development: what about the rebound effect? *Ecological Economics* 36(1): 119–132.

Bispinck, R. (2006). Germany: Working time and its negotiation. Keune, M. and Galgóczi, B. (eds). *Collective Bargaining on Working Time: Recent European Experiences*. Brussels: ETUI, pp. 111–129.

Björklund, A. (2006). Does family policy affect fertility? *Journal of Population Economics*, 19(1), pp. 3–24.

Blau, R. Kenyon, A. & Lekhi, R. (2007). *Stress at Work: A recent report for the Work Foundation's principal partners*. London: The Work Foundation.

BLS. (2012). *Employee Benefits in The United States*. March 2012. Washington, DC: Bureau of Labor Statistics.

Blyton, P. (1989). Time and Labour Relations. P. Blyton, J. Hassard, S. Hill & K. Starkey (eds) *Time, Work and Organisation*. London: Routledge, pp. 105–131.

Bojer, H. (2003). *Distributional Justice, Theory and Measurement*. London: Routledge.

Bosch, G. & Lehndorff, S. (2001). Working-time reduction and employment: experiences in Europe and economic policy recommendations. *Cambridge Journal of Economics*, 25(2), pp. 209–243.

Boulin J.-Y. Lallement M. Lefèvre G. et Silvéra R. (December 1998). 'Temps de travail et mode de vie: quelques résultats d'une enquête empirique'. *Futuribles*, n° 237.

Bourdieu, P. (1979). *Algeria 1960*. Cambridge: Cambridge University Press.

Bowles, S. and Park, Y. (2005). Emulation, inequality and work hours: Was Thorsten Veblen right? *The Economic Journal,* 115: 397–413.

Boyd, E. (2002). 'Being there': mothers who stay at home, gender and time. *Women's Studies International Forum* 25 (4): 463–70.

Brand, C. & Boardman, B. (2008). Taming of the few: the unequal distribution of greenhouse gas emissions from personal travel in the UK. *Energy Policy,* 36: 224–238.

Brand, C. & Preston, J. M. (2010). '60–20 Emission': the unequal distribution of greenhouse gas emissions from personal, non-business travel in the UK. *Transport Policy,* 17: 9–19.

Brown, S. & Pudney, S. (2005). Hours constraints and in-work poverty. *Bulletin of Economic Research,* 57 (3): 305–315.

Bryson, V. (2007). *Gender and the Politics of Time: Feminist Theory and Contemporary Debates*. Bristol: The Policy Press.

Bryson, V. (2008). Time use studies: a potentially feminist tool? *International Journal of Feminist Politics*, 10 (2).

Bryson, V & Deery, R. (2010). Public policy, 'men's time' and power: the work of community midwives in the British National Health Service. *Women's Studies International Forum,* 33: 91–98.

Burchardt, T. (2008). *Time and Income Poverty.* York: Joseph Rowntree Foundation.

Burchardt, T. (2010). Time, income and substantive freedom: A capability approach. *Time and Society*, 19(3): 318–344.

BVA. (1 December 2011). Baromètre de l'économie. Paris: BVA. Retrieved from http://www.bva.fr/gene/expe/download.php?sequence=sondage_fic he_14202e8a2aede61e7aa99af47c23b214

Carbon Trust. (2006). *The carbon emissions generated in all that we consume*. London: Carbon Trust.

Cabrita, J. (16 August 2012). Working time developments – 2011. *European Industrial Relations Observatory On-line* Retrieved from http://www. eurofound.europa.eu/eiro/studies/tn1204022s/tn1204022s.htm

Calwell, C. (2010). *Is efficient sufficient? The case for shifting our emphasis in energy specifications to progressive efficiency and sufficiency*. Stockholm: European Council for and Energy Efficient Economy.

Carlstein, T. D. Parkes & Thrift, N. (eds) (1978). (3 Vols). *I. Making Sense of Time, II. Human Activity and Time Geography, III. Time and Regional Dynamics.* London: Edward Arnold.

Carr, N. (2010). *The Shallows: What the internet is doing to our brains.* London: W. W. Norton & Company.

Carrillo-Hermosilla, J. (2006). A policy approach to the environmental impacts of technological lock-in. *Ecological Economics* 58(4): 717.

Childs, S. (2004). *New Labour's Women MPs*. London: Routledge.

Clark, P. A. (1982) *A Review of the Theories of Time and Structure for Organisational Sociology*. Birmingham: The University of Aston Management Centre Working Paper.

Clement, B. (23 February 2006)'Britons work longer hours than anyone else in Europe', *The Independent*. Retrieved from http://www.independent.co.uk/news/uk/this-britain/britons-work-longer-hours-than-anyone-else-in-europe-467467.html

Committee on Climate Change. (2008). *Building a low-carbon economy: The UK's contribution to tackling climate change. The first report of the Committee on Climate Change, December 2008*. London: The Stationery Office.

Committee on Labour Market Participation. (2008). *Towards a Future that Works: Main recommendations*. Netherlands: Committee on Labour Market Participation.

Coote, A. Franklin J. & Simms, A. (2010). *21 hours: Why a shorter working week can help us all to flourish in the 21st century*. London: new economics foundation.

Corbanie, S. & Cousin, S. (16 July 2012). New austerity measures: restrictions on 'time credit' (career breaks). International HR briefing: Belgium. *Lexology*. Retrieved from http://www.lexology.com/library/detail.aspx?g=793288a7-fb15-4029-948a-dd76ebd7d261 [Accessed August 17, 2012].

Costanza, R. Alperovitz, G. Daly, H. Farley, J. Franco, C. Jackson, T. Kubiszewski, I. Schor, J. B. & Victor, P. (2012). *Building a Sustainable and Desirable. Economy-in-Society-in-Nature*. New York: United Nations.

Cottrell, W. F. (1939). 'Of Time and the Railroader'. *American Journal of Sociology*, 4: 190–8.

Coutrot T. (February 2006). Les conditions de travail des salariés après la réduction du temps de travail. *Premières Synthèses* n° 06.3, Dares, Ministère du travail et de l'emploi.

Coutrot T. Flacher D. Méda, D. (2010). *Pour en finir avec ce vieux monde. Les chemins de la transition*. Editions Utopia.

Daly, H. E. (1977). *Steady-State Economics: The economics of biophysical equilibrium and moral growth*. San Francisco: W. H. Freeman.

Daly, H. E. (1996). *Beyond Growth: The economics of sustainable development*. Boston: Beacon Press.

Dares (1998), L'impact macroéconomique d'une politique de réduction de la durée du travail, *Premières Synthèses*, No 05–2, DARES

Davies, K. (1990). *Women and Time: The weaving of the strands of everyday life*. Aldershot: Avesbury.

Davoine, L. & Méda, D. (February 2008). Place et sens du travail en Europe:

une singularité française? *Document de travail*, Centre d'études de l'emploi, n° 96–1, p. 116.

Debacker, M. de Lathouwer, L. & Bogaerts, K. (2004). Time credit and leave schemes in the Belgian welfare state. *Work Package 6: Quality in labour market transitions: An European challenge.* Amsterdam: Royal Academy of Sciences.

DECC. (26 July 2012). Energy Consumption in the UK. UK.Gov website, retrieved from http://www.decc.gov.uk/en/content/cms/statistics/publications/ecuk/ecuk.aspx

Defeyt, P. (2010). *Pourquoi le chômage n'augmente-t-il pas plus?* Ottignies, Belgique: Institut pour un Développement Durable.

Delhey, J. (2009). From materialist to postmaterialist happiness? National affluence and determinants of life satisfaction in cross-national perspective. *World Values Research* 2(2): 30–54.

Delsen, L. & Smits, J. (2010). Does the Life Course Savings Scheme have the potential to improve work–life balance? *British Journal of Industrial Relations* 48(3): 583–604.

Devetter, F. X. & Rousseau, S. (2011). Working hours and sustainable development. *Review of Social Economy.* LXIX(3): 333–355.

Devisscher, S. (20 February 2004). The Career Break (Time Credit) Scheme in Belgium and the Incentive Premiums by the Flemish Government. Discussion Paper. Retrieved from http://www.mutual-learning-employment.net/uploads/ModuleXtender/PeerReviews/7/Discussion%20paperBEL04.pdf

Devisscher, S. and Sanders, D. (2007). Ageing and life-course issues: the case of the career break scheme (Belgium) and the life-course regulation (Netherlands). *Modernising social policy for the new life course*, edited by D'Addio, A. C. & Whiteford, P. Paris: OECD. pp. 117–132.

DfT. (September 2010). National Travel Survey. *Notes and definitions*. National Archives website. Retrieved from http://webarchive.nationalarchives.gov.uk/20110509101621/dft.gov.uk/pgr/statistics/datatablespublications/nts/

DfT. (2009). *Transport Statistics Bulletin: National Travel Survey 2008.* National Archives website. Retrieved from http://webarchive.nationalarchives.gov.uk/20100514175047/http:/www.dft.gov.uk/adobepdf/162469/221412/221531/223955/32274311/NTS2008.pdf

Douglas, M. (1976). Relative Poverty, Relative Communication. A. Halsey (ed) *Traditions of Social Policy*. Oxford: Basil Blackwell.

Druckman, A. & Jackson, T. (2008a). *The Surrey Environmental Lifestyle MApping (SELMA) framework: development and key results to date.* RESOLVE Working Paper 08–08, University of Surrey, Guildford. Retrieved from http://resolve.sustainablelifestyles.ac.uk/sites/default/files/RESOLVE_WP_08-08_0.pdf

Druckman, A. & Jackson, T. (2008b). Household energy consumption in the UK: a highly geographically and socio-economically disaggregated model. *Energy Policy* 36(8): 3167– 3182.

Druckman, A. & Jackson, T. (2009a). The carbon footprint of UK households 1990–2004: a socio-economically disaggregated, quasi-multiregional input-output model. *Ecological Economics* 68 (7): 2066–2077.

Druckman, A. & Jackson, T. (2009b). *Mapping our carbon responsibilities: more key results from the Surrey Environmental Lifestyle MApping (SELMA) framework*. RESOLVE Working Paper 02–09, University of Surrey, Guildford. Retrieved from http://resolve.sustainablelifestyles.ac.uk/ sites/default/files/RESOLVE_WP_02-09_0.pdf.

Druckman, A. & Jackson, T. (November 2010). *An Exploration into the Carbon Footprint of UK Households*. RESOLVE Working Paper Series 02–10, University of Surrey, Guildford. Retrieved from http:// resolve.sustainablelifestyles.ac.uk/sites/default/files/RESOLVE_ WP_02-10.pdf

Druckman, A. Chitnis, M. Sorrell, S. & Jackson, T. (2011). 'Missing Carbon Reductions? Exploring rebound and backfire effects in UK households'. *Energy Policy* 39: 3572–3581.

Druckman, A. Buck, I. Hayward, B. & Jackson, T. (2012). *Carbon and time: A study of the carbon implications of British adults' use of time*. RESOLVE Working Paper Number 01–12. Guildford, UK, University of Surrey. Retrieved from http://resolve.sustainablelifestyles.ac.uk/sites/default/ files/resolve_wp_01-12.pdf

Elchardus, M. (1991). Flexible Men and Women. The changing temporal organisation of work and culture: an empirical analysis. *Social Science Information* 30: 701–726.

Equality and Human Rights Commission. (2009). *Working Better: Fathers, families and work – contemporary perspectives*. Research Summary 41. Retrieved from http://www.equalityhumanrights.com/uploaded_files/ research/41_wb_fathers_family_and_work.pdf

Equality and Human Rights Commission. (2011). *Close to Home. An Inquiry into Older People and Human Rights in Home Care*. Retrieved from http://www.equalityhumanrights.com/uploaded_files/homecareFI/ home_care_report.pdf

Ehrlich, P. R. & Holdren J. P. (1971). Impact of population growth. *Science* 171, (3977) (March 26): 1212–1217.

Esquivel, V. (2011). Sixteen years after Beijing: what are the new policy agendas for time use data collection? *Feminist Economics*, 17 (4).

Estrade, M.-A., Méda, D. & Orain, R. (2001). Les effets de la réduction du temps de travail sur les modes de vie: qu'en pensent les salaries un an après? *Premières Synthèses*, n° 21.1, MES, Dares.

Estrade, M.-A. et Ulrich, V. (2002). La réorganisation des temps travailles avec les 35 heures: un facteur de segmentation de la main-d'œuvre? *Travail et Emploi*, n° 92, pp. 71–94.

Evans-Pritchard, A. (24 March 2005). France to abandon the 35-hour week. *Telegraph*, p. 38.

Evans-Pritchard, E. E. (1969/1940). *The Nuer.* Oxford: Oxford University Press.

Everingham, C. (2002). Engendering time. Gender equity and discourses of workplace flexibility. *Time and Society*, 11 (2/3): 335–351.

Fisher, M. (2009). *Capitalist Realism: Is there no alternative?* Ropely, Hants: Zero Books.

Fouarge, D. J. A. G. & Baaijens. C. (2004). *Changes in working hours and job mobility: the effect of Dutch legislation.* Tilburg.

Frank, R. (1985). *Choosing the right pond.* New York: Oxford.

Freyssinet, J. (October 2010). *Tripartite Responses to the Economic Crisis in the Principal Western European Countries.* Geneva. International Labour Organisation (ILO). Retrieved from http://www.ilo.org/wcmsp5/groups/public/---ed_dialogue/---dialogue/documents/publication/wcms_158356.pdf

Future Foundation. (2006). *The Changing Face of Parenting: Professional Parenting, Information and Healthcare.* London: An Experian Company.

Galinsky, E. Bond, J. T. Kim, S. S. Backon, L. Brownfield, E. & Sakai, K. (2004). *Overwork in America: When the Way we Work Becomes Too Much.* New York: Families and Work Institute, Executive Summary.

Gauthier, A. (2007). The impact of family policies on fertility in industrialised countries: a review of the literature. *Population Research and Policy Review*, 26(3), pp. 323–346.

Gershuny, J. (2003). Time, through the lifecourse, in the family. ISER Working Paper number 2003–3. Essex: Institute for Social and Economic Research.

Gershuny, J. (2005). Busyness as the badge of honour for the new super-ordinate working class. *Social Research*, 72, 2: 287–314.

Gershuny, J. (12 September 2011). Time use surveys and the measurement of national well-being. ONS and University of Oxford Centre for Time Use Research. Retrieved from http://www.ons.gov.uk/ons/rel/environmental/time-use-surveys-and-the-measurement-of-national-well-being/article-by-jonathan-gershuny/index.html

Ghertner, D. A. and Fripp, M. (2007). Trading away damage: Quantifying environmental leakage through consumption-based, life-cycle analysis. *Ecological Economics* 63: 563–77.

Giddens, A. (1981). *A Contemporary Critique of Historical Materialism. Power, Property and the State.* London: Macmillan Press.

Global Footprint Network. (2010). *Ecological Footprint Atlas 2010.* Oakland, CA: Global Footprint Network.

Godbey, G. (1996). *No Time to Waste: Time Use and the Generation of Residential Solid Waste*. PSWP Working Paper #4. New Haven, Connecticut, Yale School of Forestry and Environmental Studies.

Godbey, G. Lifset, R. & Robinson, J. (1998). No Time to Waste: an Exploration of Time Use, Attitudes Toward Time, and the Generation of Municipal Solid Waste. *Social Research* 65(1): 101–140.

Goffman, E. (1984). *The Presentation of Self in Everyday Life*. Harmondsworth: Penguin [originally published in 1959].

Goffman, E. (1972). *Relations in Public*. Harmondsworth: Penguin.

Golden, L. (2009). A brief history of long work time and the contemporary sources of overwork. *Journal of Business Ethics*, 84: 217–227.

Golden, L. (2012). *The Effects of Working Time on Productivity and Firm Performance: A Research Synthesis Paper*. Conditions of Work and Employment Series No. 33. Geneva: International Labour Organisation.

Goodin, R. E. (2010). Temporal Justice. *Journal of Social Policy* 39(01): 1–16.

Goodin, R. Rice, J. Parpo, A. & Eriksson, L. (2008). *Discretionary Time: A new measure of freedom*. Cambridge: Cambridge University Press.

Gorz, A. (1994). *Capitalism, socialism, ecology*. New York and London: Verso Books.

Gough, I. Adbdallah, S. Johnson, V. Ryan-Collins, J. & Smith, C. (2011). The distribution of total greenhouse gas emissions by households in the UK, and some implications for social policy. LSE STICERD Research Paper No. CASE152. London: Centre for Analysis of Social Exclusion, London School of Economics and new economics foundation.

de Graaf, J. (2010). Reducing Work Time as a Path to Sustainability. *State of the World 2010: Transforming cultures from consumerism to sustainability*. New York: W. W. Norton & Co, pp. 173–177.

de Grazia, S. (1974). *Of Time, Work and Leisure*. New York: Anchor Books.

Gregory, L. (2009). Change takes time: exploring the structural and development issues of time banking. *International Journal of Community Currencies* 13: 19–36.

Gregson, N. Metcalfe, A. & Crewe, L. (2007). Identity, mobility and the throwaway society. *Environment and Planning D: Society and Space*, 25: 682–700.

Griffin, J. (May 2010). *The Lonely Society?* Mental Health Foundation. Retrieved from http://www.mentalhealth.org.uk/publications/the-lonely-society/

Groenendijk, H. & Keuzenkamp, S. (2010). 2.19 The Netherlands. Moss, P. (ed) *International Review of Leave Policies and Related Research 2010, Employer Relations Research Series*. London: Department for Business, Innovation and Skills. pp. 161–168.

Grossin, W. (1969). *Le Travail et le Temps: Horaires-durees-rhythmes*. Paris: Editions Anthropos.

Grossin, W. (1974). *Les Temps de la Vie Quotidienne.* Paris: Mouton.

Grossin, W. (1992). Technological evolution, working time and remuneration. *Time & Society* 2: 159–178.

Grossman, L. (1 April 2010). Do we need an iPAD? A TIME Review. Retrieved from http://www.time.com/time/magazine/article/0,9171,1977106,00. html.

Grünell, M. (28 February 2000). Part-time Employment Act seeks to promote combining work and care. *European Industrial Relations Observatory On-line.* Retrieved from http://www.eurofound.europa.eu/eiro/2000/02/ feature/nl0002182f.htm

Gyes, G. V. (28 July 2009). Reducing working time as anti-crisis measure. *European Industrial Relations Observatory On-line.* Retrieved from http:// www.eurofound.europa.eu/eiro/2009/06/articles/be0906029i.htm

Hägerstrand, T. (1975). *Dynamic Allocation of Urban Space.* Farnborough: Saxon House.

Hall, E. T. (1983). *The Dance of Life: The Other Dimension of Time.* London: Doubleday.

Hamilton, C. (2010). Consumerism, self-creation and prospects for a new ecological consciousness. *Journal of Cleaner Production* 18(6): 571–575.

Hantrais, L. (1993). The Gender of Time in Professional Occupations. *Time & Society*, 2: 139–57.

Harvey, D. (1989). *The Condition of Postmodernity.* Oxford: Blackwell.

Hassard, J. (1989). Time and Organisation. Blyton, P. Hassard, J. Hill S & Starkey, K. (eds) *Time, Work and Organisation.* London: Routledge. pp. 79–104.

Hay, M. and Usunier, J. C. (1993). Time and strategic action: a cross-cultural view. *Time & Society* 2: 313–34.

Hayden, A. (1999). *Sharing the work, sparing the planet: work time, consumption and ecology.* London: Zed Books.

Hayden, A. (2006). France's 35-hour week: attack on business? Win-win reform? Or betrayal of disadvantaged workers? *Politics and Society*, 34(4), pp. 503–542.

Hayden, A. & Shandra, J. M. (2009). Hours of work and the ecological footprint of nations: An exploratory analysis. *Local Environment: The International Journal of Justice and Sustainability*, 14: 575–600.

Hayden, A. (2010). *From growth to sufficiency? A political-economic analysis of climate change responses in the UK and Canada.* Ph.D., Boston College, Department of Sociology.

Hertwich, E. G. (2005). Consumption and the rebound effect. *Journal of Industrial Ecology* 9, (1–2): 85–98.

Hertwich, E. G. & Peters, G. P. (2009). Carbon footprint of nations: a global, trade-linked analysis. *Environmental Science & Technology* 43(16): 6414–6420.

Hill, S. (1989). Time and Work: an Economic Analysis. P. Blyton, P. Hassard, J. Hill, S. & Starkey, K. (eds) *Time, Work and Organisation*. London: Routledge. pp. 57–78.

HM Government. (2008). *Climate Change Act 2008*. London, UK, The Stationery Office Limited.

Hofstetter, P. Madjar, M. and Ozawa, T. (2006). Happiness and sustainable consumption: psychological and physical rebound effects at work in a tool for sustainable design. *International Journal of Life Cycle Assessment* (Special Issue 1): 105–115.

Hong, S. Oreszczyn, T. and Ridley, I. (2006). The impact of energy efficient refurbishment on the space heating fuel consumption in English dwellings. *Energy and Buildings* 38: 1171–1181.

International Labour Organisation (ILO). (2004). *Working time and productivity*. Geneva: International Labour Organisation.

ILO. (2011a). Database of Conditions of Work and Employment Laws. Geneva: Retrieved from ILO http://www.ilo.org/dyn/travail/travmain. home [Accessed 21 June 2013].

ILO. (2011b). *Working time in the twenty-first century*, Geneva: International Labour Organisation.

Jackson, T. (2009). *Prosperity Without Growth? The transition to a sustainable economy*, London: Sustainable Development Commission.

Ingold, T. (1995). Work, Time and Industry. *Time & Society*, 4 (1), 5–28.

Jackson, T. (2009). *Prosperity Without Growth: Economics for a Finite Planet*. London: Earthscan.

Jackson, T. Papathanasopoulou, E. Bradley, P. & Druckman, A. (2006). *Attributing Carbon Emissions to Functional Household Needs: a pilot framework for the UK*. International Conference on Regional and Urban Modelling, Brussels, Belgium. 1–2 June 2006.

Jackson, T. and Papathanasopoulou, E. (2008). Luxury or Lock-in? An explanation of unsustainable consumption in the UK: 1968 to 2000. *Ecological Economics* 68 (1–2): 80–95.

Jackson, T. & Victor, P. (2011). Productivity and work in the 'green economy': some theoretical reflections and empirical tests. *Environmental Innovation and Societal Transitions*, 1, pp. 101–108.

Jacobs, J. A. and Gerson, K. (2005). *The Time Divide: Work, family and gender inequality*. Cambridge, MA: Harvard University Press.

Jahoda, M. Lasarsfeld, P. F. and Zeisl, H. (1972/1933). *Marienthal: The sociology of an unemployed community*. London: Tavistock.

Jalas, M. (2002). A time use perspective on the materials intensity of consumption. *Ecological Economics* 41(1): 109–123.

Jalas, M. (2005). The everyday life context of increasing energy demands: time use survey data in a decomposition analysis. *Journal of Industrial Ecology* 9(1–2): 129–145.

Jalas, M. (2006). *Busy wise and idle time*. PhD Thesis. Helsinki: Helsinki School of Economics.

Jalas, M. (2009). Time-use Rebound Effects: an Activity-based View of Consumption. Herring, H. & Sorrell, S. (eds). *Energy Efficiency and Sustainable Consumption*. Basingstoke, Hampshire: Palgrave Macmillan.

Jaques, E. (1982). *The Form of Time*. London: Heinemann.

Jin, W. Joyce, R. Phillips, D. and Sibieta, L. (2011). *Poverty and Inequality in the UK: 2011*. London: Institute for Fiscal Studies.

Kabat-Zinn, J. (2004). *Wherever You Go, There You Are: Mindfulness meditation for everyday life*. London: Piatkus Books.

Kahneman, D. & Tversky, A. (2000). *Choices, Values and Frames*. New York: Cambridge University Press.

Kanavos, P. Ostergren J. & Weber M. A. (2007). *High Blood Pressure and Health Policy: Where we are and where we need to go next*. Ruder Finn Inc.

Kasser, T. (2006). Materialism and its alternatives. Csikszentmihalyi, M. & Csikszentmihalyi, I. S. (eds). *A life worth living: Contributions to positive psychology*. Oxford: Oxford University Press. pp. 200–214.

Kasser, T. & Sheldon, K. M. (2009). Time affluence as a path toward personal happiness and ethical business practice: empirical evidence from four studies. *Journal of Business Ethics*, 84: 243–255.

Kern, S. (1983). *The Culture of Time and Space 1880–1919*. London: Weidenfeld & Nicolson.

Keynes, J. M. (1930). Economic possibilities for our grandchildren. *Essays in Persuasion*. New York: W. W. Norton and Co. pp. 358–373.

Knight, K. W. Rosa, E. A. & Schor, J. B. (2012). *Does Working Less Reduce Pressure on the Environment? A Cross-National Panel Analysis of OECD Countries, 1970–2007*. Unpublished.

Knight, K. W. Rosa, E. A. & Schor, J. B. (2012). Reducing growth to achieve environmental sustainability: the role of work hours. Pollin, R. & Wicks-Lim, J. (eds). *Capitalism on Trial: Explorations in the tradition of Thomas Weisskopf*. Cheltenham: Edward Elgar.

Knijn, T. C. Martin, & J. Millar. (2007). Activation as a common framework for social policies towards lone parents. *Social Policy and Administration* 41(6): 638–652.

Kodz, J. Davis, S. Lain, D. Strebler, M. Rick, J. Bates, P. Cummings, J. & Meager N. (2003). *Working Long Hours: a review of the evidence. Volume 1 – main report*. Employment Relations Research Series no. 16. London: Department of Trade and Industry.

LaJeunesse, R. (2009). *Work time regulation as sustainable full employment strategy*. Abingdon, Oxon: Routledge.

Lalive, R. & Zweimüller, J. (2009). How does parental leave affect fertility and return to work? Evidence from two natural experiments. *Quarterly Journal of Economics*, 124(3), pp. 1363–1402.

Lancaster, K. (1966). A new approach to consumer theory. *Journal of Political Economy*, 74, (2): 132–157.

Landes, D. S. (1983). *Revolution in Time*. Cambridge: Harvard University Press.

Larabee, M. (7 June 2008). Portland's walking neighborhoods seen as guide to future. *Oregon Live*. Retrieved from http://www.oregonlive.com/news/oregonian/index.ssf?/base/news/121280911730720.xml&coll=7.

Layard, R. (2006). *Happiness: Lessons from a new science*. New York; London: Penguin Books.

Leccardi, C. & Rampazi, M. (1993). Past and Future in Young Women's Experience of Time. *Time & Society*, 2: 353–80.

Lee, T. & Piachaud, D. (1992). The Time-Consequences of Social Services. *Time and Society*, 1: 65–80.

LeFeuvre, N. (1994). Leisure, work and gender: a sociological study of women's time in France. *Time & Society* 3/2: 151–179.

Le Goff, J. (1980). *Time, Work and Culture in the Middle Ages*. Chicago: University of Chicago Press.

Lehndorff, S. (2011). Before the Crisis, in the Crisis, and Beyond: The upheaval of collective bargaining in Germany. *Transfer*, 17(3), pp. 341–354.

Leijnse, F. Goudswaard, K. Plantenga, J. & van den Toren, J. P. (2002). *A Different Attitude to Security: Life course, risk and responsibility*. The Hague: Ministry of Social Affairs and Employment.

Lubbers, R. (Autumn 1997). 'The Dutch Way'. *New Perspectives Quarterly*, pp. 14–15.

Lynch, K. and Walsh, J. (2009). Love labouring: nurturing rationalities and relational identities. Lynch, K. Baker, J. & Lyons, M. (eds). *Affective Equality: Love, Care and Injustice*. Basingstoke: Palgrave Macmillan. p. 49.

McGrath, J. E. & Rotchford, N. L. (1983). Time and Behaviour in Organisations. *Research in Organisational Behaviour*, 5: 57–101.

McNeil, N. (June 2010). A twenty minute neighbourhood for bicycles? Retrieved from http://nathanmcneil.files.wordpress.com/2010/05/mcneil20minuteposter2.pdf

Maffesoli, M. (2003). *L'instant éternel: Le retour du tragique dans les sociétés postmodernes*. Paris: La Table Ronde.

Mandl, I. (2010). *Extending Flexicurity – The Potential of Short-time Working Schemes: ERM Report 2010*, Dublin: European Foundation for the Improvement of Living and Working Conditions.

Marx, K. (1977/1844). *Economic and Philosophical Manuscripts*. Moscow: Progress.

Marx, K. (1973/1857). *Grundrisse*. Harmondsworth: Penguin.

Marx, K. (1976/1867). *Capital, Volume I*. Harmondsworth: Penguin.

Meadows, D. H. Meadows, D. L. Randers, J. & Behrens W. W. (1972). *The Limits to Growth*. New York: Universe Books.

Méda, D. (2001a). Les 35 heures dans l'histoire séculaire de la réduction du temps de travail. Brunhes, B. Clerc, D. Méda, D. & Perret, B. (eds). *35 Heures: Le Temps du Bilan,* Paris: Desclée de Brouwer, pp. 13–20.

Méda, D. (2001b). Travailler moins pour vivre mieux? Brunhes, B. Clerc, D. Méda, D. & Perret, B. (eds). *35 heures: Le Temps du Bilan,* Paris: Desclée de Brouwer

Méda, D. (1995). *Le Travail. Une valeur en voie de disparition,* Paris, Aubier, Coll. Alto, 1995, rééd. Paris, Champs-Flammarion, 1998, p. 358.

Méda, D. & Orain, R. (April 2002). Transformations du travail et du hors-travail: le jugement des salariés sur la RTT. *Travail et Emploi,* n° 90.

van der Meer, M. & Leijnse, F. (2005). *Life-Course Savings Schemes and Social Policy Reform in the Netherlands: On the relationship between the welfare state, social pacts and the management of new social risks.* Amsterdam: SISWO/Social Policy Research.

Merla, M. & Deven, F. (2010). 2.4 Belgium. International Review of Leave Policies and Related Research 2010, *Employer Relations Research Series.* Moss, P. London: Department for Business, Innovation and Skills, pp. 59–64.

Messenger, J. C. (2009). Work Sharing: A strategy to preserve jobs during the global jobs crisis. Geneva: International Labour Organisation.

Ministry of Social Affairs and Employment. (2011). Life-course savings scheme. Retrieved from http://www.government.nl/ministries/szw/documents-and-publications/leaflets/2011/10/20/q-a-life-course-savings-scheme.html

Minx, J. & Baiocchi, G. (2009). Time-use and sustainability. Suh, S. (ed). *Handbook of Input-Output Economics in Industrial Ecology.* Dordrecht, the Netherlands: Springer.

Mishel, L. Bernstein, J. & Shierholz, H. (2009). *The State of Working America 2008/2009. An Economic Policy Institute book.* Ithaca, NY: Cornell University Press.

Moore, W. E. (1963). *Man, Time and Society.* New York: John Wiley & Sons.

Moriarty, P. & Honnery, D. (2010). A human needs approach to reducing atmospheric carbon. *Energy Policy* 38(2): 695–700.

Morrison, C. M. & Gore, H. (2010). The relationship between excessive internet use and depression: a questionnaire-based study of 1,319 young people and adults. *Psychopathology.* 43: 121–126.

Moss, P. (2012). International Review of Leave Policies and Related Research 2012. International Network on Leave Policies and Research.

Mumford, L. (1955/1934). *The Human Prospect.* Boston: Beacon Press.

Nassen, J. Larsson, J. & Holmberg, J. (2009). The effect of working hours on energy use: a micro analysis of time and income effects. ECEEE Summer Study.

Nguyen, D.T. (1992). The spatialisation of metric time: the conquest of land and labour in Europe and the United States. *Time & Society,* 1: 29–50.

Nowotny, H. (1989/1986). The public and private uses of time. *In Search of Usable Knowledge*. Frankfurt: Campus Westview, pp. 29–36. First published 1986 in Balbo, L. & Nowotny, H. (eds) *Time to Care in Tomorrow's Welfare System*. Vienna: Eurosocial.

Nussbaum, M. (2011). *Creating Capabilities: The Human Development Approach*. Cambridge, Massachusetts: Harvard University Press.

O'Malley, M. (1992). Time, Work and Task Orientation: A Critique of American Histiography. *Time & Society*, 1: 341–58.

OECD. (Updated 4 April 2013). Glossary of Statistical Terms. Retrieved from http://stats.oecd.org/glossary/detail.asp?ID=285

OECD. (2006). *Babies and Bosses: reconciling work and family life*. Paris: OECD.

OECD. (2010). *Employment Outlook 2010: How does Germany compare?* Paris: Organisation for Economic Co-operation and Development.

OECD. (7 March 2011). *Greening Household Behaviour: The Role of Public Policy*. OECD Publishing. Retrieved from http://dx.doi.org/10.1787/9789264096875-en

OECD. (21 June 2013). Incidence of involuntary part time workers. OECD. Retrieved from http://stats.oecd.org/Index.aspx?DatasetCode=INVPT_I

OECD. (11 July 2012). Part-time employment % of total employment. OECD iLibrary. Retrieved from http://www.oecd-ilibrary.org/employment/part-time-employment_20752342-table7

Ofcom. (August 2010). *The Communications Market Report*. Retrieved from http://stakeholders.ofcom.org.uk/market-data-research/market-data/communications-market-reports/cmr10/

ONS. (2006). *The Time Use Survey 2005*. London: Office for National Statistics.

ONS. (2006). *Input-Output (I-O) Supply and Use Tables (SUTs)*. Retrieved from http://www.ons.gov.uk/ons/guide-method/method-quality/specific/economy/input-output/archive-data/uk-i-o-analyses--2006-edition/index.html

ONS. (Spring 2008). *Environmental Accounts*. Retrieved from http://www.ons.gov.uk/ons/rel/environmental/environmental-accounts/spring-2008/index.html

ONS. (Autumn 2008). *Environmental Accounts*. Retrieved from http://www.ons.gov.uk/ons/rel/environmental/environmental-accounts/autumn-2008/index.html

ONS. (2011). *Statistical Bulletin: Families and households*. United Kingdom, 2001–2011. Retrieved from http://www.ons.gov.uk/ons/rel/family-demography/families-and-households/2011/stb-families-households.html

Otterbach, S. (2010). Mismatches between actual and preferred work time: empirical evidence of hours constraints in 21 countries. *Journal of Consumer Policy*, 33: 143–161.

Patterson, C. J. (2000). Family Relationships of Lesbians and Gay Men. *Journal of Marriage and Family* 62(4): 1052–1069.

Paul, A. T. Wiedmann, J. Barrett, J. Minx, K. Scott, E. Dawkins, A. Owen, J. Briggs, & I. Gray. (2010) *Introducing the Resources and Energy Analysis Programme (REAP)*. Stockholm: Stockholm Environment Institute.

Philippon, T. (2007). *Le Capitalisme d'Héritiers. La Crise Française du Travail.* Paris: Seuil.

Plantenga, J. (2005). Dutch debates: Modernising social security by introducing the life course as a frame of reference. de Gijsel, P. & Schenk, H. (eds). *Multidisciplinary Economics: The birth of a new economics faculty in the Netherlands.* Dordrecht: Springer. pp. 53–64.

Plantenga, J. (2005). The life course and the system of social security: Rethinking incentives, solidarity and risks. *European Journal of Social Security* 7(4): 301.

Pouwels, B. Siegers, J. & Vlasblom, J. D. (2008). Income, working hours, and happiness. *Economics Letters*, doi: 10.1016/j.econlet.2007.05.032.

Pullinger, M. (2011). *Greening Our Working Lives: The environmental impacts of changing patterns of paid work in the UK and the Netherlands and implications for working time policy.* Edinburgh: University of Edinburgh.

Rawls, J. (1971) *A Theory of Justice.* Oxford: Oxford University Press.

Ray, R. & Schmitt, J. (2007). *No-Vacation Nation.* Washington DC: Center for Economic and Policy Research.

Rees, W. E. (2006). Ecological Footprints and Bio-Capacity: Essential Elements in Sustainability Assessment. Dewulf, J. & van Langenhove, H. (eds). *Renewables-Based Technology: Sustainability assessment.* Chichester, UK: John Wiley and Sons. pp. 143–158.

Reisch, L. (2001). Time and wealth: the role of time and temporalities for sustainable patterns of consumption. *Time & Society* 10(2/3): 367–385.

Reynolds, J. (2004). When too much is not enough: actual and preferred working hours. *Sociological Forum,* 19(1): 89–120.

Rigaudiat, J. (1996). *Réduire le Temps de Travail.* Syros.

Rinderspacher, J. P. (1985). *Gesellschaft ohne Zeit: Individuelle Zeitverwendung und soziale Organisation der Arbeit.* Frankfurt am Main: Campus Verlag.

Rinderspacher, J. P. (1989). Mit der Zeit arbeiten: Über einige grundlegende Zusammenhänge von Zeit und Ökonomie. Wendorff, R. (ed.) *Im Netz der Zeit.* Stuttgart: Universitas/Hirzel. pp. 91–104.

Robinson, T. J. C. (2006). *Work, Leisure and the Environment: The vicious circle of overwork and over consumption.* Cheltenham: Edward Elgar.

Ropke, I. & Godskesen, M. (2007). Leisure activities, time and environment. *International Journal of Innovation and Sustainable Development* 2: 155–174.

Rosnick, D. & Weisbrot, M. (2006). *Are shorter hours good for the environment? A comparison of US and European energy consumption.* Washington, DC: Center for Economic and Policy Research.

RTL. (23 March 2012). Chômage: au niveau le plus bas depuis 20 ans. *RTL info*. Retrieved from http://www.rtl.be/info/belgique/societe/865551/chomage-au-niveau-le-plus-bas-depuis-20-ans

Rubin, J. (2012). *The End of Growth*. Toronto: Random House Canada.

Sachs, W. Loske, R. & Linz, M. (1998). *Greening the North: A post-industrial blueprint for ecology and equity*. London: Zed Books.

Sachs, W. & Santarius, T. (eds). (2007). *Fair Future: Resource conflicts, security and global justice*. London: Zed Books.

Sanne, C. (2002). Willing consumers or locked-in? Policies for a sustainable consumption. *Ecological Economics* 42(1–2): 273–287.

Schmitt, J. (2011). *Labor Market Policy in the Great Recession: Some lessons from Denmark and Germany*. Washington, DC: Center for Economic and Policy Research.

Schor, J. B. (1991). Global inequality and environmental crisis: an argument for reducing working hours in the north. *World Development* 19, (1): 73–84.

Schor, J. B. (1992). *The Overworked American: The unexpected decline of leisure*. New York: Basic Books.

Schor, J. B. (1995). Can the north stop consumption growth? Escaping the cycle of work and spend. in Bhaskar, V. and Glyn, A. (eds). *The North, the South and the Environment*. London: Earthscan.

Schor, J. B. (2005). Sustainable consumption and work time reduction. *Journal of Industrial Ecology* 9(1): 37–50.

Schor, J. B. (2010). *Plenitude: The New Economics of True Wealth*. New York: The Penguin Press.

Schor, J. B. (9 August 2010). The work sharing boom: exit ramp to a new economy? *Yes! Magazine*.

Sen, A. (1985.) *Commodities and Capabilities*. London: New Holland.

Sen, A. (1999.) *Development as Freedom*. Oxford: Oxford University Press.

Shackle, G. L. S. (1967). *Time in Economics*. Amsterdam: North Holland Publishing Company.

Sharp, C. (1981). *The Economics of Time*. Oxford: Martin Robertson.

Simms, A. Johnson, V. and Chowla, P. (2010). *Growth Isn't Possible*. **nef**. Retrieved from http://dnwssx4l7gl7s.cloudfront.net/nefoundation/default/page/-/files/Growth_Isnt_Possible.pdf

Solnick, S. J. & Hemenway, D. (1998). Is more always better? A survey on positional concerns. *Journal of Economic Behavior and Organization*, 37: 373–83.

Sorrell, S. (2007). The Rebound Effect: An assessment of the evidence for economy-wide energy savings from improved energy efficiency. London: UK Energy Research Centre.

Spangenberg, J. H. Omann, I. & Hinterberger. F. (2002). Sustainable growth criteria: minimum benchmarks and scenarios for employment and the environment. Ecological Economics 42(3): 429–443.

Speth, J. G. (2008). The Bridge at the Edge of the World: Capitalism, the environment, and crossing from crisis to sustainability. New Haven, CT: Yale University Press.

Speth, J. G. Costanza, R. Hassol, S. J. & Kasser, T. (10 December 2007). Some convenient truths: scaling back our energy-hungry lifestyles means more of what matters, not less. Grist. Retrieved from http://www.grist.org/article/scaling-back-our-energy-hungry-lifestyles-means-more-of-what-matters-not-le

Starkey, K. (1988). Time and work organisation: a theoretical and empirical analysis. Young, M. & Schuller, T. (eds). The Rhythms of Society. London: Routledge. pp. 95–117.

Stier, H. & Lewin-Epstien, N. (2003). Time to work: a comparative analysis of preferences for working hours. Work and Occupations, 30(3): 302–326.

Strongman, C. (8 April 2012). Copenhagen really is wonderful, for so many reasons. *Observer*. p. 29.

Sullivan, O. & Gershuny, J. (2004) Inconspicuous consumption: work-rich, time-poor in the liberal market economy. Journal of Consumer Culture, 4: 79–100.

Summerfield, A. J. Lowe, R. J. Bruhns, H. R. Caeiro, J. A. Steadman, J. P. & Oreszczyn, T. (2007). Milton Keynes Energy Park revisited: changes in internal temperatures and energy usage. Energy and Buildings 39(7): 783–791.

Théret, B. (2010). Réduction du temps de travail et développement démocratique. Coutrot, T. Flacher, D. Méda, D. (eds). Pour en Finir avec ce Vieux Monde : Les Chemins de la Transition, Editions Utopia.

Thompson, E. P. (1967). Time, work-discipline and industrial capitalism. *Past & Present*, 36: 57–97.

Thompson, C. J. & Coskuner-Balli, G. (7 November 2007). Enchanting ethical consumerism: the case of community supported agriculture. *Journal of Consumer Culture*. 3: 275–303.

Truc, O. (8 May 1998). Ces Danoises qui préfèrent le temps à l'argent. *Libération*.

Ulrich V. & Zilbermann, C. (January 2007). La réduction du temps de travail: révélateur et source de développement des relations professionnelles en entreprise. *Premières Synthèses*, n° 03.2, DARES, Ministère du Travail et de l'Emploi.

United Nations (UN). (2005). Classification of Individual Consumption According to Purpose (COICOP). United Nations Statistics Division.

UN Environment Programme. (2008). Green Jobs: Towards decent work in a sustainable, low-carbon world. Nairobi: United Nations Environment Programme.

UN Framework Convention on Climate Change. (2008). Kyoto Protocol reference manual on accounting of emissions and assigned amount. Bonn: United Nations Framework Convention on Climate Change.

Unruh, G. C. (2002). Escaping carbon lock-in. *Energy Policy* 30(4): 317–325.

Victor, P. (2008). *Managing Without Growth: Slower by design, not disaster.* Cheltenham, UK, and Massachusetts, USA, Edward Elgar.

Victor, P. 2011. Growth, degrowth and climate change: A scenario analysis. *Ecological Economics.* In Press, Corrected Proof.

Vringer, K. Benders, R. Wilting, H. Brink, C. Aalbers, E. Nijdam, D. & Hoogervorst, N. (2010). A hybrid multi-region method (HMR) for assessing the environmental impact of private consumption. *Ecological Economics,* 69 (12): 2510–2516.

Walker, T. (2002).'The'lump-of-labor' case against work sharing: populist fallacy or marginalist throwback?' *Working Time: International trends, theory and policy perspectives,* Lonnie Golden, L & Figart, D. M. (eds).

White, J. & Goulet, D. (April, 1998). Contemplating the Four-Day Week: Lessons from Bell Canada. *Policy Options,* pp. 30–32.

Woodroffe, J. (2009.) *Not having it all: How motherhood reduces women's pay and employment prospects.* London: Fawcett and Oxfam. Retrieved from http://www.equality-ne.co.uk/downloads/445_NotHavingItAll.pdf

Wolf, M. (16 June 2011). Britain's curiously continental job market. *Financial Times,* p. 9.

Woo, N. & Baker, D. (May 2012). States could save $1.7 billion per year with federal financing of work sharing. *Issue Brief.* Washington, DC: Center for Economic Policy and Research.

Working Families. (2011). *Working and Fathers: Combining family life and work.* Lancaster University Management School. p. 5. Retrieved from http://www.workingfamilies.org.uk/admin/uploads/WF_WorkingAndFathers-Report-FINAL.pdf

Yaker, H. Osmond, H. and Cheek, F. (eds). (1972). *The Future of Time.* London: Hogarth Press.

Yang, H. (2006). Work hours and self-reported hypertension amongst working people in California. *Hypertension,* 48, 4: 744–750.

York, R. Rosa, E. A. & Dietz, T. (2003). STIRPAT, IPAT and ImPACT: Analytic tools for unpacking the driving forces of environmental impacts. *Ecological Economics* 46: 351–65.

York, R. Rosa, E. A. & Dietz, T. (2009). A Tale of Contrasting Trends: Three Measures of the Ecological Footprint in China, India, Japan, and the United States, 1961–2003. *Journal of World-Systems Research,* 15(2): 134–146.

Žižek, S. (2010). *In Defence of Lost Causes.* London: Verso.

Žižek, S. (2006). *How to Read Lacan.* London: Granta Books.

About the authors

Barbara Adam is Emerita Professor of Sociology at Cardiff University. Her prime expertise is in social and socio-environmental time, working the time dimension into areas of conceptual and empirical social science research – including culture, education, environment, environmental economics, food, globalisation, gender, health, international relations, management, media, risk, technological innovation, transport and work. She has published extensively on the social relations of time and the future and is founding editor of the journal *Time & Society*.

Valerie Bryson is Emerita Professor of Politics at the University of Huddersfield. Her research interests focus on the overlapping areas of feminist political theory, women and politics, and the politics of time. Her recent publications include 'Women and Feminization' in T. Heppell and D. Seawright (eds); *Redefining Social Justice: New Labour rhetoric and reality*, with P. Fisher (eds) (Manchester University Press, 2011); *Sexuality, Gender and Power, Intersectional and Transnational Perspectives*, with A. Jonasdottir and K. Jones (eds) (Routledge, 2011); and *Gender and the Politics of Time: Feminist theory and contemporary debates* (The Policy Press, 2007).

Tania Burchardt is deputy director of the Centre for the Analysis of Social Exclusion (CASE) and senior Lecturer, Department of Social Policy, London School of Economics. Her research interests are in: theories of social justice, including the capability approach; employment, welfare and exclusion; and equality and inequality in Britain. Her current research focuses on inequality in respect of care services; and equality, capability and human rights. She has published widely and her recent publications include 'Time, Income and Substantive Freedom: A capability approach', *Time & Society*, 19(3): 318–344 (2010); and *Social Justice and Public Policy: Seeking fairness in diverse societies* (with G Craig and D Gordon) (The Policy Press, 2008).

Molly Conisbee is co-founder of think and do tank, Bread, Print and Roses. Prior to that, she was Director of External Affairs at the Soil Association. Molly has also worked in a variety of press, research and public affairs roles for leading think tanks, the Institute for Public Policy

Research (IPPR) and **nef** (the new economics foundation) and in local government and the NHS. Molly has authored and co-authored numerous policy and campaign reports, including *Environmental Refugees: The case for recognition* (with Andrew Simms); *Walk the Line: Railways after the Beeching Axe* and *The Reconquest of Bread*. Molly is an editor and blogger on the leading political website, shiftinggrounds.org.

Anna Coote is Head of Social Policy at **nef** and a leading analyst, writer and advocate in the field of social policy. She was responsible for ground-breaking work on health and sustainable development as commissioner for health with the UK Sustainable Development Commission (2000–09). She led the Healthcare Commission's work on engaging patients and the public (2005–08) and was director of Health Policy at the King's Fund (1998–2004). Earlier posts include Senior Research Fellow and Deputy Director of IPPR from 1989–98, Editor and Producer of current affairs television for Diverse Productions (1982–86), and Deputy Editor of the *New Statesman* (1978–82). Anna has written widely on social policy, sustainable development, public health policy, public involvement and democratic dialogue, gender and equality. She is co-author of *21 Hours: Why a shorter working week can help us all to flourish in the 21st century*, with A. Simms & J. Franklin (**nef**, 2010).

Mark Davis is Associate Professor of Sociology at the University of Leeds. He is the founder and director of the Bauman Institute, an international research and teaching centre established to meet the challenge of creating fairer, more resilient, and more sustainable societies around the world. He was the UK's lead academic participant in the Expert Advisory Group to the Council of Europe (2008–11) that drafted the European Charter of Shared Social Responsibilities, which was launched with Members of the European Parliament in Brussels in March 2011. His research on the social and political consequences of global consumerism is a key part of the 'Building Sustainable Societies' research programme at Leeds and he is a consultant in this area for national think tanks in the UK, including **nef** and Compass. He is currently researching the concept of 'community resilience' and the role democratic finance can play in promoting greater levels of social cohesion. Dr Davis is also a Fellow of the Royal Society of Arts.

Angela Druckman is Senior Lecturer in the Centre of Environment Strategy at the University of Surrey. After reading engineering at the University of Cambridge, and gaining Chartered Engineer status through working in electronics research and development, Angela now is a leading researcher on the environmental impacts of household consumption.

She has published widely and has a particular interest in exploring the links between the carbon footprint of different types of lifestyles and UK households.

Jane Franklin is a researcher in the social policy team at **nef**. She is a policy analyst and political sociologist whose research interests include critical engagement with neoliberal policy discourses; equality and social justice in Britain; and feminist theory and politics. She has worked at the Institute for Public Policy Research (1989–97); London South Bank University (1997–2007), and the Young Foundation (2007–08). She is co-author of *21 Hours: Why a shorter working week can help us all flourish in the 21st century*, with Anna Coote and Andrew Simms (**nef**, 2010).

Anders Hayden is Assistant Professor in Political Science at Dalhousie University in Halifax, Canada. His primary research interest is the social and political responses to climate change, particularly the evolving balance between efforts to promote ecological modernisation ('green growth') and sufficiency-based challenges to the endless growth of production and consumption. He is the author of the book *Sharing the Work, Sparing the Planet: Work time, consumption and ecology*. He previously worked as research and policy co-ordinator for 32 Hours, a Toronto based group committed to a reduction and redistribution of work time.

Bronwyn Hayward is a senior lecturer in the School of Social and Political Sciences at the University of Canterbury, New Zealand and a visiting fellow with the Sustainable Lifestyles Research Group, University of Surrey. Her research focus is democracy and youth in periods of environmental, social and economic change. Her most recent book is: *Children, Citizenship and Environment: Nurturing a democratic imagination in a changing world* (Earthscan/Routledge, 2012).

Tim Jackson is Professor of Sustainable Development at the University of Surrey. From 2006 to 2009 he led the Sustainable Development Commission's Redefining Prosperity programme and authored the controversial report, later published by Earthscan as *Prosperity without Growth: Economics for a finite planet* (2009–11). Tim's research interests at Surrey have focused on the relationship between lifestyle, well-being and the environment, with the Economic and Social Research Council (ESRC) Research Group on Lifestyles, Values and the Environment (RESOLVE) and the Sustainable Lifestyles Research Group (SLRG) funded by Defra, the Scottish Government and the ESRC. He has also been awarded an ESRC professorial fellowship to study Prosperity and Sustainability in the Green Economy (PASSAGE). This project includes – in collaboration with Professor Peter Victor (York University, Toronto) – the development of the Green Economy Macro-Model and Accounts (GEMMA). Tim has published widely in his field.

Dominque Méda is Professor of Sociology at the University of Paris-Dauphine and Chair of Ecological conversion, work, employment, and social policy' at the Collèges d'Études Mondiales. Her work has focused on the value and meaning of work, on issues of gender equality and finding a better balance between work and family life for men and women, as well as improving the position of women in employment. Her current work focuses on the balance between work, social and environmental policy and she has recently published *Redefining progress in the light of the ecological crisis* (Veblen Institute for Economic Reforms, 2012).

Martin Pullinger is an ecological economist, whose research looks at the interactions between environmental sustainability and human well-being, focusing on how these two can be combined. His work seeks to produce new insights into how different everyday practices and working patterns influence household carbon footprints, energy and water use, and well-being. He has contributed to research into the design of policies and interventions to promote well-being and more sustainable lifestyles, practices and behaviours. He currently works on the IDEAL home energy advice project at Edinburgh University.

Juliet Schor is a professor in the sociology department of Boston College. Her scholarly interests are consumer society and consumer culture; working hours and lifestyles; environmental degradation; the emergence of a sustainable consumption and production sector, including political consumption and the new sharing economy, and alternative, sustainable economies and societies. Her 'work and spend' cycle is an integrated approach to production and consumption which emphasises the sociological dynamics that determine spending. Most recently she is working on issues of sustainable consumption and production, with particular emphasis on political consumption, new patterns of time use, and alternative economic structures. As a member of a MacArthur Research Network she is studying the emergence of collaborative consumption. She is widely published in her field, and noted publications include *The overworked American: The unexpected decline of leisure* (Basic Books 1992); 'Sustainable Consumption and Work time Reduction', *Journal of Industrial Ecology*, Special Issue on Sustainable Consumption, 9(1): 37–50, 2005; and *True Wealth: How and why millions of Americans are creating a time rich, ecologically light, small-scale, high satisfaction economy* (Penguin, 2011). Schor is a co-founder of the Center for a New American Dream, and the organiser of the Summer Institute in New Economics – a programme in new economics for graduate students.

Andrew Simms is the author of several books including the bestselling *Tescopoly*. He is a fellow of **nef** and was its policy director for a decade. He trained at the London School of Economics and was described by *New Scientist* magazine as, 'a master at joined-up progressive thinking.' Andrew is a long-standing campaigner who coined the term 'Clone Towns' in work on local economic regeneration, co-authored the ground-breaking Green New Deal, was one of the original organisers of the campaign to cancel poor country debt, co-founded the climate campaign *onehundredmonth.org* and devised 'Ecological Debt Day'. After witnessing at first hand over two decades of failed international efforts to solve critical problems ranging from extreme poverty to climate change, his latest book *Cancel the Apocalypse: The new path to prosperity* (2013) is the result of a search for something better.

Robert Skidelsky is Emeritus Professor of Political Economy at Warwick University. His three-volume biography of John Maynard Keynes (1983, 1992, 2000) won five prizes. A single volume abridgment appeared in 2002. A revised edition of his book on the current crisis, *Keynes: The Return of the Master*, was published in September 2010. He was made a member of the House of Lords in 1991 (he sits on the cross-benches) and was elected a fellow of the British Academy in 1994. He is a non-executive director of Rusnano Capital and formerly of Janus Capital and Sistema JSC. His most recent book, *How Much is Enough? The love of money and the case for the good life*, co-written with his son Edward, was published in July 2012.

Index

Locators for information found in tables are indicated in **bold**, and those for information in figures are indicated in *italics*.